The War I Survived
Was Vietnam

The Nation.

June 12, 1995 $2.50 U.S./$3.50 Canada

SPRING BOOKS

CAROL BRIGHTMAN & MICHAEL UHL
On McNamara's War

JESS MOWRY
On Banks's Runaway

EDUARDO GALEANO'S
Windows

ARTHUR C. DANTO
On Morrisroe's Mapplethorpe

GORE VIDAL
On Kopkind's Dispatches

JOHN LEONARD
On García Márquez

CARLIN ROMANO
On Meyers's Wilson

MAURICE ISSERMAN
On American Communists & Russian Archives

LESLIE MARMON SILKO
On Alexie's Indian Experience

ERIC FONER
On Democracy's Prospects

ILAN STAVANS
On Bianciotti's Argentina

© ART SPIEGELMAN 1995

The War I Survived Was Vietnam

Collected Writings of a Veteran and Antiwar Activist

MICHAEL UHL

Foreword by Steve Rees

McFarland & Company, Inc., Publishers
Jefferson, North Carolina

ALSO BY MICHAEL UHL

Vietnam Awakening: My Journey from Combat to the Citizens' Commission of Inquiry on U.S. War Crimes in Vietnam (McFarland, 2007)

Frontispiece: Art Spiegelman's cover art for the review of McNamara in *The Nation*.

LIBRARY OF CONGRESS CATALOGUING-IN-PUBLICATION DATA

Names: Uhl, Michael, 1944– author.
Title: The war I survived was Vietnam : collected writings of a veteran and antiwar activist / Michael Uhl ; foreword by Steve Rees.
Description: Jefferson, North Carolina : McFarland & Company, Inc., Publishers, 2016. | Includes bibliographical references and index.
Identifiers: LCCN 2016036954 | ISBN 9781476666143 (softcover : acid free paper) ∞
Subjects: LCSH: Vietnam War, 1961–1975—Personal narratives, American. | Vietnam War, 1961–1975—Veterans—United States. | Vietnam War, 1961–1975—Protest movements—United States. | Post-traumatic stress disorder. | Uhl, Michael, 1944–
Classification: LCC DS559.5 .U353 2016 | DDC 959.704/3092—dc23
LC record available at https://lccn.loc.gov/2016036954

BRITISH LIBRARY CATALOGUING DATA ARE AVAILABLE

ISBN (print) 978-1-4766-6614-3
ISBN (ebook) 978-1-4766-2580-5

© 2016 Michael Uhl. All rights reserved

No part of this book may be reproduced or transmitted in any form or by any means, electronic or mechanical, including photocopying or recording, or by any information storage and retrieval system, without permission in writing from the publisher.

Front cover image of unidentified participants in a November 6, 1971, antiwar march in San Francisco © 2016 by photographer Steve Rees

Printed in the United States of America

*McFarland & Company, Inc., Publishers
Box 611, Jefferson, North Carolina 28640
www.mcfarlandpub.com*

For Avalee

Acknowledgments

I wish to thank all those who willingly and cheerfully granted permission to reprint the previously published works that appear herein.

My old friend Steve Rees, a man whose integrity and many talents I have long admired, took time from his busy life to write the foreword, a very generous appraisal of the author and his work. I am not only deeply grateful for Steve's contribution, but ever in his debt.

I also wish to thank Art Spiegelman, and Roane Carey of *The Nation,* for permission to reprint the cover drawing Art provided for an issue of the magazine which featured the review of Robert McNamara's memoir included here.

I am likewise indebted to both Noam Chomsky and Clara Bingham whose kind and supportive words appear on the cover of this volume.

My loving wife, Susan Connery, can seldom be captured at rest. She moves from one undertaking to another like a whirlwind, as a creative force in her own right, and as caregiver extraordinaire for those fortunate enough to be in her life. And still Susan found the time and energy to take on the tedium of retyping from original texts several of the works included in this collection. Her support has been bountiful, and profoundly appreciated.

Table of Contents

Acknowledgments vi
Foreword by Steve Rees 1
Preface 7

Featured Articles

Searching for Vietnam's M.I.A.s 14
Vietnam's Shadow over Abu Ghraib 21
The Wall: Entering the Aura of the Dead 26
The Spat-Upon Vet Revisited 29
Annals of the New Left: Dissing Golub 34

Poetry

Introduction 39
Black Silks, Black Mud 40
Dignum et Justum Est 41
Shades 42
War Birthed Me 43
It's Hard to Tell Sometimes… 44

Criticism and Reviews

Bombing for the Hell of It (Michael Uhl and Carol Brightman) 46
  • *Excerpt from an Interview with Robert Strange McNamara* 52
Revising the Meaning of the Vietnam War 54
The Problematic: Penny Lewis Repairs Some Misconceptions
  About the Vietnam War 58

Apocalypse Now? The Strange Jeremiads of Christopher Hedges	64
Déjà Vu All Over Again: Notes on a Jonathan Schell Review	69
An Enfant Terrible Stumbles Upon the Vietnam War	75
• *Veteran War Crimes Testimony, 1969-1971: An Annotated Clipping File*	82
Meeting the Enemy: A Marine Goes Home	93
Combat and Reconciliation: A Vietnam Vet Returns to Heal Old Wounds	96
Armed with the Facts	99
A Skillful Chronicle of Kerry's Conflicts	102
War and Remembrance	105
Warrior's Honor and the Ordeal of Survival	108
That's Vietnam, Jake	112
The Jaws of Victory: A Historian Argues We Could Have Won—and Nearly Did Win—the Vietnam War	121
War and Madness	124
Obsessed by Vietnam	127
How We Bombed in Laos	130
On the Lam from Vietnam	133
Travels with Charlie	137
The God That Resigned	144
Letters Home	149
Gung Ho	152

The Chosen: An Essay

Some Notes on Being a Veteran in America	156

PTSD

The Politics of PTSD	174
PTSD from the Inside Out	177
Surviving PTSD	181

Table of Contents   ix

In My Activist Voice

Heeding the Call	184
With Paul and Do' at My Lai	187
VFP Agent Orange Delegation in Vietnam	190
Kerry and the Year of the Veteran	193
Warriors for Peace	195
Antiwar Vets Raise Their Voices	197
Vets Bite War	203
Occupying the Contested Zones of Meaning	207

With Tod Ensign

Introduction	209
Soldier as Workers	212
Changes in U.S. Army Mean Soldiers May Unionize	217
A Union of Soldiers	221
Support Still Strong for Military Union	226
Prospects for a Military Union Setback	228
Coalition Organizes Against Senate Bill	231
Unorganizing GIs	233
A Victim of the Tests	236
Blowing the Whistle on Agent Orange	238
Excerpt from *G.I. Guinea Pigs: How the Pentagon Exposed Our Troops to Dangers More Deadly Than War*	244
• Introduction	244
• Chapter 7—The Ranch Hands: "Only We can Prevent Forests…"	247
• Chapter 10—The VA Fiddles while Agent Orange Burns Vets	265
Appendix: Author's Testimony Before the House Committee of Government Operations Hearings on the Phoenix Program	279
Index	287

Where dissent is blunted by the conventions of compromise … it is tempting to conform. We need people who make a virtue of opposing mainstream opinion.

—Tony Judt, *Ill Fares the Land*

Foreword by Steve Rees

How far from the big moments in our lives must we wander before we pause to review, reevaluate and, at times, rewrite them? And how close to the end of our lives must we approach before we're prompted to take stock of the lives we've lived?

Michael Uhl has been immersed in both of these moments at the same time, and I have a hunch that this has given him the energy and endurance to look again with his eyes and mind wide open at the artifacts of his very full life. What makes him unusual is not that he has, in his sixties, paused to write his memoir, or that in his early seventies agreed to his editor's prompting to assemble an anthology of his writing. What makes him unusual is his capacity for critical self-reflection, his graceful prose, and his grasp of the historical significance of the events of his time. I should note that he is also unusual in that he is an activist, a citizen of his times who has made a deep mark on world events.

Many writers get off easily when they come to write their memoirs because they never documented their first impressions in print. Michael Uhl gets no such free pass. Because he wrote scores of articles, and co-authored two books, he has no way to escape comparing the written record of his first impressions with the richer perspective of historical distance. Without embarrassment, he is ready to face the evidence of his younger self, and share with his readers his self-critical reflections. Few of us, I would hazard a guess, are brave enough to share memories of our younger, more impulsive selves with our children sitting by our side. Michael Uhl has shared this with strangers in writing.

Not that his anthology contains anything less than evidence of a life well lived. What's notable to me is that while Michael Uhl has much to be proud of, he does no bragging. In fact, his stance as an author is characterized by a humorous, self-effacing voice and a graceful humility. This is in contrast to the combat ready stance he has taken in the world as dissenter and activist, both of which require fortitude and confidence. How rare it is to find these qualities combined together in one person.

Finally, this collection shows us an author who is navigating a moral path through a world filled with immorality and amoral pathways galore. The Vietnam War thrust him into a series of unwelcome circumstances—assigned to a counter-intelligence unit in a decidedly unintelligent bureaucracy; responsible as a lieutenant must be for the command of a platoon; unwitting witness to interrogators using electrical shock to compel submission. His memoirs, *Vietnam Awakening* and *Safe Return* (a work in progress near completion) relate both those moments where he strayed off the path he was charting toward the moral high ground, and those moments where he succeeded at charting his way. This collection of articles and selections from his books are of the moment. They do not convey the author's reflections in the manner of his memoir. But they do reflect the degree to which his moral compass and his tenacity enabled him to do remarkable deeds and imagine powerful ideas that would spark others to strive to do more of the same.

"Daddy, what did you do in the war?"

Michael Uhl's answer would confuse any child prepared only for simple symbols of good and bad. His answer would state that he enlisted to fight in a war that he quickly came to oppose, and once he was discharged, helped men who quit the military and left the United States return home again. And he encouraged those men, who many called deserters, to feel proud of their refusals, as a moral act in the face of an immoral war.

We Americans are too often like children, steeped in moral tales that lack complexity and nuanced meaning. Through the 1980s, President Reagan and scores of establishment historians reinterpreted the Vietnam War as a noble cause, and celebrated the sacrifices soldiers made in fighting that war. Those who asserted these sanitized explanations of the war tried to mend a rift in the American social fabric. They may have patched the rift for some, but it has not mended. Michael Uhl's writings issue an appeal to begin the real healing by calling a spade a spade, a defeat a defeat, and a crime a crime. Michael Uhl's answer—that deserters were honorable men—might be hard for a young man of 20 today to grasp, who having been born in the mid–1990s has only known his country to be at war with one or two countries continuously, and whose wars seem justified to them, in the defense of American security and people's peace of mind.

Our American naiveté is compounded by the geographic fact that we are an island people. Only one war has been fought on our soil, and in that war own countrymen fought each other. Never has America been invaded. So war for us is something that happens elsewhere. When we fight in wars, our soldiers go elsewhere. This, too, makes Michael Uhl's writing all the more important.

His writing, and the life he lived from the New York City suburb of Babylon, to Vietnam and back, embody one man's experience of the second American civil war. The opposition to the Vietnam War ran so deep and so wide that it divided institutions as big as the Army and Navy, as well as social institutions as familiar as families and churches. Families were ruptured when its members could not agree whether their sons should submit to the draft, or move to Canada. Universities were ruptured when their mainstream students occupied research buildings dedicated to military contracts, went on strike, refused to go to classes pretending that what was normal was acceptable. Churches were ruptured when their ministers and their congregations took opposing stands on the profoundly moral questions the war posed. City councils erupted when challenged by council members to vote to provide sanctuary for those refusing the draft or walking away from military service. Even the civil rights movement was fractured when, on April 4, 1967, Dr. Martin Luther King, Jr., preached at Riverside Church about the inseparability of the fight for racial equality and the fight for peace in Vietnam ("Beyond Vietnam: A Time to Break Silence").

Even inside the war-making institutions, divisions were evident at all levels. Johnson's cabinet was split on the commitment of combat troops. Congress was split. Most interesting, however, were the divisions of opinion within the command itself. From the Joint Chiefs of Staff down to field generals, the military command was far from unified, either on strategy or tactics. Beyond the three most visible opponents of the war—Gen. James Gavin, Gen. Matthew Ridgway and Marine General David M. Shoup—was a broad band of commanders who strongly opposed a combat role for U.S. forces in Vietnam. While their political reasons varied, their shared advice to the President was to limit the U.S. military to an advisory and support role. "Do not get involved in a land war in Asia" was the message they conveyed.

Michael Uhl's writings are in my view a living testimony to the depth and breadth of the second American civil war prompted by the war in Vietnam. In his life, he entered the military believing in the truths our parents tell us, and hoping to do good as we take our place in the world. (See "War Birthed Me" in the poetry section.) And as he encountered evidence of the falsehoods through the course of his time in service, he grew up. It was the end of childhood, not just for Michael Uhl, but for me and millions like us who were born close to the end of World War II, who were school age children taught to duck under our desks to survive World War III, and who came of age at the start of the Vietnam War.

However, we all enter the grown-up world differently. Michael Uhl entered it with a fierce energy and an intellectual and moral commitment that was matched to the intensity of his times. His transition to post-college adulthood was marked by a discovery of betrayals by the larger institutional authorities in his life. Perhaps his anger at these betrayals helped him maintain his energy for a very long time, in a political environment that was often fractious, impractical and self-absorbed. The decline of the antiwar movement after 1971 looked at times like a pedantic child throwing temper tantrums. Level-headed, pragmatic activists, who maintained an adult's consistency in both principles and action, grew increasingly rare as the decade of the 1970s unwound. Michael Uhl, together with his close comrade, Tod Ensign, continued to defend veterans and advocate for the safe return of self-retired exiles, maintaining a quality of work that is evident in the articles in this collection.

Range of Topics, Range of Audiences

The range of Michael Uhl's writing is worth noting. In this anthology, readers will find poetry, film reviews, personal recollections, opinion essays, magazine articles and polemics. The publications that brought his writing to a larger public included the *Boston Globe, The Nation, GEO Magazine, House Beautiful, The Progressive,* and *Travel and Leisure.* In addition, he is author of four *Frommer's* travel guides, and co-author of *GI Guinea Pigs,* published by Playboy Press. Clearly, this is a man whose pen is both his sword and his livelihood. He wields that pen to criticize and praise; to guide others to gain more meaning from their travels; to call attention to deserving works that have received little attention, and to debunk works that have received an excess of attention and praise.

Take, for example, his review of Penny Lewis's book, *Hardhats, Hippies and Hawks: The Vietnam Antiwar Movement as Myth and Memory* (Cornell University Press, 2013). Here is a work that had enjoyed reviews only in the press of the New Left, and apparently no mainstream recognition, positive or negative. As of December 2015, it ranked #1427 on Amazon's list of sociology books. Yet, Michael Uhl, duly skeptical of popularity rankings, discovered much value in Penny Lewis's fresh look at the blue collar opposition to the war in Vietnam. He also called attention to the author's courage in stretching the conventions of higher education scholarship in order to advance a contrary notion.

In contrast, Michael Uhl and his co-author and former partner, Carol Brightman, wrote a review of Robert McNamara's book, *In Retrospect: The Tragedy and Lessons of Vietnam.* The essay, titled "Bombing for the Hell of

It," appeared in the June 12, 1995, issue of *The Nation,* and probed for meaning where others were either cheering McNamara or booing him. Summoning up the words of Hannah Arendt and the larger question of the legality of the war itself, these two brought to their review questions much larger than whether McNamara's *mea culpas* were proportional to his sins. In calling on Telford Taylor's comments of January 1971 about the consequences of applying Nuremberg Doctrine to LBJ's cabinet, Uhl and Brightman questioned whether McNamara would be tried for war crimes.

It is the gift of persistence the two of them share that led them to go beyond the book, and interview McNamara himself. They enriched their book review with an admission of a remarkable sort—without commenting on the legal question of whether Vietnam was formally one or two countries, McNamara, under relentless questioning by Michael Uhl, declared that the war "…wasn't primarily a war of aggression [from the North].… In a very real sense, I believe we invaded a country that was in the process of a civil war." Michael Uhl pressed his questioning further, asking if Vietnam was, then, in effect one nation. McNamara replied, "In the sense that the people wanted to unite, I think probably yes."

The 40 Year Lag Factor

It took decades for Robert McNamara to reevaluate his wartime judgment, and it has been 40 years since the U.S. exodus from Vietnam (itself the subject of a review in this collection of Rory Kennedy's film, "Revising the Meaning of the Vietnam War"). What is it about this interval of three or four decades that brings memory alive? Uhl has been sparked to collect his writing for this anthology in a propitious moment. Is it a moment of commercial promise for the book? Is Michael Uhl himself prompted to collect his writing as he advances into his seventh decade, more aware of the fact that, in the end, we are all visitors here? Is it the annual reminders of America's blind spots, as our country wages war in one or two countries at a time, moving the dollar cost of war "off budget" and the human cost of war out of sight? How long does it take for us to wake up to the significance of our choices and the meaning of our deeds?

Ours is not the only country to face a lag factor of several decades, a long sleep, indeed. These questions prompted me to revisit the French people's moments of reckoning with Vichy, and the evidence of broad collaboration with their Nazi occupiers. Marcel Ophuls' 1969 film, *Sorrow and the Pity,* was made and released 23 years from the end of World War II. In reading reviews whose authors range in their opinions of Ophuls' 270 minute documentary, they agree that the film ended an extended period of silence about collaboration during the reign of the Vichy government. The film's interviews centered on the citizens of the small French city of Clermont-Ferrand, only 20 miles from Vichy. There, Ophuls' team interviews subjects on all three sides: Nazi sympathizers, members of the Resistance and those who simply went along with the new Vichy government (what we now call "collaborated"). This third group was by far the largest numerically of the three, and the film probes more fully the motivation of these passive collaborators.

Although the film was commissioned by French national television, on seeing the work in progress, they refused to complete their funding of it. So it was only with the support of English and German and Dutch television that the film was completed. The film was shown widely in these countries, but not screened on French television. It did enjoy a theatrical release in 1971.

The echo of this moment followed 13 years later, when Klaus Barbie was indicted for crimes against humanity. A jury found him guilty in 1987. In 1993, the Vichy official Rene Bousquet was assassinated while awaiting trial for the same crime. In 1994, Paul Trouvier was convicted of crimes against humanity, and in 1998, another infamous Vichy official, Maurice Papon, was tried and convicted of identical charges. Perhaps it is coincidence that it took the French a little more than 23 years to face the mirror to their own history, and another 20 or so before their prosecutors dared bring charges against the guiltiest of the guilty. But that is close to the 40 year interval of time it has taken us in America to face the question of what we have done, what havoc we have wrought, and why.

I would like to believe that Michael Uhl's book is part of a national awakening, an end to a collective amnesia. We are at that 40-year point, after all. While I don't harbor a hope that Samuel Huntington (the academic who designed the strategy of saturation bombing to result in what he called "forced urbanization") will be tried as Klaus Barbie was in France, I do harbor a hope that we will come to see America take a more humble place in this world. Small signs of this possibility are visible, with a younger generation of voters favoring a foreign policy less eager to stray outside our shores.

Michael Uhl's writing and his work have again and again pushed these fundamental questions in front of us to answer. Our collective reply is not yet audible. But I believe we are closer to issuing that reply because writers like Michael Uhl provide us with steady and artful reminders.

Steve Rees was a photographer and activist in the civil rights, student and antiwar movements from 1964 to 1980. His experience and training in the underground press has led to a long career in publishing. He lives in San Francisco, and his photographs can be seen at www.sixties-photos.com.

Preface

The body of work assembled in this collection falls largely within the tradition of how wars are remembered, and written of, by their surviving veterans. The war I survived was Vietnam, and my writing about it, excepting a few poems, has been confined to the staples of non-fiction, which is to say, memoir, reporting, criticism, commentary, and the like.

To lead off I've placed several articles that are personal favorites. There's an investigative piece about the extraordinarily high numbers of Vietnamese soldiers and civilians missing in action after the American military withdrew its forces in 1973, and which I only became aware of in 1994 on my first return to Vietnam since serving there almost three decades earlier. Next is an essay that telescopes ahead to our succeeding generational war in Iraq where I compare how allegations of torture by Americans during Vietnam are compared with similar revelations at Abu Ghraib.

The two pieces which follow honor fellow Vietnam war veterans by reflecting on, first, the mythic appeal of the Vietnam Veteran Memorial in Washington, D.C.—the Wall—the sacred shrine that unites all surviving veterans of that war, however they have come to think of it in their postwar lives, and second, my take on a persistent urban legend known as "the spat-upon vet."

The final selection in these featured articles narrates an adventure into the world of art and politics, and one of the more madcap episodes of a New York–based non-profit I co-founded called the Safe Return Amnesty Committee [in Support of Self-Retired Veterans].

Only occasionally have I been summoned by the Muse to express myself poetically, yet it was a poem written while on patrol through the rice paddies of Vietnam's Quang Ngai Province, and reprinted here, that became my first published work. But even for the occasional poet, the poems add up with the years, and from my stash, some published, some not, I've included a very small sampling here.

Taken individually, works in the genre of criticism by far dominate this volume. The *New York Times* book critic, John Simon, who was also my editor on one occasion at *The Nation,* told me that every book review is a signed editorial. If, therefore, the critic must be a writer of strong and pointed opinions, I am guilty as charged. There is, moreover, a deeper justification than opinion-mongering behind my attraction to this medium. It's no accident that every one of these reviews was written after my years of full time antiwar activism which extended throughout the '70s and into the early '80s. By that time, the Vietnam War, at least chronologically, was well behind us; but the battle over how that conflict would be recorded by history was just beginning. An engagement with this mission would preoccupy much of the politicized writing I produced over the ensuing decades.

Heading the list is a review I can take only partial credit for, co-authored with the writer and biographer Carol Brightman. Together we took under examination the memoir, *In Retrospect*, by former Secretary of Defense, and prime architect of American Vietnam policy, Robert Strange McNamara. Of all the war's managers no one was more aptly named. At the end of his career in public service, leaving the World Bank and still at the pinnacle of the global power structure, McNamara chose to break his long silence about Vietnam to explain why his war was a "terrible mistake," and yet he proved incapable of expressing the slightest remorse for his own role in its savage consequences.

The articles which follow, numbering some twenty-odd pieces, are ordered in reverse chronology, the last, and oldest, dating from 1986, when I took James Fallows to task for his romance with the projection of American force, as if the only lesson to be drawn from the Vietnam debacle demanded that a retread of counterinsurgency doctrine replace the discredited battlefield of overwhelming fire power.

I have thereafter welcomed every opportunity to make a record of my own views on the Vietnam experience, and with particular relish where they have differed from the views of other public commentators. Around fine points of analysis, my left political bent notwithstanding, I have been no less sparing of fellow progressives, who promote one-sided critiques of American evil, than of rightwing apologists, who preach on behalf of nationalist doctrines of American economic hegemony and military domination.

When the former war correspondent, Chris Hedges, reinvented himself as an evangelist of antiwar opposition in the Iraq/Afghanistan era, I was quick to point out that his apocalyptic prescription for resistance in the face of genuine threats to American civil liberties in the era of mass terrorism was not only misguided but essentially hysterical. And, in responding to Jonathan Schell's historically deflated and wide-eyed endorsement of Nick Turse's claim to having unearthed in a musty archive the true scale of American atrocities against the people of Vietnam, I reminded Schell, himself the author of some of that war's most insightful reporting, what he had apparently forgotten. That story, about the ubiquity of U.S. war crimes in Vietnam, far from being untold, had been paraded before the American media years before by veterans like myself. To substantiate that claim, I have included a long list of newspaper citations which reported nationwide on the war crimes testimony made public by these veterans.

I then scored Turse for not only having appropriated that historical episode as his own discovery, but for inexcusably minimizing the impact of the most effective popular resistance to an unpopular war that the world has ever seen. And, as I demonstrate in "The Problematic," it was precisely the disappearance from public memory, mass culture, and high school text books of that unique generational event—the unprecedented resistance and opposition to the Vietnam War—which confronts an incredulous anti-Iraq war activist when she learns what has been erased from the past.

Much of this critical writing traces the careers of returning veterans, some with high profiles in national public life, like John Kerry and Bob Kerrey, others, known and less-known, who have recorded their war and readjustment stories in memoirs, novels and poetry; and also in tales of return to the places in Vietnam where they had once been soldiers.

There are several reviews as well of historical works whose authors— both pro and antiwar—accuse those in high places, whether Washington or Hanoi, of selling out their cause. I call particular attention to "The God that Resigned," my review of a seminal work by the historian Gabriel Kolko. And in my notes on a memoir by David Harris, probably the best known draft refuser of his day, I highlight his central point about Vietnam that echoed my own as an intelligence officer exposed to prisoner interrogations, and which drove my antiwar activism above all else: "I believed that Nazis tortured, not Americans."

Perhaps the most controversial of these pieces of criticism, "That's Vietnam Jake"—at least within the small community of antiwar veterans— was my scathing review in *The Nation* of a book purporting to be a history of the Vietnam veterans' movement. Angry letters were traded back and forth between the outraged author and the uncharitable reviewer; they can be easily found in that magazine's digital archive.

My observations of the war's legacy on the outer events of its veterans' lives is balanced to some small degree by a series of three personal essays on the combat-variation of an ailment that only in recent years has become widely known through its acronym, PTSD—post-traumatic stress disorder. For one who suffers that disability, these articles were difficult to write, and remain at least as difficult for me to re-read. Yet, however far they fail to reach and reveal the elusive genie that drives this illness, I nonetheless believe their inclusion might be of interest to a given reader.

I have written my share of polemic over an activist lifetime in a voice with no claim to impartiality. And since that exercise has occupied me so frequently, I could not fail to include a sampling of how an impulse to right or publicize an injustice often sped me to my keyboard. The bulk of this writing presented here has been of more recent vintage, and focused on either the revival of the veterans' peace movement since the American invasion of Iraq in 2003, or in looking back at unfinished business still of relevance to the Vietnam War.

"The Chosen," an essay of middling length, rambles over my reflections on what it means to be a veteran of military service in the United States, and into a cross-cultural comparison on the social construction of the veteran identity in several Western countries; and from there onto the evolution of a social policy in a unique American context of disability entitlements that combines a nation's genuine gratitude for sacrifice with the pragmatism of political patronage.

Long before I took up the trade of freelancing for a paycheck, I had been honing my craft in the non-profit environment, first with the Safe Return Amnesty Committee, and later, Citizen Soldier, when in both environments every work I published was co-authored with my comrade, Tod Ensign. The small sample of our joint output included here documents, with a series of articles, the rise and fall of our campaign to unionize the U.S. armed forces in the late 1970s. This is followed by two chapters from our book, *GI Guinea Pigs: How the Pentagon Exposed Our Troops to Dangers More Deadly than War* (Playboy) on how we helped lay the groundwork of a successful effort to win recognition for veterans with health problems caused by exposure in Vietnam to deadly herbicides like Agent Orange. A brief introduction to the material collected under the heading "With Tod Ensign" provides additional information on our collaboration.

I have placed the final entry for this volume in an Appendix. It is a transcript from the Congressional Record of testimony I gave under oath before a committee of the House of Representatives that had undertaken an investigation of the Phoenix Program, an intelligence-driven assassination program sponsored by the CIA that ran amok in Vietnam. I provide an account from the vantage point of a counterintelligence officer operating in the field of why that was the case.

In revisiting each of the works for this collection—the majority of them chosen for their relevance to my experiences with Vietnam or as an activist antiwar veteran—I have become aware that, in many cases, I might yet improve them, not just the content, but the style. Such is a writer's vanity. But these are the works I actually produced in real time, often constrained by word counts and deadlines, and always within the boundaries of my own limitations and strengths, while being buffeted by the garden variety of life's pressures we all feel, if we are fortunate enough to not suffer worse. I have been fortunate.

It's not enough to claim that these works are the products of a sincere mind, and my views honestly stated. Clearly where politics is concerned, I cannot hope to find a single person with whom I am in perfect agreement. Indeed, quite the opposite is true, for it is in the nature of opinions that everybody has one; and it is in the nature of opinions that they are meant to differ. The only claim I can make is that the views I have put forth in these works are entirely, authentically mine. If they provoke thought in whoever reads them, I will be profoundly satisfied.

Featured Articles

Searching for Vietnam's M.I.A.s

*Brother, nothing belongs to you
not one blade of grass.
This hill covers much land,
but you don't even have a grave*[1]

As happy as I was to leave Vietnam twenty-five years ago, even by stretcher, I was just as glad to go back this past July with my family for a month to gather materials for a book. My exposure to Vietnam under wartime conditions had been intense but necessarily narrow, so I looked forward to broadening my firsthand knowledge of the country and its people under these more relaxed circumstances. Four of us would be traveling to many places whose names were intimately familiar to me, but where a young American lieutenant assigned to a combat brigade in central Quang Ngai Province had little reason, and less opportunity, to visit in 1968 and 1969: Hue, Nha Trang, Saigon (Ho Chi Minh City) ... much less Hanoi. The very citadel of the former "enemy," where we were to make our first stop.

A monsoon was sweeping the region, and a day after our arrival, the heavy rains trapped us for an entire morning in Hanoi's Army Museum. As I stood for some time before a diorama of the battle of Dien Bien Phu, pondering the military stupidity of the French, my partner, Carol Brightman, who'd been exploring elsewhere, reappeared. She'd just seen an American military man in a small room, way off in some corner; he had something to do with M.I.A.s. In a brief conversation, Carol had asked him why he thought Americans were so hung up about the P.O.W/M.I.A. issue, to which he unexpectedly responded, "Because we lost. We're sore losers."

Being of a similar mind, I immediately went off to meet this uniformed heretic, and found a trim muscular Air Force master sergeant sitting behind a large table, bent over a laptop computer. The room was filled with shelves of bound documents, and served, he said, as the Hanoi-based archive of the Joint Task Force—Full Accounting—the official name of the U.S. sponsored venture involving Vietnam, Laos, Cambodia and China in the search for the remains of American M.I.A.s.

We made small talk for a few minutes, which led nowhere; the man, having said his piece, perhaps to his regret, seemed tense, evasive. So I backed off, but just as I was about to leave, my eyes came to rest on a chart near the door. Columns of numbers listed Vietnam's victims from the "American War," nearly 1 million military fatalities, and below that, two figures totaling the 282,405 Vietnamese who are recorded as missing in action. That's more than a hundred times the number of American M.I.A.s. I didn't need to be reminded of the enormous suffering we had inflicted on the Vietnamese and their land, but I hadn't a clue there were so many Vietnamese M.I.A.s: like most Americans, I had never thought to ask.

Over the next month, however, I never stopped asking. For two weeks in and around Hanoi, we enjoyed a series of productive meetings with Vietnamese officials, learning a good deal in the process about the "new" Vietnam. But whenever I tried to dig into the question of the Vietnamese M.I.A.s, I would hit ledge; time and again officials would sidestep my question and drift into ceremonial never-never land. In the most irritating instances, the spokesperson would actually shift the focus of my question 180 degrees and start talking about Vietnam's policy toward American M.I.A.s: how the country was bending over backward to help provide *us* with a "full accounting': and how the Vietnamese people felt great sympathy for the American families. I frankly didn't give a hoot about the American M.I.A. issue, at least not in that mawkish, sentimental way. And I resented being dealt with as if I were some boneheaded Rotarian from Podunk who could see only the American side of things.

I am not insensitive to the pain American and Vietnamese families have suffered in not being able to recover the remains of their combat dead, or worse, not knowing where and how their husbands, wives, sons, daughters or siblings came to their end. But my sudden interest in Vietnamese M.I.A.s was political, I began to see the scale of Vietnam's M.I.A problem as something of a reality check for the folks back home, an antidote to the cynical way the American M.I.A. issue has been manipulated to overshadow the plight or the thousands of surviving Vietnam War veterans whose lives have been ruined by the war. Furthermore, every administration since Richard Nixon's has wielded the P.O.W/M.I.A. issue as a crude ideological weapon to perpetuate hostile public opinion toward the Vietnamese and deny them the multibillion-dollar reparations we agreed to after the Paris Peace Accord of 1973 (see H. Bruce Franklin, "M.I.A.sma," May 10, 1993).

But the message behind my interest wasn't getting through to the Vietnamese, and their message, whatever it was, wasn't getting through to me. My persistent inquiries were beginning to cause consternation among my hosts, and embarrassment to my companions, who thought I was being impolitic, if not boorish. The resistance was cultural, I was cautioned.

Still I plodded on because no one we met with, least of all our sponsors at the Vietnam/United Stares Association (founded in 1947 by Ho Chi Minh to express solidarity with the American people), would come right out and say that there could be no discussion about Vietnamese M.I.A.s. Instead, I was just patronized, promised a briefing, told that documents would be provided before I left for home and that, indeed, a meeting with an "M.I.A. family" had been added to our itinerary.

That "M.I.A. family" turned out to be a sympathetic old man who had come north with the Vietminh in 1954, and whose wife at the time had remained in the south with their five small children, four of whom were subsequently killed during the war but were not among the missing, and none of whom, including the former wife and the surviving daughter, the man had set eyes upon since his departure with the rebel forces forty years before.

Before leaving Hanoi, I hit on another tactic to get answers to my questions. By asking officials directly about their personal lives, whether they had anyone in their own families who was still among the missing, I began to piece together a rough account of how deeply the M.I.A. issue has rent Vietnamese society over the past two decades.

A Vice Minister for Labor, Invalids and Social Affairs, an honored war heroine and former leader of a female militia that had shot down many American planes over the strategic Ham Rong Bridge south of Hanoi, presided over a disappointingly didactic presentation of her ministry's responsibilities for the social welfare of those who had been impoverished or otherwise disadvantaged by the war. But when I posed my M.I.A. question, her tone softened briefly as she told us that her own brother was among the missing, and that she still had no solid leads as to the whereabouts or his grave.

Later that night, at a farewell dinner given us by our hosts, a senior staff member of the Central Committee of the Communist Party who had dazzled us earlier in the day with a briefing on the future of socialism in Vietnam, momentarily chilled the convivial table talk when I asked if there was anyone in his family among the missing. "My father-in-law," he said, his expression shading hard as he added, almost *sotto voce*, "I will put the war aside, but I will not forget."

The next morning, just hours before we left the city, I rushed over to the offices of *Vietnam News*, a lively English language daily published by the government, hoping that someone there could help me sort out why it was that my inquiries about Vietnamese M.I.A.s were causing so many bad vibrations. Luckily, I ran into an Australian journalist named Terry Hartney, who'd just come by to peck out his weekly column for the paper on an old Remington manual.

A large, gentle man, Terry thought there could be something to the idea that I was running up against a cultural taboo, "an, 'it's our sorrow, not yours,' kind of thing." Two of the seven employees in his own office at the Vietnam Overseas News Agency had M.I.A. family members, and it had taken Terry months to learn their stories "on the run, a few bits and pieces at a time." Whenever he brought up the topic of American M.I.A.s, the Vietnamese would nod and say, "with a subtle underscore in their tone of voice, 'We know what they're talking about.'"

There was nothing understated, however, about the active presence their missing relatives continue to play in their own lives. These same two Vietnamese colleagues, Terry said, were constantly going off, following leads from various sources, both private and government," to track down battlefield graves so the remains of whomever they were searching for might be re-interred in family plots among their ancestors.

According to Terry, most Vietnamese are "fatalistic" about the chances of ever finding their missing relations; and well they might be, because, as I have since learned, many of the mass graves where Americans and their allies buried enemy dead were bulldozed or carpet-bombed into oblivion. And yet, he continued, "people clutch at any straw," even bringing piles of dirt to fortunetellers who claim the power to communicate with a spirit whose corporeal traces might be mingled therein. And every day, Vietnamese newspapers carry ads with photos of missing soldiers, seeking information on their fates and resting places from former comrades, while periodic news accounts report the unearthing of human remains at some site, near or remote, throughout the country.

That afternoon, we left Hanoi and traveled south for the next three weeks, from Hue to Ho Chi Minh City. I continued to bring up the question of Vietnamese M.I.A.s in all official and casual encounters, adding new accounts of those touched by the M.I.A. tragedy with every stop. It was. ironically in the little coastal town of Duc Pho, the district capital where my own brigade had been based during the war, that we received the most detailed briefing about how the national effort to account for the missing is being carried on at the grass-roots level throughout Vietnam.

Apparently, each province had been ordered or encouraged by the Prime Minister's office in Hanoi to conduct, on a district by district level, surveys of the nation's war victims in various categories, including M.I.A.s. Due Pho was the only district among the half-dozen or so where we had made official stops where such a survey had actually been carried out, resulting in a preliminary count of 125 M.I.A.s out of a wartime population of roughly 68,000 people. It was a lack of resources, not interest, we were told over and over, and that prevented other locales from implementing this directive.

Mid-August arrived, and it was time for us to leave for home. Yet I was still no closer to understanding why those we consulted among the higher echelons of Vietnams leadership, in what was otherwise an atmosphere of openness, candor, even warmth, had been so reluctant to discuss this issue. Only since our return have I slowly begun to disentangle the complexities behind the politics of silence surrounding the "other" M.I.A.s.

The picture emerging from my research and interviews suggests that the M.I.A, issue in Vietnam—the political question, as opposed to the widespread grass-roots activities carried on more or less spontaneously by the population since the end of the war—has evolved along two separate tracks that have intersected, perhaps with something of a shock, only very recently.

One path can be traced to negotiating sessions beginning in the mid-1980s, when U.S. delegations in Hanoi were trying to gain permission for American experts to lead the search within Vietnam for American M.I.A. remains. In those negotiations, the Vietnamese leadership did indeed, and continuously, call their former adversary's attention to the gravity and scope of their own M.I.A. problem. If we help you, the Vietnamese seemed to be saying, what will you do for us?

But by the time the first recovery operation at a B-52 crash site was actually conducted in November 1985. Hanoi seemed to have fully grasped that the P.O.W./M.I.A. issue was a millstone Washington had hung around its own neck; if it were to be removed so that relations between the two countries could be normalized, Vietnam would have to seize the initiative. Thus, by recognizing that they faced a conundrum peculiar to the inscrutable side of domestic U.S. politics, one therefore immune to any genuinely reciprocal negotiations, the leadership in Hanoi came to distinguish between the M.I.A. issue's deeply emotional impact on the American public and the manner in which it had long been manipulated by successive U.S. administrations to punish Vietnam for America's humiliating setback in Indochina. On this basis, Vietnam ultimately agreed to the creation of a joint task force as a purely "humanitarian" gesture. In Hanoi it was understood, of course, that Washington needed to save face.

By 1991, according to Lewis Stern, a U.S. government specialist on Southeast Asia who spoke on the subject of Vietnamese M.I.A.s before a U.S.–Vietnam trade group at Georgetown University this past July, there were signs that the problem of Vietnamese M.I.A.s was being raised in Vietnam, not only by Hanoi as a "negotiating ploy" to gain diplomatic leverage in talks with America but more urgently among "veterans and party organizations within the military in commenting on the draft platform for the [7th] National Party Congress," which took place in June of that same year.

In other words, just as agreement was being reached to open a U.S. P.O.W./M.I.A. office in Hanoi by July 1991, concern, and perhaps even resentment, was mounting among lower level cadres that their party and government were not doing everything they should to account for Vietnam's own M.I.A.s. In cooperating so closely with the very high-profile, spare-no-expense American recovery teams operating throughout Vietnam—like the most recent episode this September, in which eighty-eight American P.O.W./M.I.A. experts were searching for the remains of eighteen U.S. M.I.A.s at thirteen sites spread over six Vietnamese provinces—Vietnam's government has unwittingly raised the expectations of its own population that an intensive, multimillion-dollar, high-tech campaign to recover remains of their own M.I.A.s would not be an unreasonable undertaking.

Or, as Terry Hartney told me in Hanoi, the pressure for a "full accounting" was being expressed even more broadly through "a new public recognition in Vietnam since the lifting of the American economic embargo last February that resources being used to search for and recover the remains of American M.I.A.s will now be used to help find Vietnamese M.I.A.s as well."

When I ran this assumption by a U.S. military spokesman at Joint Task Force—Full Accounting headquarters in Hawaii, it was strenuously denied. That officer, at least, was quite anxious to dispel any impression "that our efforts aren't directed 100 percent toward the recovery of US M.I.A.s." Despite this disclaimer, it is no secret at the Pentagon that considerable cooperation occurs informally in the field, especially in cases where information, or recovered remains, might help the Vietnamese identify their own missing.

Such actions seem to reflect a growing sensitivity to Hanoi's dilemma among those American institutions most concerned with the M.I.A. issue, the Pentagon and at least one American veteran's organization, that the need for "face-saving" has shifted to the other side. This awareness has been expressed in the last year by two important initiatives.

In 1993, a decision was made by a U.S. interagency group to turn over to Hanoi a full set of the "captured document series," some eighteen miles of unindexed microfilm containing letters, diaries and official papers taken from Vietcong and North Vietnamese soldiers on the battlefield, whether dead or alive. (Apparently, the Reagan Administration had offered Hanoi copies of these same documents in the early eighties, but they were refused by the Vietnamese, who, I was told by a well-informed Vietnam-watcher, were embarrassed because they lacked the resources to process the materials and pass on relevant information to next of kin.)

A second significant action was the campaign inaugurated in 1993 by the Washington-based Vietnam Veterans of America. V.V.A. has requested that its membership relinquish all battlefield souvenirs and memorabilia that might aid the Vietnamese in identifying their M.I.A.s. To date, V.V.A. has sent two delegations to Hanoi with a variety of documents and artifacts, identification papers, weapon serial numbers, and maps of enemy burial sites recalled from memory, all of which may help Vietnam recover the remains of as many as 3,300 missing soldiers.

Considering the enormity of the problem, however, such gestures are largely symbolic. Even to approximate a viable solution, the United States must finally pay Vietnam the long overdue reparations we promised in 1973. (Call it "foreign aid" if we can't stomach the truth; but first we must establish full diplomatic relations with Hanoi, since such aid is currently prohibited by U.S. law.) Then cash-strapped Vietnam might be able to distribute a modicum of meaningful relief, not only to its M.I.A. families, but to the millions of other victims who continue to suffer from the war of aggression our official scribes so glibly diminish and dismiss as a "mistake."

The Nation, **November 14, 1994**

Notes

1. From "In Pham Thiet," a poem by Huu Thinh. Translated by Nguyen Ba Chung and George Evans. *Compost* #4, 1994, an independent journal published in Brookline, Massachusetts.

Vietnam's Shadow Over Abu Ghraib

What Did Sy Hersh Know ... and When Did He Know It?

In reading the Abu Ghraib articles Seymour Hersh wrote for the *New Yorker* in May 2004, what struck me about the revelations of abuse and torture was the similarity in detail to what I experienced in Vietnam 35 years ago. The one major difference has been the media's willingness to embrace in 2004 a story that they shunned in 1970, when returning veterans attempted to inform the American public of widespread atrocities, including the routine killing and torture of prisoners, committed by American forces in Southeast Asia.

Only certain episodes of the widespread Vietnam veteran war protests throughout 1970 and into 1971 are well-known, like the April 1971 veterans' encampment in Washington. Scores of former combatants—with John Kerry in a visible position of leadership—threw their service ribbons and medals of valor over a barrier in the direction of the Capitol steps. But one has to dig far deeper to recover and stitch into a coherent narrative an account of the precise issue—U.S. war crimes in Indochina—that motivated much of Vietnam veteran antiwar activism in those times. With the exception of the My Lai massacre—made public in the U.S. under Seymour Hersh's byline more than a year and a half (November 1969) after it had occurred (March 1968)—Vietnam war crimes, which often included torture, never attained the level of media validation and public recognition afforded to the events at Abu Ghraib.

I've often wondered why Hersh never demonstrated more interest during Vietnam in the larger war crimes issue, of which My Lai was only the most dramatic component. Perhaps unfairly, I've concluded that, for the investigative reporter, the scoop is at least as important as the story. Had Hersh investigated the "systematic" nature of American war crimes during the Vietnam War as thoroughly as he is investigating the "systemic" presence of torture during interrogations in Iraq and Afghanistan, he might have instructed his readers and his colleagues that the murder, torture and abuse of prisoners is military business as usual.

Some of the parallels between what I witnessed in Vietnam as leader of a small military intelligence team, and the details reported by Hersh about Abu Ghraib, reflect, in my view, disturbing patterns of American military practice over decades that the American public would prefer not to know about. As one of Hersh's informants puts it, "The process is unpleasant. It's like making sausage. You like the results, but you don't want to know how it's made." The more serious of these wartime parallels have grievous consequences for both victims (typically civilian non-combatants) and perpetrators, who in time reenter the U.S. population as damaged veterans.

But even some of Abu Ghraib's more ordinary occurrences are reported by Hersh as if they were without precedent. In two of his three New Yorker articles, for example, Hersh, adds a shade of cloak and dagger intrigue describing military intelligence (MI) personnel at Abu Ghraib who appeared in "sterile" uniforms, unmarked by rank, or, when entitled to not wear military uniforms, were dressed in mufti. Some interrogators, he writes, used "aliases."

My first assignment in 1967, fresh from Army counterintelligence school (preceded by Infantry Officer School), was as titular head of a Corps level counterintelligence (CI) office at Fort Hood, Texas. Provided a snub-nosed .38 and a set of "box tops" (badge and credentials), I was styled a Special Agent and wore civilian clothes on duty. Even my small motorcycle with its green civilian sticker was "undercover."

The man who met me at the airstrip when I arrived at the 11th Infantry Brigade in Duc Pho, South Vietnam, to become officer-in-charge of the 1st Military Intelligence Team (1st MIT) wore unmarked jungle fatigues. He had a "U.S." pinned where the insignia of rank normally appeared, as did all members of counterintelligence on the MI team, including me. Months later in Quang Ngai City, I ran into a fellow Georgetown undergrad, also with Army military intelligence, dressed in khakis and a bright button-down broad cloth shirt—my uniform in college, and his still in Vietnam. Like the OSS operatives who preceded us in World War II, certain special agents routinely posed as civilians in designated contexts, and some had occasion to operate under noms de guerre. This practice was SOP, standard operating procedure. It was not something exotic or irregular.

The 11th became infamous as the Calley brigade, a reference to Lt. William L. Calley, the platoon leader who led the mayhem at My Lai and was later convicted by court-martial of murder. The My Lai massacre took place eight months before I arrived at the 11th in November '68. It was my good fortune to never witness anything to compare with such a horror, though just over one year later as a veteran activist in the antiwar movement I would have a hand in exposing massacres that other Vietnam veterans had seen or participated in. What I witnessed personally were many acts of abuse and torture while on patrol, or within our own team's IPW (Interrogation Prisoner of War) section located on the brigade base camp; and once, following the bizarre hunt for Viet Cong cadres operating in a nearby hamlet, I stood alone in preventing the murder of a prisoner captured in the field.

One obvious parallel between Iraq and Vietnam that is a clear violation of the conventions of war is the treatment of civilian populations. In both wars, civilians have been subjected to omnibus rounds-ups, arbitrary incarceration under brutal conditions, severe deprivations and acts of physical abuse, and, in some cases, interrogation under torture. In his New Yorker article of May 10, Hersh writes that a "lack of proper screening also meant that many innocent Iraqis were wrongly being detained—indefinitely ... in some cases ... [with] more than sixty percent ... deemed not to be a threat to society." The modus operandi of rounding-up resistance suspects and confining them, no doubt differs widely in Iraq from what occurred in Vietnam. But the net effect on that majority of innocent civilians is the same, and it is this practice of unjustified population removal followed by brutal incarceration that very likely constitutes a war crime.

The 1st MIT interrogation section in Vietnam was often swamped with Vietnamese rural villagers who were dragnetted by infantry units on their sweeps of the countryside and delivered to the brigade base camp as "VC suspects." Once in our custody, there was enormous pressure from the intelligence command to classify detainees as "civil defendants (CDs)," adjudged by American interrogators, despite our obvious lack of competency, to have broken the laws of South Vietnam. As a CD, the "suspect," without the slightest evidence of being either a VC cadre or a criminal, might then be turned over to the local South Vietnamese police, whose methods of persuasion were even less gentle than ours.

The most prized classification aspired to by the IPW section was that of PW, prisoner of war, but this required that the detainee be captured with a weapon, an infrequent occurrence. The category CD, therefore, became a functional substitute for the more valued PW designation, in that the number of CDs also counted toward the MI teams' performance and productivity in the manner of a "body count." And, whereas in Iraq, males who are indeed apparently of fighting age formed a large percentage of the Abu Ghraib detainee population, the demographics in Vietnam differed greatly.

There we were dealing primarily with women of child-bearing age, seniors, and late teens. It was assumed that all the draft age male inhabitants of a given locale were already fighting on one side or the other, or were off somewhere hiding whenever American forces were operating in their area. Ironically, it was only these latter military-aged males whom the South Vietnamese government considered "draft dodgers." They were most likely local force guerrillas living outside the Saigon government's control whom the IPW interrogators might have legitimately designated "CDs" on strictly legal grounds. And they were the one group we rarely saw.

Hersh might have drawn other instructive comparisons between Iraq and Vietnam. One is the defensive manner in which the sitting administration in Washington responded to the battlefront atrocity. George W. Bush, when finally forced to respond to a scandal that persisted in headlines around the world, said, according to Hersh, that "the action of a few did not reflect on the conduct of the military as a whole." The media, for the most part, seemed to reject this wan excuse, and news accounts began referring to the ever-widening exposure of abuse at Abu Ghraib and elsewhere as "systemic." At the same time, such expressions of skepticism have by no means translated into any deeper criticism of the Iraq war within the media mainstream. For his part, Richard Nixon, following the revelation of My Lai back in 1969, called the perpetrators "a few bad apples," and the massacre itself was termed an "aberration." Antiwar veterans had a different spin: My Lai was just the tip of the iceberg, we claimed, and the torture of prisoners, "systematic." When it came to Vietnam, it was Nixon's message, not the veterans' that history recorded.

Hersh writes with justifiable outrage in his May 10 article that the "wrongdoing" at Abu Ghraib reflects a "failure of Army leadership at the highest levels." At the same time, one of his anonymous sources reminds the reporter that, far from distributing real responsibility up the chain of command, the "army is attempting to have these six soldiers [American MP guards at Abu Ghraib prison] atone for its sins." And in his piece of May 24, Hersh quotes another unnamed "insider" that the operatives from elite intelligence units are "vaccinated," and that "the only people left to prosecute are those who are undefended, the poor kids at the end of the food chain." Affixing primary responsibility for atrocities that are hardwired into modern wars of "counterinsurgency" onto the lowest-ranking soldiers, those tasked with carrying out the dirty work, while limiting the culpability of the command, is yet another echo from the My Lai massacre that resonates with Abu Ghraib.

Thirty-five years ago, antiwar Vietnam vets demanded that the Pentagon not scapegoat a few low-ranking GIs for atrocities that could be traced to the nature of an aggressive war conducted against an entire people, designed and carried out at the highest levels of the American government and its military establishment. A similar view was expressed by then Senator George McGovern when commenting on the conviction of Lt. Calley in March 1971: "I think it's a mistake to make one man the scapegoat for a mistake in national policy. It's policy that's wrong." To which antiwar vets amended, "GIs in the field do not make policy." As for "command responsibility, " then as now, a few senior officers in direct positions of command had their wrists slapped, ending or sidetracking their military careers (with full pensions), but without the stigma of conviction and prison time that their enlisted subordinates will carry for life.

Not surprisingly, the former spooks and military professionals in Hersh's pieces attempt to obscure the trail of amoral practices institutionalized in the intelligence community from the Cold War to the present. We read that, at Abu Ghraib, "fundamentally good soldiers—military intelligence guys—[were] told that no rules apply," because "since 9/11, we've [the government apparatus responsible for intelligence oversight] changed the rules ... and created conditions where the ends justify the means." And so, instead of seeing Vietnam's shadow over Iraq, readers may conclude that torture and abuse in Iraq are unique in the recent annals of American warfare, or, as Nixon said when speaking of My Lai, "an aberration."

Of course, Seymour Hersh's disinterest in drawing comparisons between Iraq and Vietnam may be perfectly valid. He may see historical analogies as an unnecessary distraction from the urgency and gravity of the subject at hand; why muddy the waters? The reason history matters here, however, is because the valuable lessons of Vietnam, which have deterred the U.S. from the unilateral application of major force over the past three decades to achieve its hegemonic foreign policy objectives, have been severely undermined by Iraq. It now appears that Bush II may have succeeded in finally putting the country's "Vietnam Syndrome," so intolerable to the war party, behind us.

Antiwar.com, July 31, 2004

The Wall: Entering the Aura of the Dead

I knew two of the men whose names are engraved on the Vietnam Veteran Memorial. The first, Artie Klippen, I saw a lot of that season in '63 when we both played Lacrosse at Georgetown. We had one of those anarchic undergraduate arrangements where we briefly shared a car, a beat-up old Chevy with the gear shift on the steering column. Compared to so many guys at that age who are callow and two-faced, Artie was a straight-up, warm and friendly guy, qualities that make him continue to stand out in my memory, even though we never got to know each other well. After that year, I seldom saw Artie again. I had been in Brazil all of '64, but came back with too few credits to graduate with my class in '65, the year Artie did. Having completed ROTC, Artie got his lieutenant's butter bar along with his sheepskin. I was still at Georgetown, having stuck around an extra year in ROTC myself to avoid the draft, when I heard Artie had bought it in Nam while leading a convoy unit.

I read somewhere that the odds of getting killed in Nam were a thousand to one. On average. The life expectancy for an LT in a vulnerable job like Artie's was averaged against that of a chaplain's assistant in the rear, a two-star general well behind the wire in his air conditioned trailer, a spoon in the mess hall who hugged an M-16 at night in a bunker to guard the perimeter, or a spook like me patrolling in harm's way by day, but generally secure overnight in a base camp. So Artie already faced poorer odds compared to most of us. But a soldier's superstition held that, no matter where you found yourself in Nam, if there was a bullet in Hanoi with your name on it, you weren't coming home. We called that blind luck, and Artie didn't have it.

I don't recall how Artie died exactly. It might have been a bullet; more likely a booby trap. In Vietnam, where you stepped, or drove, and where you didn't, made all the difference. But given the routinely barbarous acts American GIs perpetrated on innocent Vietnamese civilians, I feel confident that Artie made his unit play by the rules of engagement to whatever degree that was even possible in a peoples' war. He would not have been gung ho or reckless. Artie would have put a premium on the welfare of his men, even as he had the moxie to lead them in a deadly encounter. And if I were to learn Artie died bravely to ensure someone else might live, that would be consistent with the character of the man I knew. Even in an evil war like Vietnam, I want to believe a man like Artie Klippen could be a hero.

The other young man I knew whose name is on the Wall, wasn't even close to being a hero. But he was a tragic loss, and just as chosen by misfortune as anyone else whose name is inscribed there. I believe that Stanley Reed was not yet twenty when he died, right in line with the nineteen year, ten month average age of all American soldiers who served in Vietnam. Stanley was average in other ways too, I guess. An average smart ass, authority-allergic American teenage white boy, likely from a blue collar background in which a college deferment was not an option, and who enlisted for four years to avoid being drafted into the infantry for two. The Army trained Stanley to be an interrogator.

When I took command of the 1st Military Intelligence Team of the 11th Infantry Brigade, Stanley was already there in the interrogation unit. I had been trained as an infantry officer at Ft. Benning, then in a school for spooks in a compound near the Baltimore harbor. In the MI team, I ran the counter-intelligence unit, while interrogation was under the supervision of another lieutenant junior to me. The interrogation center was off site from our compound, so I seldom dealt directly with the interrogators, except after hours when all the team members filled our little club to drink beer over cards or ping pong.

I recall getting a whiff of Stanley's attitude a couple of times when he attempted to bait me in some childish test over authority. It was irritating, and I probably put him in his place. But I didn't spend a lot of time defending my military dignity. I detested the Army. Moreover I did not relish being officer-in-charge of anything, much less a team of fourteen American intelligence agents and as many South Vietnamese Army interpreters. In my mind I wasn't supposed to end up anywhere near the Infantry. It was a fluke. Like Stanley, I had joined something bad to avoid something worse. But here we both were anyway on LZ Bronco with the 11th Infantry.

My section, CI, was out in the bush a lot, working the fringes of the Phoenix Program. But the interrogators had no business going on patrol. Stanley got restless I suppose. Said he didn't want to go home without having some small taste of the field. When the squad came back at dusk, I got the news. They'd made contact. In the fray, Stanley had been wounded, maybe a rocket from one of our own gunships, friendly fire. After a few days a couple of us flew down from Duc Pho to Qui Nhon to visit him at the evacuation hospital. The damage to some internal organs was serious, but he was expected to recover. Stanley was in good spirits, and he and I actually made real contact. I look back on that moment as redemptive. Two weeks later, the land line buzzed in my office tent when my colossal asshole boss up at Division called to tell me Stanley was dead.

That night Charlie pounded us relentlessly with mortars and rockets. The team huddled in the bunker to escape the shrapnel. Otherwise we were well protected from anything but a stray round, since the enemy's main target was the landing strip to our front. The news of Stanley's death had cast a spell of fatalism over all of us. No one felt safe that night. No one talked. No one played cards. Each individual was preoccupied with his private grief, his private thoughts. Who next among us might be disgraced by fortune? If Stanley could buy it, then why not me?

We who served in Vietnam and came home, stand before our Wall as survivors, and we are drawn inescapably into the world of our comrade spirits. Entering the aura of the dead, our faces melt in tears. It is not strange or exceptional to witness two aging men hugging each other, sobbing, shamelessly, inconsolably. They are still grieving the fate of a fallen brother, reliving the horrors of their war, crushed by the heaviness of the wound of survival they will carry to their graves. Me too. I have seldom wept as powerfully, as involuntarily, as profoundly intimately, exposing my most deeply buried existential sadness, as when I have stood before the Wall. In one sense, that's what it means to have beaten the odds.

This letter was part of a 2015 Memorial Day event, Letters in Support of Vietnam Full Disclosure.

CounterPunch, April 17, 2015

The Spat-Upon Vet Revisited

Back in mid–April, the phone rang one evening. You have a call from Bob, the woman's voice said. I was in end-of-day mode, not the best time for a tele-scammer to invade my home life. I hung up, and the phone rang again almost immediately. That dance took two more turns, before I switched to sardonic. Bob's not here, I answered in my most blandly convivial voice, but she insisted. It's a call *from* Bob.

The next call I let the answering machine pick up. The good nurse must have finally figured, "screw the privacy policy," and she gave Bob's last name, and a call back number. Like I said, end of the day, I'm in fade out. Unless you're identifiably one of my closer friends or a family member, and you want the verbal me, you gotta call before six, after which I'm mixing my martini, and starting to prepare for dinner and an evening that does not include talking on the phone.

Anyway, I snapped to. Christ, what a jerk I'm swearing at myself, as I rush to the phone. It's *Bobby*, a dear friend, old comrade from the day, the GI project in Wrightstown outside Fort Dix, and then part of our activist circle on the deserter amnesty issue before he took the union buy-out and fled to the hills of Vermont. Bobby, who took his first plane ride at 19 en route to Vietnam, schlepped an M-60 all over the Delta with the 9th Division. He was third generation printer's union at the *Daily News*, and had barely ever traveled from Brooklyn past Manhattan—maybe a time or two over to Jersey. Bob is one of those rare Brooklyn Yankees' fans, worshiped the Mick, day dreamed about playing center field in the house that Ruth built while gazing out the window in grammar school until Sister Mary Malpractice put a knuckle sandwich upside his head.

Bobby wasn't much of a student. If he survived Nam, there was Charlotte, his HS sweetheart waiting at home in Sheepshead Bay, and the union card as a legacy from his grandfather's own bashed head when the newspaper workers battled the publishers' goons for the right to organize. It was one of those womb-to-tomb life plans, and if that wasn't the American Dream for the average working stiff, nothing was. I don't need to tell you that Nam pretty much put a major crimp in that scenario for my friend Bob. As I dialed the phone, I feared the worse. But the voice was the same old Bob, and it's not that we've ever been out of touch for very long since the early 70s, never more than a couple of months at a time. Sometimes he'd come to Maine, or I'd go see him.

The news was that Bob was in the psych ward at the VA in White River Junction, about an hour and a half from his place in Vermont's so-called Northeast Kingdom. PTSD became a ratable service-connected disability by the VA in the early 80s, and it wouldn't surprise me if Bob had been among the first to get his diagnosis and his hundred percent. He's been through all the substance programs, the in-patient clinics, with their twin accents on group therapy and meds.

Alcohol is how Bob deals with his demons. And dames. Charlotte divorced him, but they remained neighbors and stayed close; when a brain tumor took her, Bobby lost his best friend, the one he could always lean on to regain some semblance of balance after each bounce off the wagon, and each prolonged binge into oblivion that followed. Bob tried and tried to build another relationship. But he smothered women with kindness—No, Michael, really, this is the one, I know it—and in succession, they would flee, breaking his heart and, in some cases ripping him off in the bargain. It was the latest broken heart that sent him back to White River Junction, that and the open casket funeral of a local boy one town over who'd been killed in Afghanistan.

I'd always get on his case about his thing with women. Take it slow, I'd say. Don't try to rescue her and the two kids, or get involved with the scum bag dead beat dad, all in the first month. Or whatever. About the dead kid in the casket, that registered on me. Bobby is a sweetheart and a funny, sensitive guy, a softy. But when he offered that dead boy as causa prima for his latest bout with the deep, deep blues, it caught in my throat too, and I could feel the mist starting to rise. It's that deep, unappeasable thing that makes a Nam vet bawl whenever he goes to the Wall in DC.

Anyway, Bob hadn't tried to hurt himself. I was thankful for that. He was feeling better and was going to check himself out in a day or two against the advice of his keepers, but that was to be expected. None of them can imagine, given their own far less turbulent heads, how any of these toxic grade PTSD guys ever survive from one day to the next. But I knew Bob's resilience, and could hear in his voice that he'd landed on his feet again, and still had some rounds left in him.

A couple of days later Bobby called to tell me he was back home. He became uncharacteristically talkative about his time in Nam. All the years I've known him, he'd never go into detail, not even with me. He didn't have to. I could read between the lines. The 9th Infantry Division was based in the northern Mekong Delta, some forty miles below Saigon. Till the late sixties, American units only operated sporadically there, and the South Vietnamese Army hardly at all. This warren of waterways, rice paddies and canopied woodlands was densely populated and traditionally a stronghold of the Vietnamese resistance, the guerrilla forces of the Viet Cong. I always figured Bob had gotten into some heavy shit, and just couldn't bring himself to talk about it.

Suddenly, I couldn't get him off the phone. He'd started looking through old boxes he'd dragged from the barn to his living room, mostly articles Charlotte had clipped every day while waiting for her soldier to get home, from the *Daily News* and the *Times*, particularly if they mentioned the 9th. Bob was rambling on about some home coming parade involving his unit, and how they'd been attacked by antiwar protesters.

Bob, I interrupted, what the hell are you talking about. That welcome home shit was something Reagan's people manufactured trying to get Americans to stop feeling bad about Vietnam so they could stick it to the rebels in Central America, go from covert to overt, which the public wasn't buying. There were a lot of cry-baby vets, who couldn't get their dad's "good" war out of their imaginations, and who knew goddamned well that Vietnam was no noble cause, the pap Reagan was doling out, but who couldn't make the emotional break because to them, if the war was bad, it meant they were bad too. The hat vet organizations like the Legion and the VFW are filled with vets who think like that—or who don't do a lot of independent thinking about their war experiences, or the world in general, is the way I view it.

No, no, no.... Michael, Bob persisted, we had a parade. I've got it right in front of me. They jeered at us, it says. Again, I jumped his train of thought, onto a digression about how the whole spat-upon vet thing was an urban myth. No documented evidence has been produced, and besides, I said, how did all those GI-hating hippies get on the tarmac of a U.S. air base to sling their spit at guys just getting back to the World? And even when you out-processed, and left the base, it's not like you were in uniform, even if you hadn't been discharged yet. The average GI hated the uniform by then, and couldn't wait to get it off when on his own time. But Bob was still adamant. He just couldn't string it out in a way that made any sense. Finally, I said, make some copies of what you're talking about, and send them to me, okay? And, listen man, those clips sound interesting; they should go to a library.

When the clips came I could see immediately that Bob had sent me something important. It was a copy of a very brief AP story, only three paragraphs, datelined Seattle July 10, 1969, under the heading, "Returning GIs, Hailed, Jeered." The other clips Bob included tell the whole story.

In the '68 presidential run up, Richard Nixon promised, if elected, to begin withdrawal of American troops from active combat in Vietnam, to be replaced by the forces of South Vietnam. This strategy quickly became dubbed in the media as, "changing the color of the corpses," because the American Air War, and presumably the war itself, was on the books to continue indefinitely. Nixon, in fact, would fulfill this promise, and, in doing so, unwittingly set the stage for the victory of the Vietnamese people and the reunification of their country.

To implement Nixon's policy, the Pentagon chose a battalion of the 9th Division to play the public role of being the first homecoming unit, first among 25,000 U.S. troops that would be rotated home over a seven week period. On July 8, 1969, 814 GIs, "draped in leis and grinning broadly," stood at attention for two hours at Tan Son Nhut air base just outside Saigon, participating in a farewell ceremony that saw them harangued by the commander of U.S. forces in Vietnam, General Creighton Abrams, as well as South Vietnam's president, Nguyen Van Thieu, "a late arrival," according to the story in the *Times*.

After the ceremony, the GIs boarded the giant C-141 transports that would, after 18 hours, return them to the World. A few GIs are quoted in clippings from the New York papers. The men are understandably ecstatic, since for many of them it means cutting short, if only by a month in one case, their one year combat tours. Most of them have seen heavy action in the Delta, which is also described in many articles Charlotte had saved for Bob. And I know from my own experiences, some of horrors they'd dealt with, and, one guys says it all, "I'm just lucky to be getting home alive."

When the transports landed at McCord Air Force Base in Tacoma, another dog and pony show awaited the returning heroes, 3000 people, some of them relatives, and a brass band. The men off the first plane got a hand shake from former Vietnam commander, now Army Chief of Staff, General William Westmoreland. The South Vietnamese Ambassador to the U.S. is also there, as are 100 little leaguers in uniform. The battalion is due to be deactivated, and many of the men will be discharged. But not quite yet. Two days later there's an official home coming parade in downtown Seattle. And that's where it happens. The AP story reports "the jeers of anti-war protestors who demanded, 'Bring them all home now.'" So, it appears from the slogan quoted that the protestors weren't "jeering" at the GIs, but at the likes of Secretary of Army Stanley Resor, and the other pro-war officials, who watched them march past from the reviewing stand.

Now, here's the tough part. Bob felt like he was being jeered, and I'll bet that was how most of the other GIs that day felt too. When we talked Bob told me that, not only had his unit been verbally abused by protestors in Seattle, but he'd experienced similar treatment when he went to Fort Hamilton, Brooklyn to report for his induction physical. But Bob, I reminded him, that happened everywhere. The antiwar movement was all over the inductions centers, in the major cities anyway. They were protesting the war and the draft, not the draftees. Besides, I added weakly, you weren't even in the Army yet.

I was missing the point. Most of the protestors had enough middle class privilege to avoid military service. Blue collar guys like Bob didn't get that option; they went to war. The fact that Bob misunderstood the words the protestors were yelling that day in Seattle is disturbing; what's even more disturbing is that he's still misinterpreting them after all these years. Class resentment runs deep and gets tragically misplaced in this society, while divide and rule fuels the myth that vets were spat upon, even when they weren't.

InTheMindField, **May 16, 2011**

Annals of the New Left: Dissing Golub

The following story is intended as a commentary on the political culture of the New Left during the Vietnam War era; it is also intended to amuse.

Tod and I sat in the reception area sipping from containers of takeout coffee and traded last minutes strategies for the meeting with Bernie Mazel, Direct Mail Czar of left-wing causes in the U.S. Bernie wore two other power hats, publisher of Mazel Books, high quality texts for the medical profession and Business Manager of the *New York Review of Books*, of which he was one of several co-founders. Bernie was also a tough, cigar-chomping New York Jew with the gruff manner of the Garment Center, and you'd better have your shit together if you showed the chutzpah to approach him with a deal.

If Bernie wasn't a wide eyed Left romantic, neither were Tod and I. We ran our Safe Return Amnesty Committee like a small business.[1] By the early seventies we'd established the group as a 501 c3 tax exempt foundation—Alternatives to Militarism (ATOM, Inc.)—which opened the way to spread our funding base by getting into the mails at the then preferential rate of 2.4 cents per unit. Bernie had seen one of our early mailings, sent a critical note, but offered to teach us the ropes. We responded that we wanted his help, but that we already had a plan.

When Bernie finally called us in we started to make nice and he told us to skip the bullshit. "Whadda ya want," he snapped, through the side of his mouth not corked by the ubiquitous half-smoked stogie. So we laid out the scheme. I. F. Stone was about to merge his weekly newsletter—some 33,000 names—with the *New York Review*, but first Izzy had agreed to give us a one-time use of the subscription list for a fund raising letter under his signature. We had a line of credit with a mail house and a printer, but nothing close to the twenty-five hundred bucks needed for postage. Would Bernie front the money?

Came then the proverbial pregnant pause as Bernie locked his eyeballs onto ours. "Alright," he barked, following some private set of calculations sizing up the odds of getting repaid. "But you'll pay it back from first receipts." We agreed, shook on it and left before he had a chance to change his mind. Bernie did this, not just from a long standing commitment to progressive causes, but to promote the benefits of Direct Mail, a funding tool much employed by the Right, but avoided in New Left circles—some puritanical hang-up about business, associating the risks inherent in any venture with a form of gambling.

When the returns started pouring in it took Tod and I all morning the first week or two to open the stack of BREs—business reply envelopes— and enter the checks onto deposit slips. Izzy Stone's list was dirty—lots of bad addresses—but none of our subsequent direct mail campaigns ever did as well as this one—netting a 5% return. Suddenly we were rolling in dough, but we retained a prissy New Left edge of our own. Safe Return's staff of two, sometimes three or four—including Tod, a lawyer—continued to subsist on Movement wages, and in my case, on my disability from Vietnam. There were a few modest cultural dividends. We got some vicarious jollies raking in contributions from Hollywood liberals whose sympathy for the Left we had never expected. Leonard Nimoy, fifty bucks. Dennis Weaver, a hundred. We even got a check from Helen Gahagan Douglas, who Nixon had dubbed the Pink Lady and defeated in the 1950 campaign for the U.S. Senate. But the high point came one morning when I slit the flap of a BRE and a check for $500 popped out signed by Alexander Calder.

I was so ignorant of the art world that I didn't even know who Calder was; Tod was a bit savvier. He suggested I write Calder immediately, not only to acknowledge his generous gift, but to request a meeting that summer of '74 when I planned to travel in Europe coordinating political actions with American servicemen in what remained of the GI resistance there. Tod's idea was to have Calder donate a painting from which we could design a poster for amnesty. The artist responded with a two or three line hand written note inviting me to his home south of Tours; I should come down in July, he wrote, when my business in Germany and Paris was completed.

The suburban station servicing Calder's village was shut down for the French midday siesta when my train arrived. Undaunted, indeed inspired by an anecdote of how Friedrich Engels once trekked across Europe before assuming control of his father's Manchester mill, I shouldered my pack and schlepped the remaining nine kilometers on foot, my first exposure—innocently decontextualized to the unparalleled beauty of the French Chateaux country.

One approached the Calder complex—several sprawling grey-sided structures spread over acres of grassy rolling fields—from a road that passed a diminutive village square crisscrossed by narrow cobble-paved lanes and alleys, hemmed in tightly by stone dwellings and commercial houses dating from the Middle Ages. Gracing the epicenter of the tiny common was a scaled-down Calder stabile, amazingly harmonious with its ancient surroundings.

Calder's son-in-law—an American expat living in Paris—welcomed me into the home-studio and introduced me to the artist and his wife, Louisa, both well into their seventies. They were seated at a long trestle table of polished roughhewn timber adjacent to the kitchen. The interior of the building was entirely open, some three to four thousand square feet, with the work space where Calder painted and designed his sculptures at the opposite end from where I now stood. Approaching the table I passed a large box under glass displaying dozens of the playful circus figurines in twisted wire, another of Calder's celebrated talents.

The three men, Calder, the son-in-law and I clustered toward one end of the table, while Louisa—a stern and formidable presence, looking very much the Pennsylvania Quaker lady she most probably was—sat knitting at the other. A recent stroke had deprived Calder of his speech; his few words were barely intelligible. So while I explained my mission and the work of the committee, Calder listened intently and the son-in-law posed questions about our politics. Like many progressive liberals Calder had a hard time with the revolutionary rhetoric that peppered the idiom of New Leftists; it was an old tick about communists held over from the thirties, I guess. Calder wanted to be assured that he wasn't dealing with the acolyte of some disciplined Leninist sect.

When it came out that I myself was a veteran of the war, Calder's doubts evaporated and he led me over to the work space, showing off a collection of *gouaches* he'd recently completed, gesturing for me to select one. I could pick it up, the son-in-law suggested, in New York that fall when the artist and his family returned for their annual visit to the States. Back at the table, Calder turned festive and reached for a second bottle of Bordeaux, since we'd already killed the first one. Louisa looked up and spoke for the first time. "Sandy, don't use this as an excuse to get drunk." With the only clear words he was to utter in my presence that afternoon, Sandy replied, "Don't need no excuse."

Back in New York, Calder's painting became the centerpiece of an Art Benefit Tod and I had organized for the early winter of the following year. And here I should point out that, aside from this foray into the upper heights of the American art world, and despite our mutual involvement with the cultural scenes of jazz and theater, neither Tod nor I had any contact with contemporary artists in the city life. We looked upon artists as petit bourgeois dilettantes who indulged vanguardist fantasies of the more-left-than-thou variety, despite the fact that so many veterans of the antiwar movement also continued to describe themselves in one flavor or another of antiimperialist politics. This topic, alas, touches the many variations of self-destructive sectarianism that riddled the New Left in those days, complicated in my own case by a suspicious personality and intensified further by the wounding of my psyche in Vietnam.

The art fund raiser went on as planned. We secured donations of works from the likes of Jasper Johns, Robert Motherwell, Andy Warhol, Judith Krassner, Robert Rauschenberg, Claes Oldenburg, Nancy Graves, Alex Katz, Frank Stella, to name a few, as well as from some artists long associated with the Left, like Leon Golub, then relatively unknown.

A friend in SoHo lent us her loft and secured as well the space of the adjacent, well established, Onasch Gallery. Lucy Lippard, a powerful voice in the art community even then, volunteered to hang the show with my assistance. As we worked quickly and in silence, a large, hirsute man in bib overalls entered the space, holding a manila envelope. His manner was rude and overbearing. "I'm Carl Andre," he announced, demanding that I produce rubber cement, which he spread on the wall just inside the door, then slapped an 8 × 10 sheet of white paper, covered with a geometric pattern of typescript, onto the adhesive. "This," he said, handing me the envelope, "is the original." Turning on his heels he left without another word, shooting me a disgusted look over one shoulder when I called after him, "How much should I ask for *this*?"

Andre, you may recall, was tried in New York several years later for the murder of his wife, who tumbled from their 34th floor apartment off Mercer Street. The way the rumor circulated in the city was that, despite the testimony of neighbors who had heard shouts of "No, no, stop," and experts who maintained that, in similar cases, suicides don't customarily yell out, Andre was acquitted.

Since Lippard had only a few free hours that Saturday she took off before hanging the entire show. One of the pieces remaining against the wall was Leon Golub's, a four foot square of Masonite where the artist had stenciled slogans like "Hands Off Chile," and "CIA Assassins Killed Allende," in a style similar to placards one would see at demonstrations, against a background of day glow orange paint. Good politics, Lippard and I had agreed, but dubious art.

With so many details to attend before the opening, I left soon after Lippard without putting up the remaining works, asking Penelope, the loft's owner, to complete the task if she could.

Only when the guests were already arriving the next afternoon did I realize that Golub's work was nowhere to be seen. Fearing the artist might show up and make a scene, I spotted Penelope across the room. "Where's the Golub," I mouthed, rushing over to her. Tod told me that Penelope's psychiatrist boyfriend was pumping her with heavy psychotropics in those days to curb her allegedly wild, unfocused energy. A devilish expression curled her smile as she led me to a corner where the wine and cheese were spread. Lifting the white table cloth to reveal a Masonite edge, she snickered, "It's right here."

Postscript: I was informed by Bernie Mazel's son that under no circumstances did his father ever smoke a cigar. I only have my memory to go by.

InTheMindField, **April 9, 2011**

Note

1. Safe Return: Committee in Support of Self-Retired Veterans [Deserters] played an important leadership role in the left-based movement to win Universal, Unconditional Amnesty for all resisters to the Vietnam War, whether draft or military, and to redress the issue of less-than honorable discharges given to more than half a million GIs during that era.

Poetry

Introduction

In 1972, a trio of American military veterans of the Vietnam War embarked on a unique publishing venture. They collected scores of poems by fellow veterans, and produced *Winning Heart and Minds* (WHAM), a volume of poetry reflecting their wartime experiences.

The collection was widely recognized for its quality and the authenticity of its collective antiwar message throughout the mainstream of U.S. print media, to include favorable reviews in the prestigious *New York Times Sunday Book Review*, and *The Nation* magazine.

The project had received its editorial impetus from poet Jan Barry Crumb, aided by his fellow poet/editors Larry Rottmann and Basil T. Paquet. WHAM's initial success led to its immediate republication in hard cover and paperback editions by McGraw Hill, one of the major publishing houses in the U.S.

A second edition of veteran poetry, *Demilitarized Zones*, was then assembled by Mr. Crumb, and W.D. Ehrhart, who has been called, "one of the foremost figures of literature of the Vietnam War."

My own career in writing has been essentially in prose, but I am honored that a poem I wrote in 1968 while on patrol in Quang Ngai Province, "*Black Silks, Black Mud*," appears in *WHAM*, a copy of which I presented to former Premier Pham Van Dong during a visit to Vietnam in 1994. Two of my poems also appear in *Demilitarized Zones*.

Two additional works from among my other published and unpublished poetry are also included here. One is war-related, the other nostalgic.

Black Silks, Black Mud

Black silks, black mud, knee deep they work
                                  the rice
Bamboo plow furrows through the rows, a black
                                  wake behind
Simple thought and lives—the targets of
                              our progress
    "Let me till my rice
    This is my only plea
    I trade my fragile body for this
                              fragile plant
    And when black night comes
                                      my thatched hut
    Calls me to an island hamlet."

**From *Winning Hearts & Minds: War Poems
by Vietnam Veterans*, McGraw-Hill, 1972**

Dignum et Justum Est

A nail in a yellowed wall holds
   the icon I carried into battle
The blue-silver virgin clashes sharply
   with its companion on the chain
Metallic dog-tags fastened with
   adhesive tape
Symbols of a faith and a love
   even then I bore with confusion
Hanging now as on some museum wall
   dusty relics, some illusion

Shades

Shades are my fishbowl,
my consolation.
The three-mile limit
where anything goes.
There I walk secure
among my faceless peers.
There I hide my tears.

From *Dimilitarized Zones: Veterans After Vietnam*, East River Anthology, 1976

War Birthed Me

War birthed me
As a babe I was swaddled in it
Rocked by fission
Wise men reeled like drunks
when I was just learning to smile
By the time I was six
war was as familiar as my mother's voice
War was always becoming
winding itself around me like a fine wire
Growing up was to arm
I expected a war of my own
and was not to be disappointed
Still, my mind was a bundle of tricks
when chance recruited me
Moral instinct not mute
only buried
In uniform I was awkward
knew shame
And yet
I carried war in my blood
In or out of service
I was at war
Even today
every day war explodes in my brain

It's Hard to Tell Sometimes…

(For Bill Drury)

It's hard to tell
sometimes
where you are
Main Street
an island
off season
could be P-town
Far Rockaway
Ocean Beach
all seep in from memory
even Babylon home
the slanty colonial lines
flourish of a Mansard roof
large square buildings sag
on wooden frames
along the waterside
of a working harbor
and you climb a gentle hill
to an obelisk for war dead
pride of the locals
library in stone
the band shell
speaks
of home grown entertainments
and boarded sidewalks
steamers up from Boston
of an Italian stonecutter
Odd Fellow
who played the coronet
in Sunday bands
quarried granite
all week long
his monument
a mighty caisson
two floors high
well sheltered in
its open-sided shed
but no one
on the village square
speaks
for those who cut cobblestones
three-pennies each
on Green's Island

In *New Labor Forum* Summer 2006

Criticism and Reviews

Bombing for the Hell of It
(Michael Uhl and Carol Brightman)

In Retrospect: The Tragedy and Lessons of Vietnam
(by Robert S. McNamara)

Poor Bob. He picked the year thousands of Americans are celebrating the Good War in Europe to break a silence of three decades and explain how that other war, the bad one in Southeast Asia went "wrong, terribly wrong." However belated, the refutation of strategic judgments by a man of Robert McNamara's stature is a rare event in American political life. And so our penitent from the Pentagon has rekindled the flames of controversy which are now synonymous in the popular mind with the word Vietnam.

Robert Strange McNamara's critics span the ideological spectrum, though the burden of their indignation differs according to whether they believe his moral failure lies in the past for not having spoken out sooner, or in the present for having spoken at all. For others, ourselves for instance, McNamara is guilty of a more insidious, featureless crime, and thus, for all its deadly consequences in Indochina, more difficult to bring home. It is to this man, more than any other, that Americans owe the dangerous integration of foreign-policy-making with defense planning, procurement and spending that is current today. McNamara's approach to "organizing human activities" (his phrase) was developed at Harvard, honed in the Army Air Corps' statistical control office in 1942–45 and applied at the Ford Motor Company before being taken into government. "Put very simply," he explains in his memoir, *In Retrospect,* the task was to define a clear objective for whatever organization I was associated with, develop a plan to achieve that objective, and systematically monitor progress against the plan.... The objective of the Defense Department was clear to me from the start: to defend the nation at minimal risk ... cost, and, whenever we got into combat, with minimal loss of life.

Simple, clear, systematic, minimal risk, cost—these are the buzzwords of the bureaucratic model of reality, against which, in Vietnam, the hard, stubborn facts of history, politics, geography and the sheer determination of people fighting for things of real value refused to submit.

To this great refusal, we owe the fall of Saigon in 1975 (another landmark in the year of looking backward), as well as McNamara's unexpected memoir. Far more illuminating—with all its lacunae—than critics have allowed, *In Retrospect* is a case study of what Hannah Arendt, in her 1971 review of the Pentagon Papers, "Lying in Politics," called the "defactualization" of the policy making process. But it is also a reconstruction of four major turning points of the war, and demonstrates that on each occasion not only was the decision to escalate made without illusions about the odds for success but evidence of the progressive *deterioration* of the American position was invariably near at hand.

In *Retrospect*, which can be read as a sequel to the Pentagon Papers—an appendix, so to speak, containing material that McNamara himself ordered kept out or the original record (along with taped White House conversations he hadn't known about)—is pertinent for another reason. It offers fresh evidence that the war in Vietnam, far from being a "mistake," a "triumph of the politics of inadvertence," as Arthur Schlesinger suggests, incubated in American strategic thinking for more than twenty years before the Marines landed at Danang in 1965.

Vietnam was our Asian Berlin, whose partition in 1945, in each case, was imposed to maintain big-power harmony. In Berlin, Washington and Moscow stood eyeball to eyeball, locked in a confrontation that remained largely symbolic because of a shared reliance on nuclear weapons for defense. "Massive retaliation," the doctrine was called, and when he came to work for Kennedy in 1961, it was McNamara's job to dismantle it.

"President Kennedy said we had put ourselves in the position of having to choose in a crisis between 'inglorious retreat or unlimited retaliation,'" McNamara writes, in the limpid prose of the memorandiist. "We decided to broaden the range of options by strengthening and modernizing the military's ability to fight a nonnuclear war." The new doctrine was called "flexible response," and the theater was Indochina. Kennedy's comeuppance, of course, like Johnson's and Nixon's after him, was that in Vietnam, where each president believed he was fighting a proxy war with the Soviet Union and/or China, the United States faced an indigenous revolutionary army, flush with victory over another Western power that had tried, and failed, to crush it.

To this fundamental miscalculation of its adversary, we owe the substitution of image for concrete goals that became the hallmark of America's

Vietnam objectives. Thus, it hardly mattered that the bombing of North Vietnam failed to stem the flow of troops and supplies to the South—a failure accurately predicted by CIA assessments of the "largely decentralized" and "essentially self-sustaining" Northern economy—when the bombing's ulterior objectives, especially the "graduated air attacks directed against the will of the DRV" (Maxwell Taylor), transcended counterarguments from the field. American goals in this instance were matters of faith, part of what McNamara called in a telephone interview with us, "the theology of containment ... a theology accepted almost without debate."

The bombing's initial objective—to prevent "a collapse of national morale in the South"—was already moot when the first two missions were canceled early in 1965 because of palace coups in Saigon. Indeed, the initial premise underlying U.S. involvement—shoring up a non-Communist regime capable of resisting encroachment from the North—was lost by March 2, 1965, when the air war began, if not by November 2, 1963, when, with the assassination of Diem, Washington forfeited its stake in an independent South Vietnam. By McNamara's account, that is.

In fact, American goals in Vietnam were doomed from the start, founded as they were on the multiple illusions that the South was a separate state—much less an anti-Communist one—and the North a puppet of China that was in turn aligned with the Russian bear. The fatal illusion was the presumed vulnerability of guerilla forces to U.S. firepower, especially air power. As both the Pentagon Papers and *In Retrospect* make clear, only the CIA had any sense of the determination and capabilities of the opposing armies, and that knowledge was not absorbed by the rest of the bureaucracy until late in the war.

In his book, McNamara concedes that the postwar policy or containment never should have been applied to Indochina. "Our misjudgments of friend and foe alike," he admits, "reflected our profound ignorance of the history, culture, and politics of the people in the area." In our interview, he told us, "We looked on Ho Chi Minh as an associate of Stalin and a believer in Khrushchev, whereas I think he was probably an Asian Tito."

This and other post-publication concessions are more specific than the general critique of the containment model made in the book—as is the surprising statement, offered in response to our question about the legality of the Johnson Administration's "aggression from the North" thesis. The war, McNamara said, "wasn't primarily a war of aggression [from the North].... "In a very real sense. I think we invaded a country that was in the process or civil war." Was Vietnam then one nation? "In the sense that the people wanted to unite," he answered. "I think probably yes."

The civil war thesis is itself debatable; a more informed view holds that regional political and cultural differences distinguishing the former French protectorates of Tonkin and Annam from the wealthy French colony of Cochin China in the South gave way (though not necessarily forever) to the unifying impulse unleashed by the need to repel a foreign invader. But McNamara's point is significant, for it lays the groundwork for questioning whether the United States, in invading a sovereign state, committed a crime of aggression under prevailing international and domestic law governing the justification for war, as well as the manner in which it is conducted.

McNamara is not unaware of these implications. "Well, again, I'm not a lawyer," he chuckled nervously when we presented him with Telford Taylor's statement that in January 1971, that if the standards of Nuremberg (where Taylor was chief counsel for the prosecution) and at the Manila trial of Gen. Tomoyuki Yamashita were applied to former Secretary of State Dean Rusk, Defense Secretary Robert McNamara, and special assistants McGeorge Bundy and Walt Rostow, "there would be a very strong possibility they would come to the same end he (Yamashita) did."

"I can't respond in legal terms whether the people you mention should be tried, or whether they would be declared guilty," McNamara said, proposing instead "the more pertinent question.... Why did they do what they did?" Not, surely, "simply because they were criminal.... We're not going to have a lot of criminals running our country, in the future." (This was a reference to McNamara's oft-stated aim in the book to study the mistakes of the past to avoid repeating them in the future.) Speaking of his "associates," he could only say they were "highly intelligent, well-educated, dedicated servants of their country and people [who upheld] the values and principles of the country"—not "criminals" but "misguided individuals." A strange response, it is typical of McNamara's tendency to speak out or both sides of his mouth, as if penitent and apologist are grappling for control.

It wasn't ignorance of geopolitical realities or "misjudgments of friend and foe alike," however, that caused the Vietnam disaster. As Telford Taylor pointed out in *Nuremberg and Vietnam*, U.S. economic and military missions had been in Vietnam for too long "to attribute the blunders that accompanied the massive buildup to lack of information." Meanwhile, reading *In Retrospect* alongside the angry reviews, editorials and counter editorials it has generated, together with transcripts of interviews and television appearances that show McNamara yielding ground on bedrock questions avoided in the book, one senses that the war-crimes issue may not be purely the rhetorical charge it once seemed. Sometime in the not too distant future the architects of our Vietnam policy may very likely be called to account in some institutional setting (if by then mostly in absentia) for crimes of aggression in Vietnam.

McNamara has opened the door to a serious examination of the motives and working methods of the governing elites responsible for the war. True, he shuts it before answering the question "Why did they do what they did?" But the question hangs in the air, and will not go away.

In his memoir, McNamara nowhere admits the possibility that American attempts to suppress what Kennedy saw as the "forces of subversion, infiltration ... indirect or nonovert aggression," and so on, represented anything more than the byproduct of a misdirected crusade against Communism. And yet there is something bogus about this harping on how "deeply frightened we were by the potential for Communist aggression."

If American leaders really believed that the Soviet Union and China had supplanted Nazi Germany and Japan, as McNamara insists they did (having acquired their worldview in service during World War II), then why did they show so little interest in the actual relations between Communist powers? How could they *not* have known about the deep animosity between Stalin (and later Khrushchev) and Mao, or the fragmented character of the Communist movement following the war, or the centuries-old conflicts between China and Vietnam, when so many people outside government did? And if they did know, why didn't they try to exploit the conflicts through diplomatic and commercial channels?

Why did successive administrations ignore the testimony of OSS officers, such as Archimedes Patti *(Why Vietnam? Prelude to America's Albatross)*, who were based in southern China and Vietnam in 1945–46 and knew firsthand of Ho Chi Minh's repeated attempts to enlist American support for an independent and nonaligned Vietnam? The Pentagon Papers reports a cable from an American diplomat in Hanoi about the letters Ho wrote President Truman requesting the United States "to support the idea of Annamese independence according to the Philippines example," a startling proposition that might have extended to Vietnam the semiautonomous status of a client state in the American orbit. The letters were never answered.

Vietnam, whose affairs were then covered by the French desk in the State Department, did not absorb American intentions until after France proved itself incapable of keeping its errant colony in the Western fold. And even then, after the United States had supplanted the French, its role was primarily as gendarme. "We do not require that it [South Vietnam] serve as a Western base or as a member of a Western Alliance," McNamara told a Congressional committee in 1964. In early 1967, he testified that there was no longer any reason to "contain China." So what was the United States doing in Vietnam?

The argument that U.S. involvement was motivated by a lust for Vietnamese tin and tungsten died a hard death in the antiwar movement, but the fact is that in Indochina the United States has never demonstrated much interest in the traditional booty of imperial conquest—not in the 1940s, not in the 1960s and not now either. Speaking of his seven years in government during the war, Pentagon analyst James Thomson told a Vietnam conference in 1964 that he "never saw in writing nor heard in discussion in the most secret and confidential documents or meetings, any allusion whatsoever to our need for the raw materials or other products of Indochina—or indeed for access to an Indochina market." Contemporary Vietnam may remind businessmen quoted in *The Wall Street Journal* after the embargo was lifted last year of "a land rush in the old West," but as one added, it's "the Japanese, Taiwanese and French [who] all have their wagons moving," not the United States.

That is not to say that the United States wasn't pursuing a global policy with imperialist overtones. Behind Kennedy and McNamara's flexible-response doctrine there existed a drive to open new corners of the globe to American influence, especially in the stripped territories and broken-backed colonies sloughed off by the old empires. Here, at least, one might expect that the United States, squaring off with its Communist competitors, would attempt to divide in order to rule the outcomes of the independence struggles under way in the Third World. But when Mao Zedong and Zhou En-lai approached Roosevelt as early as January 1945, "trying to establish relations with the United States in order to avoid total dependence on the Soviet Union" (as a State Department document later reported), there was no response. This interesting event, picked up by Hannah Arendt in her 1971 review, was discussed at a Senate Foreign Relations Committee hearing in 1969 when China scholar Allen Whiting testified that information about the overture was suppressed because it contradicted "the image of monolithic Communism directed from Moscow."

Speaking of Vietnam policy, Arendt was struck by "the divergence between facts—established by the intelligence services, sometimes by the decision-makers themselves (as notably in the case of McNamara), and often available to the informed public—and the premises, theories, and hypotheses according to which decisions were finally made." Perhaps the "image" of a monolithic Communism, existing apart from the facts, was really a premise in disguise, a pivot on which policies turned that would otherwise be indefensible.

No wonder that 70 percent of the commanding officers interviewed by Douglas Kinnard in *The War Managers* reported they never understood what U.S. objectives in Vietnam were. What McNamara's book teaches us is that at the highest levels of government, our leaders weren't sure what those objectives were either.

Bombing for the hell of it, one might call the ultimate rationale they reached at the end of 1964 when Washington opted for a land war in the South and an air war against the North. Once combat troops were introduced, the military logic for bombing the North, to eliminate the guerrillas' sanctuary, was set. But it was Maxwell Taylor's final argument that mattered most: "[We] are presently on a losing track and must risk a change," he warned, "because to take no positive action now is to accept defeat in the fairly near future." *Risk, change, action* were the alternate catchwords of decision-making, and broke the spell of defeat when the bureaucratic models fell.

In scale, and in the end, Vietnam was a world war. Jonathan Schell is right to suggest, as he did in a conversation with us after our interview with McNamara, that "in Vietnam, they thought we were fighting World War III. This was a doable war." If any credo comes close to articulating the nightmare vision, it is Rusk's: "The integrity of the U.S. commitment is the principal pillar of peace throughout the world.... If that commitment becomes unreliable, the Communists would draw conclusions that would lead to our ruin and almost certainly to catastrophic war." And so they soldiered on, to "save: face" and "keep our word," after *losing* both—masking aggression and *lese-majeste* behind a tissue of myths.

The Nation, June 12, 1995, by Carol Brightman and Michael Uhl

Excerpt from an Interview with Robert Strange McNamara

In the course of research for the above review of In Retrospect, *I conducted a telephone interview with former Secretary of Defense, Robert S. McNamara on April 27, 1995. I record here an excerpt of some historical significance from that interview:*

Michael Uhl: It's a rather lengthy question, so... According to the Juridical Memorandum submitted to the Senate Foreign Affairs Committee on March 4, 1966, the Johnson Administration claimed that American intervention in Vietnam merely constituted aid to the Saigon government against aggression from the North. A rival assumption, widely held around the world, if not in the United States, is that Vietnam at the time of American intervention was one nation, and as such, could not be seen as committing aggression against itself. If future historians, examining the evidence, find this second interpretation persuasive—and I think they will—they will have to conclude that the United States invaded Vietnam, and, in consequence, committed a crime of aggression within the meaning of statutes binding on us at the time of the invasion. Given that you've written about the Saigon government's lack of a political base, and the ease with which the NLF [National Liberation Front, aka, Viet Cong] recruited adherents in the South, who were, after all, fighting for reunification, do you still believe that we possessed a legal base for military intervention in Vietnam?

Robert McNamara: Well, I'm not a lawyer. It is a very interesting point, because, Dean Rusk till the day he died—he died December 20th last year, you know—and his son, by the way, has just written an extraordinary appraisal of what his father believed at the time. And I think that Dean, were he alive today and sitting with me at this table, would say we had a legal right to intervene. And the legal right was based upon the protocol to the SEATO Treaty, the Southeast Asian Treaty, under which we assumed a responsibility to defend the states protected by that treaty, including the states mentioned in the protocol, which included Vietnam, against aggression. Dean, to the day he died said yes, we had a legal right. I don't know. I'm not a lawyer, I can't...

Uhl: So we conferred a legal status on South Vietnam as being a State.

McNamara: Yes we did. And I'm not arguing that that is the correct interpretation. I'm not qualified to discuss the legalities of it. But we did believe that the North was seeking to commit aggression against the South, destroy the State, and take it over, as a base for further communist aggression in Asia. Now, I think we were wrong on several points. Forgetting the legalities for the moment, I am absolutely convinced today that largely—not solely—but largely, the conflict was a civil war.

Uhl: So you would say, looking back...

McNamara: In a very real sense, I think we invaded a country that was in the process of a civil war, and took the side of one party.

Uhl: Would you then, looking back, say that there was one nation? Since you're saying it's a civil war, I suppose you would be saying that Vietnam was a single nation?

McNamara: I don't want to say that from the point of view of legality, because I really don't know. But in the sense that the people, I think, wanted to unite, I think probably yes. But I just look today upon it as a civil war.

Revising the Meaning of the Vietnam War

Last Days in Vietnam (a documentary film by Rory Kennedy)

With "Last Days in Vietnam," a full length documentary film contending for an Oscar in 2015, comes the disturbing realization that the spirit of the age has finally flipped the lessons of the Vietnam War from a progressive cautionary tale of longstanding, to a simplistic recitation of half-truths designed to nurture the turn toward reaction that grips the public mind today. That a polemic supporting such a perversion of the record ushers from the artistic, ahistorical, politically muddled imagination of the daughter of a man who was assassinated when exposed to personal danger in 1968 as a highly visible presidential candidate in opposition to the Vietnam War, underscores my dire evaluation of the times.

Whether one views the filmmaker Rory Kennedy as a manipulator of the historical record, or as a victim of manipulation incapable of approaching a complex subject with sharper critical tools, her film objectively defies her father Bobby Kennedy's legacy in its complete failure to address even the most rudimentary contexts that led Bobby, along with tens of millions of his fellow citizens, to reject an American military adventure that would dominate world events for over a generation. In Rory Kennedy's film, the saga of Vietnam's struggle to free itself of foreign domination is reduced to a sentimental micro-historical vignette focused almost entirely on the failure of the United States in the final month of the war to evacuate members of the South Vietnamese military elite and other collaborators of the puppet regime caught in Saigon when the liberation forces finally captured the city on April 30, 1975.

One might still shed a tear for those trapped in Saigon, whether by design or circumstance, and destined to face victor's justice, and even admire the pluck of a handful of soldiers among the small contingent of Americans left as advisors in one capacity or another after the U.S. had evacuated its troops following the Peace Accord in January 1973. These men are the heroes of Kennedy's Vietnam War, and with the aid of some spectacular archival footage, she faithfully documents their acts of decency and loyalty toward South Vietnamese counterparts in the officer corps and Saigon government of Nguyen Van Thieu, moving logistical mountains—often in opposition to their superiors—to organize the means to evacuate the most compromised collaborators, or in some cases simply the family baby sitter.

Kennedy is relentless in her ridicule of the American Ambassador, Graham Martin, a man of great Southern charm we are told, and marvelously revealed through snippets of interviews in the final hours before his own departure, affirming his fantastic belief that the incompetent and uncommitted South Vietnamese military—the ARVN—would stem the advance of the armies from the north, which, incidentally, they not only outnumbered—at least on paper—but also outgunned thanks to the tons of materiel their U.S. sponsors had supplied them. Recall that Saigon had an air force, while Hanoi did not. Undoubtedly some, if not a truly significant addition, of the high and middle ranking adherents to the southern regime and their families would have made good their escape if Martin had not so deluded himself. But the fact was that the U.S. authorities had no mass evacuation plan, and the fates of their allies were sealed long before Saigon was threatened.

The two major factors, I think, confirming why that was the case were that, not only Ambassador Martin, but no one anywhere that I remember (except perhaps the Pentagon who held a calculus on ARVN ineptitude even greater than Hanoi's) had an inkling when the North Vietnamese regulars launched their offensive from I Corps within South Vietnam in March 1975, taking advantage of the post–Watergate confusion then besetting the American government, that their forces would accomplish the objective of reunification with such lightning speed; moreover, it was generally assumed that the U.S. would rally militarily to the aid of the South, and not let the ally on whose behalf it had invested nearly sixty thousands American lives and billions of dollars, simply fall.

Kennedy addresses the scenario of an American comeback directly, but she misses the play of forces that determined that outcome, citing one of the obstacles to military intervention, but not others that were equally telling. Kennedy gives the role of explainer to Henry Kissinger, if not exactly an architect of the conflict, ultimately a pro-war zealot who wielded the power of a field marshal. Now, admittedly, antiwar activists of the Vietnam generation, including many war veterans like me, harbor unkind thoughts toward the man the author of *Catch 22*, Joseph Heller, famously described as "that little fat fuck." Kissinger is an offensive presence to us, an evil mastermind, a Moriarty, a corrupter of the guileless like Rory Kennedy. Henry tells her that Gerald Ford, in office barely six months after Nixon resigned in disgrace, had asked the Congress to appropriate an emergency military funding bill of $722 million, and it failed to pass. In Kennedy's narration, this happened under pressure from the antiwar movement … allowing Henry to play the classic Dolchstoss card, the knife in the back by a Fifth Column that snatched defeat from the victory our brave combatants had deserved.

A friend of mine suggests that, in fact, "the peace movement had shriveled tremendously to the point that it did not engage in the emergency funding debate at all. The prime reason the funding did not pass was that the Pentagon opposed it." But if we parse the term "peace movement" into its component parts, we will find that the activist core of the movement remained thoroughly engaged, but was incapable at that moment of mobilizing on the street the kinds of numbers from a larger pool of non-activist opponents that would compel the immediate attention of the Congress. Thus the mass movement might have been persuasive, but on this occasion it wasn't. That said, opposition from the Pentagon was a powerful deterrent; but even without the pressure of mass demonstrations, the Congress had taken the pulse of public opinion. And if the public was done with Vietnam, then the antiwar movement could claim its share of the credit.

What fatally robs Rory Kennedy's documentary of the moral force she claims for the Vietnamese victims, despite what was clearly an American failure of responsibility—some would say disinterest—in saving them, is the arrogance or chutzpah to debut such a work during the fiftieth anniversary year of the U.S. invasion that evolved into that long, bloody and ultimately futile land war in a remote and strategically insignificant corner of South East Asia.

Futile for us, devastating for the Vietnamese, not only in the loss of life into the millions, tens of thousands of whom (take note MIA stalwarts!) still remain among the missing; not only in the persistent poisoned landscape with its attendant and tragic public health consequences resulting from the wide scale spraying of dioxin-laced herbicides like Agent Orange, or the large patches of land still saturated with unexploded ordinance which primarily punishes the natural curiosity of children playing in the dirt; but also an economy "bombed into the stone age," made infinitely worse by the postwar imposition of a vindictive American embargo, slowing Vietnam's recovery, and benefitting least those left behind who had fought or worked against reunification. In that project, as any serious history will inform you,

Hanoi always enjoyed the overwhelming support of the Vietnamese population.

You would think from Rory Kennedy's film that such a line of thinking about the events that gave rise to the devastation I describe above either pale in significance or are somehow irrelevant when compared to the personal tragedies of those in "the last days" of Vietnam who failed to get aboard the last chopper and therefore to a way of life they could not win on the battlefield.

Rory Kennedy offers that vision of "privileged freedom" as the new meaning of the Vietnam War against the stronger urge of a whole people—still mindful of its long exposure to French colonial subjugation—to resolve the national question, to expel this latest foreign invader, while failing to reference a single example of the shameful horrors that the Americans and their Vietnamese clients inflicted on an entire nation. Why, my friend Paul Cox has asked, does Kennedy "choose to ignore a vast reality, in service of a ripping good yarn? There are war stories abundant. What we need in this country is not some feel good battle flick, but a hard look at that vast reality."

If the peace movement has lost the likes of the daughter of Bobby Kennedy, can we also then not imagine a day, given the structural political shift I assert at the beginning of these comments, when one's history of opposition to the Vietnam War will become not merely unfashionable, but a potential source of overt repression? I'm not playing Chicken Little here, but, to the degree we understand that an honest telling of the history of the Vietnam War defends a broader progressive and antiwar agenda, we can better articulate why a falsification of that history best serves the war agenda of the radical Right.

Counterpunch, April 17, 2015

The Problematic: Penny Lewis Repairs Some Misconceptions About the Vietnam War

Hardhats, Hippies and Hawks: The Vietnam Antiwar Movement as Myth and Memory
(by Penny Lewis)

The Vietnam War seems to be drawing attention increasingly from researchers born during or after the tumultuous decade in which that deadly drama played out. One sees mostly this generation's higher profile works, like Fredrik Logevall's *Embers of War; The Fall of an Empire and the Making of America's Vietnam*, winner of the 2013 Pulitzer Prize for History, and Nick Turse's *Kill Anything That Moves: The Real American War in Vietnam*. More in the academic shadows, but perhaps suggestive of a wider trend in the making, is a new study by Penny Lewis, *Hardhats, Hippies and Hawks: The Vietnam Antiwar Movement as Myth and Memory*, rich in the vistas it surveys, and a seed bed for future scholars to expand on.

A reader will scan this book's quirky title in vain for a quick fix on what the work undertakes to present. Lewis, an assistant professor at City University in New York, and active in contemporary Labor and antiwar movements, devotes much of her book's narrative to the project of sharpening an outmoded analysis of the American working class, accomplished in part by locating *the class* historically within what the late *New York Times* columnist Tom Wicker once called "a very broad spectrum" of public opposition to the Vietnam War, some of it organized, some of it not.

The distinction is critical, with the organized spheres of Vietnam War opposition, as highlighted in the book's subtitle, easier to pin down and label. Lewis comes to her interest in the Vietnam antiwar narrative through disappointing efforts in the last decade to mobilize public opposition to the wars in Iraq and Afghanistan, a movement that promised much in its early stages, then, she dryly notes, "faded." Serving as a representative of her union within a Labor movement far more sympathetic to an antiwar message in 2003 than it was in 1965, Lewis, "staffing tables, working on resolutions, organizing protests ... spoke with fellow labor activists about their experiences within the Vietnam antiwar movement."

Digging through this "buried history," the author subsequently confirmed that antiwar forces in the US during Vietnam were every bit as "massive" and "dynamic" as the accounts she was hearing from her older comrades. How, then, could a post–Vietnam generation individual with Penny Lewis' credentials, a committed peace activist, a leader in her union, a solidly grounded career-bound academic, have missed that story? Apparently because, growing up, what she had absorbed about *that* war and *those* times, as "fleshed out in numerous movies, TV shows, textbooks, journalist's renderings, histories, memoirs, political speeches, and personal recollections," exposed her to what she now accurately identifies as "half-truths and, overall ... is a falsehood."

Myth holds sway in the "renderings" of this history earmarked for storage in the "collective memory," and doled out with the greatest damage, as Lewis chillingly demonstrates, in the vast majority of text books that feed young minds through mainstream scholastic channels with "[h]ostile treatments of the movement ... focused on the elite and out-of-touch nature of the protestors ... as 'spitters and haters.'" In contrast, "war supporters" during that period "are often imagined as ordinary ... people from Middle America ... who supported God, country and our boys in Nam."

Lewis sets about restoring some of the nuance to the record, framed by the sociological ground rules in force where such discussions occur in her branch of the scholarly manufactory. Fortunately she is sufficiently clear headed and graceful in expression, that the speed bumps of jargon, and occasional quoted infomercials from esteemed mentors and colleagues, shouldn't deter a general reader drawn to this subject from reaping insight and satisfaction from Lewis' summary, but deft, treatment of the twin themes she brings under investigation, class and protest.

Lewis frames correctly a chronology—too obvious to have been so often overlooked—that recognizes much attributed culturally and politically to the Sixties to have occurred or spread into the Seventies, a point of some significance when Lewis explores the demographic makeup of the opposition farther on. But the most spectacular relic rescued here by Lewis is a shining image of the Vietnam movement's voluminous mobilization of "6 million" antiwar activists ... "with another 25 million close sympathizers." Imagined visually, it's a perfect snapshot of what sustained mass organizing looks like, and it cannot be over-emphasized by interested parties seeking to defend and replicate this history in the present. Let me put it this way, there wasn't a corner of the land for a decade where an organizer couldn't find a welcome crash pad, and a public forum for whatever on-going or upcoming antiwar action he or she had come to herald.

Examining the evolving Vietnam era antiwar movement over time, Lewis could see that, until the mid-60s, when the public was finally being drawn into the debate, most of the vocal opposition had been limited to well-known figures from the Fifties' 'ban-the-bomb' network, like Dr. Ben Spock and A.J. Muste, a leading pacifist. As the American combat role in Vietnam rapidly expanded, opposition soon spread to a vanguard of precocious students on several of the nation's top campuses, and included, as well, their less privileged counterparts among young black civil rights workers in the South.

Initially, preoccupation with the war on campus was tangential to a rise in student involvement with civil rights, and demands for academic freedom. The Free Speech Movement at Berkeley in 1964 was an act of defiance against *in loco parentis* that shocked college administrators who for years had expected nothing more rambunctious from their student bodies than cafeteria food fights and panty raids. Student leader Mario Savio's name became a house hold word overnight, and the actions of the Berkeley students ignited a political charge throughout a budding youth culture that spawned a collective resistance to the draft, and militant opposition to an escalating war.

At the University of Michigan, where it had been discovered that a program to advise the South Vietnamese government served as a front for the CIA, a handful of leftwing students affiliated with the League For Industrial Democracy, broke with their timid work-within-the-system and red-baiting elders, and, in 1962, formed Students for a Democratic Society. Their impulse had a domestic focus, a desire to explore possibilities for what they called participatory democracy, which might in turn help strip some aggression from the nation's foreign policy. Then, in 1965, SDS organized the first mass anti–Vietnam war demonstration, bringing 25 thousand protestors to Washington, D.C., and, till the end of the decade, the organization inspired independent political action for a draft age generation, mostly white, middle class college students, female and male, who, as a demographic, remained the backbone of the protest movement until the war's end.

But where in this generational upheaval were working class youths not bound for college with its privileged four year deferment from conscription? The boys at least, or "proles," as James Fallows once infamously described them, overwhelmingly filled the ranks of the armed services, where their own rebellion, in Lewis' astute observation, "had as great, if not greater, an effect on the US military's ability to fight the war than did the more typical protest actions" on the home front.

Lewis is understandably perplexed that an event of such powerful impact like the GI rebellion receives almost no attention in even the best historical accounts of the movement, like Charles De Benedetti's *An American Ordeal*. Lewis has to provide an academic explanation for this mysterious oversight, arguing that studies of "social movements" are too narrowly defined to accommodate anomalous structures that don't fit this or that discipline's analytic criteria, and so forth and so on. Lewis, of course, wants to expand the scholarly strike zone. But the fact remains that the bibliography of works addressing the GI movement is so tiny and obscure that even in the heat of the hunt Lewis has failed to cite among the rare treatments two contributions of seminal importance, Matthew Rinaldi's 1974 essay for *Radical America*, "The Olive Drab Rebels," and James Lewes' *Protest and Survive*, a book length survey of the scores of underground GI newspapers that circulated during the war.

The GI Resistance combusted from many acts of spontaneous, individual defiance, although civilian organizers who recognized the importance of working with GIs provided indispensable political and logistical leadership through a network of GI coffee houses and counseling centers that sprang up outside virtually every major US military installation at home, and near many bases overseas as well. The movement in the military paralleled the civilian movement, but was in many ways dissimilar, not least in having erupted under the authoritarian environment of military discipline, and in the rice paddies of Vietnam.

Then, home from the war and discharged from the service, ex–GIs rose up en mass in 1970, energized a flagging movement, and helped to further erode whatever lukewarm public support remained for the war. Never before had veterans anywhere opposed war in such numbers, and, even more unprecedented, did so while their war remained very much in progress, its outcome still in the balance. The antiwar veterans have been studied only slightly more by movement historians, Lewis comments, than the GI resisters.

What about the working class as a whole? Where did Middle America stand on the war? Stored in the distorted memory bank described by Lewis, a white male worker stands upon a pedestal on which the word "hardhat," is engraved. An unabashed flag waver and pro-war patriot, he appeared briefly in May 1970, and beat up some long hairs demonstrating against the war in the vicinity of Wall Street.

It does not matter that this prevailing caricature obscures the existence of female and minority workers, and fails to sum up fairly where white male production workers stood on the war overall—the antiwar vets and GIs providing the most glaring rebuttal of the hardhat thesis. The bullying behavior of a battalion of jerks from the pampered and manipulated New York building trades is held up as evidence of a false and inverted reality where only elites of a leisured middle class with too much time on their hands opposed the war, while tradition-bound Archie Bunkers expected their sons to serve when called, even at the cost of coming back from Nam in a body bag.

There's no doubt that class polarization on the war existed, but leaving aside large segments of rebellious middle and upper middle class young people, the well-heeled parents who paid their college tuitions were more likely to support the war than their opposite numbers among the *Greatest Generation* in the blue collar neighborhoods. According to one comprehensive survey Lewis cites, "Opposition to the war was in fact higher among lower income than among higher income Americans." By using the locution, "in-fact," Lewis explains, this study's author "acknowledges the common misconception that the opposite was true." And yet, she muses, "…no account … explains why such a misconception exists…."

Grappling with that conundrum, Lewis says, is the essential project of her book, and she casts the net widely. Her extensive exploration of the inadequacy of the tools of contemporary social science to distinguish the structural conditions that define working class realities from contingent forces that contradict leftist notions of objective class interests, and are often manifest by workers in conservative and individualist political behavior, is easier to read than to review. As the Dude would say, it's complicated … lotta ins, lotta outs. So, around that task I invite the reader to follow Lewis first hand.

But to the degree that misconception erases the rejection of the Vietnam War by a majority of low income Americans, suffice it say that, generational differences notwithstanding, blue-collar opposition was seldom expressed or politicized in any manner resembling movement activism. Much working class skepticism of US military policy in SE Asia centered on the inability of the nation's leaders to justify the burden in blood and treasure extracted disproportionately from their communities in pursuit of war objectives that could never be adequately explained to their satisfaction. Such attitudes in Middle America, communicated as *vox populi*, seldom translated into sympathy for the more flamboyant aspects of the protest movement.

In fact, "[t]he countercultural expression of many parts of the movement challenged core values of many workers," Lewis acknowledges. Or as Notre Dame sociologist, Andrew Greeley, once quipped, "If the white ethnic is told in effect that to support peace he must also support the Black Panthers, women's liberation, widespread use of drugs, free love, campus radicals, Dr. Spock, long hair and picketing clergymen," you're unlikely to find him in the peace movement.

Greeley's observation, which echoes the witty pen of George Orwell describing eccentric Brit peaceniks of the Thirties, is likewise more parody than picture of a movement that was as eclectic as the society from which it was formed. But you don't have to be intolerant of cultural diversity to share in a critique of the infinite contradictions that riddled the organized Vietnam antiwar opposition. "Useful knowledge," Lewis proclaims, can be gained by those carrying a "desire for social change" into the future, who study the Vietnam antiwar movement for its "shortcomings" as well as its "achievements."

In *Hardhats, Hippies and Hawks* Lewis underscores two constants that link the Vietnam conflict with contemporary US military adventures in Iraq and Afghanistan. All are or were driven by similar "economic and political imperatives." And, ultimately, all three were or are rejected by the overwhelming majority of Americans. Only during Vietnam, however, did a people mobilized by an explicit antiwar agenda exercise a strong hand in bringing the war to an end. Obviously conditions differ from one epoch to the next, but it is still useful to emphasize what distinguishes a "faded" movement from a "dynamic" one.

InTheMindField, July 21, 2013
As "Beyond Spitters and Haters" in *Counterpunch*, July 26, 2013

Apocalypse Now? The Strange Jeremiads of Christopher Hedges

A Critical Take on "Hope: An Affirming Flame"
(speech, December 16, 2010)

Chris Hedges is the former *New York Times* war correspondent turned tribune for the antiwar resistance. In a series of articles and interviews over the past six months, Hedges has elaborated on his belief that former channels of democratic redress and reform, whether swift or incremental, are foreclosed in today's repressive political climate. Barack Obama in this scenario is much more than a disappointment. He is described by Hedges in a rather obscure formulation as "like Herod of old" in league with all the dark elites in our society that are driving the American people toward "bondage." For those who refuse quiet "submission" to such a fate, hope lies only in "repeated and substantial acts of civil disobedience."

The concept of *hope* looms large in the Hedges cosmology, as in the following riff-like sequence from a recent [December 2010] polemic delivered in Washington's Lafayette Park before an assembly of antiwar veterans:

"Hope now will come when we defy physically the violence of the State.... Those who resist today with nonviolence are the last thin line of defense between a civilized society and its disintegration ... all who succumb to fear ... become enemies of hope.... The more futile, the more useless, the more irrelevant and incomprehensible an act of rebellion is, the more potent hope becomes. Hope never makes sense." Here at least, neither does Chris Hedges.

The thoughts and words above, whether quoted or paraphrased, are representative of Hedges blend of mysticism and muddled thinking, sprinkled with flashes of erudition and much poetic elegance. Some of his millennial comparisons and historical readings—the simile linking Obama to Herod—elsewhere equating the U.S. political system to Egypt under Mubarak—are downright bizarre. But I'm really stuck on that startling revelation that hope's potency rests upon futile, useless, irrelevant and incomprehensible acts of rebellion. Really? Does that mean failure will make better people of us? This strikes me as stuff for the sectarian pulpit, not the public forum.

And yet I hasten to confess that, almost without qualification, I agree with Hedges' assessment of the mounting woes and blows that we as a people have grown unaccustomed to bearing during the salad years of the American Century. And, maybe, we progressives, having lapsed into complacency after the great cultural victories of the sixties and seventies, are stunned to suddenly feel more keenly the presence of Big Brother ... again. It seems very true to me, as I believe it does to Hedges, that our already imperfect democracy is growing measurably weaker right before our eyes.

Can Hedges be right that the options of fighting back through familiar social and institutional struggles are indeed "closed in advance," and that only acts of individual purification can—what? That's where he loses me. Anyway, I'm not convinced, scanning over the American past, that these are the worst of times, as opposed to exceedingly bad times for which our history presents ample precedent. For political repression and suppression of civil liberties alone, I can tick off John Adam's Alien and Sedition Acts, a blatantly autocratic attempt to silence opposition. Lincoln, our American saint, suspended *habeas corpus*. All the Haymarket Martyrs, including three who were hanged, were later found to have been innocent. What about Debs being railroaded to an Atlanta, Georgia jail cell with a ten year sentence for advocating resistance to World War I? Check out how the Espionage Act and the Palmer Raids in the teens and twenties targeted the Left and the foreign born. Domestic communist witch hunts were jump-started with passage of the Smith Act in 1940. Hedges himself is too young to have lived through the subsequent rout of American communists and their sympathizers during the McCarthy era. We no longer have a House Un-American Activities Committee, although the Honorable Pete King in the U.S. Congress today seems eager to recreate one to admonish the latest hyphenated immigrant bogeys, the Muslim-Americans.

Those repressive cycles were always superseded by popular counter-struggles, resulting that hard won victories long taken for granted have been hard wired into our social contract. But nothing is permanent. What has been won can be snatched away. When oligarchs rise and seek to erode economic and democratic gains through deception, demagoguery and repression, the tools and means available to defend ourselves—assuming average citizens can be stirred to act in their own best interest—will differ from one age to the next.

Trying to fashion those tools is the task that confronts progressive-thinking people today. Many of us who have devoted decades to antiwar politics have been frustrated to distraction by our inability to mobilize a sizeable movement to stir and focus public opposition to the wars in Iraq and Afghanistan. Even among youth privileged with higher education, few today have seen fit to make common cause with us against these wars. They have their own distractions. The economic pressures facing most Americans Hedges is quite correct to associate with an increasingly corrupt political system and an insatiably greedy class of elites who perceive their lord-of-the-world status steadily and visibly eroding in the twilight of the empire.

It is widely known that empires rise and fall. Those who study or observe such things assume that America too will one day fall. No one has the play book on how quickly we will arrive at the moment when someone looking back will be able to say, Rome, Britain, and the United States of America were all once great empires that passed from the scene. At that point, the global balance of power will have finally shifted from our shores, and my sense is that, in the absence of dystopia, those who then occupy this land may experience the transition as virtually seamless, and not necessarily cataclysmic. The point is, we're not there yet, but that the greedy plutocrats who rule us, whose fear of the inevitable decline does seem wildly heightened, are up to more looting and hoarding than usual these days.

How do we stop them? To review Chris Hedges' plan, return to the top two paragraphs.

Hedges' rise to prominence as a voice of the antiwar movement has been rapid. That he is a man of impressive accomplishments is undeniable. Hedges' top drawer education was matched by his academic excellence. As a journalist he was at the pinnacle of his profession, a war correspondent with the *New York Times*, in the historic company of Homer Bigart, Neil Sheehan, and David Halberstam, and other legendary reporters who covered world battlefields for *The Times* before him. Hedges is an enviably prodigious—not to mention successful—writer. And yet, his resume in the peace movement seems a trifle lite.

Amy Goodman interviewed Hedges on *Democracy Now!* just after the December 16, 2010, action at which he read "Hope: An Affirming Flame," which I have quoted from above. Hedges is explaining his hopeless plan of action, when, about midway through the interview, Goodman seems to shift gears. Instead of asking a question, she makes a statement: "You were actually quite muted about the government when you were at *The New York Times* [until 2005] and you were being interviewed, like by us."

"Yeah," retorts Hedges, obviously miffed, "*The Times* wouldn't consider it muted."

Point Goodman; she drops it and returns to the usual hagiographic style she reserves for movement celebrities in her interviews. From the above quote, it's impossible to really guess what Goodman had in mind. What comes to my mind is that Hedges has had no deep life experience with radical politics or mass movements, and very probably missed much in the major mass movement against war in our lifetimes that roiled the American population during Vietnam. He has a lot of experience with war, and his exposure to the disasters of war is, I sense, layers deeper than anything I went through in Vietnam, with the major exception that I carried a gun and he a pen. The resulting PTSD, which Hedges claims, does not take sides between soldiers and journalists or civilians in the crossfire. And it is in our shared burden of that malady that I locate my deepest affinity for Chris Hedges, and embrace this tender comrade as a brother veteran–victim of war.

Clearly I am not a disciple of his politics. In fact I must say that I am completely confounded by the fact that Hedges went out of his way this January to interview Ralph Nader, and then—even in light of recent events in Madison, Wisconsin—has completely failed to integrate the lessons Nader was attempting to teach him. Nader, who probably understands civil, political and corporate cultures in the U.S.—and how they interact—better than any other American political figure, does not as far as I know subscribe to the "throw our bodies into the machinery" brand of political evangelism currently being pushed by Hedges. Rather, Nader suggests an alternative imperative:

"Every major movement starts with field organizers, the farmers, unions, and the civil rights movement.... But there's nothing out there. We need to start learning from what was done in the past."

There's a surprisingly whimsical side to Nader too. He momentarily waxes poetic describing for Hedges a vision he calls the "black swan question ... whether something will erupt that is rare, extreme and unpredictable."

This is before Wisconsin, so Nader muses that it's "amazing that it hasn't happened in any pocket of the country. How much more can the oppressed take before they revolt? And can they revolt without organizers"?

Nader, with his sensitivity to rapidly changing historical currents, impatiently awaits the ever-anticipated push-back as we are witnessing now among public sector workers and nurses, firmly resisting the latest union busting challenge confronting a labor movement long in decline. Is this the 'black swan' moment? Maybe yes, maybe no. Minimally, Hedges and those who follow his doomsday strategy must concede that "repeated and substantial acts of civil disobedience" are not the only avenues of struggle available to us today. There is an opening here, an opportunity to end our wars more quickly by building support for this revived labor movement, which in turn must come to understand that obscene levels of military spending and tax breaks for the greediest are the major obstacles, not only to their interests and the popular welfare, but to democracy itself.

It's an iffy proposition. As Nader says, "You have got to have organizers, and now, we don't."

Counterpunch, **January 23, 2015**

Déjà Vu All Over Again

Notes on Jonathan Schell's Review of Nick Turse's *Kill Anything That Moves*

Jonathan Schell's probing review of Nick Turse's *Kill Anything That Moves* originated on *Tom Dispatch* and migrated to *Salon*, where it appeared under the head, "Vietnam was even more horrific than we thought."

Really? While Jonathan Schell is not accountable for the Homer Simpson–moment in *Salon*'s headline, he nonetheless seems convinced that Nick Turse's recently published book justifies such hyperbole. Schell, of course, produced some of the finest reporting to come out of the Vietnam War, and one is inclined to take seriously his views on this subject. Yet Schell immediately undermines the authority conferred by his masterly reporting during the war's earlier stages with the disclaimer that, "like so many reporters in Vietnam, I saw mainly one aspect of one corner of the war … not enough to serve as a basis for generalization about the conduct of the war as a whole."

This retroactive blind spot on Schell's part, I'd wager, did not prevent his many readers from doing precisely what he says he shied from, extrapolating from his gripping accounts the strong suspicion that the air war he witnessed so intimately in Quang Ngai Province was a template for the use of American air power and massive bombing throughout South Vietnam. It's a tangential point, but it does set up the clouded historical perspective Schell applies throughout this review.

I cannot comment here directly on Turse's book for the simple reason that I won't see the copy I ordered for another week. But, as I sit here midwinter in a small village on the coast of Maine with only limited reference materials at hand, I must take issue with some of the claims Jonathan Schell makes for this book that are independent of any future evaluations on my part concerning its quality, timeliness, and scholarly contribution.

It seems that only now with the publication of Nick Turse's book has the narrow window through which Schell says he once observed the war expanded to reveal a source that "has for the first time put together a comprehensive picture ... of what American forces actually were doing in Vietnam." What Schell had "once considered isolated atrocities, were in fact the norm."

Turse's achievement, according to Schell, is "an accurate overall picture of what ... has never been assembled ... for instance, the mind-boggling estimates that during the war there were some two million civilians killed...." This is hardly news when you consider that the Vietnamese themselves have been loudly proclaiming this carnage for decades. Nonetheless Schell goes on to argue, "It has not been until the publication of Turse's book that the everyday reality of which these atrocities were a part has been brought so fully to light." Perhaps the key word here is "fully." What Schell seems to be arguing is that, what had been and remains common knowledge to many—antiwar Vietnam veterans like myself for example—only constitutes true knowledge of the war's "everyday reality" if it is repackaged years later between the covers of a single volume in which the author is said to have formulated "the actual facts of the case."

Schell then concedes that it wasn't exactly that the "actual facts" of the war were shrouded from public view, but that they were presented within the frame of a false dichotomy. As accounts of atrocities began to accumulate dramatically after the revelation in November 1969 of the My Lai massacre, these barbarisms by the troops were presented by the government as "aberrations" and by antiwar forces as "orders from the top," which is to say, "policy." For Schell, however, "the relationship between policy and practice in Vietnam was ... far more peculiar than the two choices suggest."

American troops invading Vietnam in 1965 were, he reflects, "expecting to be welcomed as saviors." But instead they "found themselves in a sea of nearly universal hostility." Built on this observation—and presumably distilled from Turse's text—is perhaps the most convoluted passage in Schell's lengthy essay. Essentially he concludes that since Washington had not provided a "manual," which is to say clearly stated policy guidelines, "it was left to the soldiers to decide what to do." And, therefore, "to this extent, policy was indeed being made in the field." In this scenario, U.S. soldiers were trapped between the "impossible mission dictated from above (to win "hearts and minds" of a population already overwhelmingly hostile, while pulverizing their society) and locally conceived illegal but sometimes vague orders that left plenty of room for spontaneous, rage-driven improvisation on the ground."

"Locally conceived illegal but sometimes vague orders," is definitely a mouthful for any poor grunt to digest. But let's just isolate the words "vague orders" to highlight the flaw in Schell's thinking here. Well, were they orders or weren't they? Or to put it more clearly, did the troops understand them as orders or didn't they? Somehow erased from Schell's portrayal of American soldiers "in the field" is the fact that they were commanded by senior field grade officers (lieutenant colonels), and on occasion by officers of even higher rank (as in my own experience with the 11th Infantry—the My Lai brigade—under the notorious "gook hunter," Colonel John Donaldson). While I suspect these names are not overlooked by Nick Turse, there's no mention by Schell of Hatchet Hank Emerson, or George S. Patton, Jr., and other notoriously blood-thirsty battalion commanders who were constantly in the field directing and cheering on the "rage-driven" mayhem carried out by their troops.

To extricate himself from this apparent slippage in his analysis, Schell mounts a *deus ex machina* that in one magic stroke replaces an anarchic battlefield reminiscent of *Lord of the Flies* with a war suddenly and unambiguously conducted by "orders from the top." Schell cues the next scene with actual stage directions: "Enter General [Julian] Ewell and his body count." Schell's contention being that the high command has finally come to understand that counting the bodies is the only yardstick available to them in a People's War for measuring progress on the battlefield, and thus, "the improvising moved up the chain of command until the soldiers *were* following orders when they killed civilians."

The problem is that by the time General Ewell took command of the 9th Infantry Division in February 1968, the *body count* culture—*de facto* or otherwise—already had deep roots in the "search and destroy" operations that long dominated American combat tactics. Whether a given GI sometimes handed out candy to small children, or, in another mood—covered in the blood and flesh of a buddy blown sky high by a booby trap within sight of a "friendly" village—torched a hooch or abused a cringing *papasan* or worse, every grunt understood the meaning of the 'mere gook' rule. Any Vietnamese killed in an operation—and statistically that was almost always an unarmed civilian who may or may not have been a non-combatant—was declared to be one less Viet Cong and added to a unit's roster of enemy kills in a shower of praise from the "old man." The practice of awarding three day in-country R&R getaways to Nha Trang and other exotic beaches on the South China Sea to GIs who had increased their units' body count was by then well established.

Keep in mind that the My Lai massacre occurred in March of 1968, many months before General Ewell and his 9th Infantry launched the infamous Speedy Express operation Schell refers to that produced such an enormous body count and so few captured weapons, at which point Ewell becomes Schell's avatar who shifts accountability for the slaughter of civilians from the troops in the field to the policy makers in Washington and the high command of the Pentagon. The fact was, if you do the math based on two million dead Vietnamese, it's clear that Speedy Express was itself, not the exception, but the norm.

Bogged down in the untenable thesis that field policy "was left to the soldiers to decide," Schell can only move on by acknowledging that, after all, but "for the blind and misguided policies ... of the war's architects ... these infernal situations never would have arisen." The war was always intrinsically an "atrocity producing situation," Schell now realizes, citing the well-known formula coined by psychiatrist, Robert J. Lifton, an early pioneer in recognizing post-traumatic stress disorder among Vietnam War veterans. This insight of Lifton's on how atrocities became the "norm" in Vietnam is one, it now appears, that can be generalized by Schell to embrace the entire war.

Everything that Schell attributes to Turse's book in his review—which is clearly only one enthusiastic critic's précis of the work—was well known, if not during the earliest days, certainly by the late stages of the organized opposition to Vietnam. Getting out that message was precisely what scores of returning war veterans like myself were attempting, most intensely between the public revelation of My Lai in late 1969 and the by now obscure and forgotten congressional hearings on war crimes in Vietnam chaired by Congressman Ron Dellums at the end of April 1971. Schell suggests that the evidence of wide scale atrocities then in circulation was anecdotal when, in fact, Vietnam veterans in waves, representing virtually every phase of the war and every sector of the fighting, appeared in public over a period covering almost two years giving *eye witness* testimony of atrocities they had witnessed or participated in. Moreover these atrocities were consciously framed by the antiwar activists who organized these veterans as *standard operating procedure* and *de facto* policies designed by the architects and managers of the war.

Even in advance of seeing it I anticipate that, as a comprehensive study, Nick Turse's new book is an extraordinary contribution to the efforts of those of us who for decades have been fighting the battle over how our history will portray the Vietnam War. The campaign to challenge the forces aimed at re-writing or sanitizing the history of the Vietnam War has recently been injected with new urgency in the wake of President Obama's launching last Memorial Day [2013] of the Pentagon's Vietnam War Commemoration Project. This $5 million-a-year Pentagon project seeks to honor Vietnam veteran "warriors" in national and community-based ceremonies from now until 2025, while stripping away the "atrocity producing" context in which the war was executed.

Among the 30,000 titles on the Vietnam War Jonathan Schell refers to in his review, his *The Village of Ben Suc* and *The Military Half* are in the cream that floats on the top of that list. But still, I believe that Schell has oversold the groundbreaking significance of Nick Turse's book by overlooking the historical platform on which it has been constructed.

Let me be clear on several points. Nothing can justify the atrocities inflicted upon the Vietnamese people by American soldiers during the course of the Vietnam War. Probably the majority of American soldiers never committed atrocities, although I would argue that a majority witnessed them at one time or another during their in-country tours. Nor are those who did commit atrocities absolved of personal responsibility for their actions. The questions here are where the greater responsibility falls, and whether or not "soldiers in the field" ever formulated policy, even in a *de facto* sense, and whether or not the commission of these atrocities was known to be the "norm"—even if this assertion was not generally accepted by the government, the media, the public or Jonathan Schell—long before the publication of *Kill Anything That Moves*. Schell maintains that "the everyday reality" of the war was "never assembled" before Turse's book. [Appended to the following article, my review of Nicolas Turse's book, is a bibliographic clippings file that calls this view into question].

Postscript: The bibliography on what the historian and Vietnam War apologist Guenter Lewy called the Citizens Commission of Inquiry (CCI) and Vietnam Veterans Against the War's (VVAW) "war crimes industry" is short. It includes, *Standard Operating Procedure*, by James Simon Kunen (Avon, 1971); *The Dellums Committee Hearings on War Crimes in Vietnam* (Vintage, 1972), and my own memoir, *Vietnam Awakening* (McFarland, 2007).

Here's how I described the CCI in *Vietnam Awakening*:

> The CCI would play a catalytic role in building this unprecedented formation of antiwar veterans by framing an issue around war crimes that the former soldiers could address and legitimize with reference to their own experiences on the battlefield. And no one knew better from the inside out what was wrong with Vietnam than the troops who fought there. What made this mobilization of antiwar vets all the more astounding was that the war was still far from over. Moreover the vets who were eventually filtered—directly or indirectly—through CCI into Vietnam Veterans Against the War, already possessed strong needs to communicate their disillusionment to the Middle American communities from which they sprang: these same folks who President Nixon caricatured as the silent majority, a great blob of drones and tongue tied patriots, among whom, unfortunately, the message and style of the antiwar movement played with such little sympathy.

It was in linking Vietnam veterans to the powerful antiwar forces already in existence by means of a highly publicized campaign to denounce U.S. war crimes throughout Indochina that CCI's two principal coordinators,

Jeremy Rifkin and Tod Ensign, made their considerable contribution—though largely overlooked in accounts of the times—to organized antiwar opposition during its later stages from 1970 through 1971.

What I present as evidence in the "clipping file," is, as we used to say about the My Lai massacre, just the tip of the iceberg. A reader might conclude, however, even based on this limited sampling, that Americans were hearing and reading on a regular basis in the mainstream media, certainly after November 1969, the widely published message from elements of the antiwar movement, and from war veterans themselves, that atrocities in Vietnam were in fact the norm, and the direct outcome of U.S. government policies and "orders from above," however explicitly or implicitly delivered. If that message failed to be heard, that's another thing entirely.

InTheMindField, **January 22, 2013**
Counterpunch, **January 23, 2013**

An Enfant Terrible Stumbles Upon the Vietnam War

A Review of Nick Turse's *Kill Anything That Moves*

> "...the most unjust war ever waged by a stronger against a weaker nation."
> —Ulysses S. Grant (speaking of the Mexican War).

Comes now Nick Turse, forty years after the signing of the Paris Peace Accords, with *Kill Anything That Moves: The Real American War in Vietnam*, a compendious retelling of the horrors once inflicted by the United States of America against a tiny South East Asian adversary and its entire population. As a foundation for this grisly retrospective the author has assembled hundreds of sources, virtually all of which date from the time of the original telling, and to which he has joined the testimony of veterans and veteran observers along with the voices of Vietnamese victims unavailable for interview until long after the war had ended.

The impulse to resurrect *en masse* the record of this dirty war, what Turse characterizes as its "hidden history," resulted from an epiphany the author experienced in 2001 at the National Archives. As a graduate student "researching post-traumatic stress disorder among Vietnam veterans," Turse confides that he "stumbled upon ... the yellowing records of the Vietnam War Crimes Working Group ... more than 300 allegations of ... atrocities that were substantiated by army investigators." The files, Turse says, were "long hidden away and almost forgotten."

Well, yes and no. A decade earlier, these same files had been scanned and duly cited by Michael Bilton and Kevin Sim, whose *Four Hours in My Lai* was motivated by a similar premise, that the notorious massacre of March 16, 1968, had suffered from "twenty years of cover-up and willed forgetfulness." Nick Turse, quite rightly, goes much farther in applying his indictment of "forgetfulness" to the entire Vietnam conflict, where, in the once familiar mantra of antiwar veterans who had witnessed these horrors first hand, and then publically condemned them, *My Lai was just the tip of the iceberg*. But by now, Turse laments, "The other atrocities perpetrated by U.S. soldiers have essentially vanished from popular memory."

Come to think of it, what hasn't? "Popular memory," assuming the concept isn't completely spurious, is at best a labile thing. Moreover, what can one expect the popular memory to retain? We might with some charity assign a collective D—to the powers of retention of historical detail—informed or otherwise—by our fellow Americans. The comic genius Groucho Marx devilishly exhibited this national deficiency on his television quiz show in the Fifties. When a pair of contestants failed to answer a single question correctly on some current or iconic historical topic, Groucho offered them a consolation prize if they could tell him who was buried in Grant's Tomb, or what was the color of Washington's white horse; sometimes they couldn't.

The example may seem trivial, but the point still holds. Can Vietnam hope to fare any better if we are to depend on popular memory to remind us of its truths? What if anything beyond the most abbreviated commonplaces does popular memory recall of our prior "Vietnams"—the Indian Wars, the Mexican War, the Spanish American War in Cuba and the Philippines, Central America for over a century—our dark tradition of turning superior fire power against weaker nations we target for the sake of our *destiny* to dominate and pillage? As for Iraq and Afghanistan, the public didn't even catch them the first time around.

A fellow Vietnam veteran and memoirist, John Ketwig, relays an anecdote that illustrates the problem sharply. Ketwig wrote me of "a long ago conference at Gettysburg College [where] … the audience and presenters consisted of professional soldiers from the nearby Army War College at Carlisle, PA." During the morning session Ketwig, "along with W.D. Ehrhart and other prominent Vietnam [War] authors," served up the by-then familiar inconvenient truths about the criminal nature of the war they'd recently been fighting. After which, Ketwig recalls, "an old lifer Sergeant Major spoke, pointed to us and very specifically stated, 'These whining, complaining Vietnam veterans will die off. I want to assure you, we have written the history of the Vietnam war your grandchildren will read.'"

If the Old Lifer imagined he was addressing History-with-a-capital-H, clearly his prediction was overwrought by wishful thinking. The bibliographic catalog is well stacked against the diehard apologists, not least the self-justifying screeds by those who cheered and managed the debacle and their revisionist disciples who have followed. The real whining would come, of course, from the likes of Robert J. McNamara. No amount of breast beating about dangers born of Cold War tensions has made what lies beneath the My Lai iceberg suddenly vanish from the historical record, to which *Kill Anything That Moves* now provides a striking addendum.

Obviously Nick Turse's ambition for this book ranges far beyond serving scholarly mills, or reaching whatever limited market this subject still commands among its core readers. Turse intends *Kill Anything That Moves* as mass-shock treatment to override the public's amnesia, aggressively demanding that we re-examine Vietnam's horrors with even greater intensity today than we did forty to fifty years ago. But how does this agenda square with the public mood? That query returns us to the chilling side of that Old Lifer's prophesy, because the views on the Vietnam War our millennials are forming today suggest strongly that the indoctrination he boasted of is well underway.

Citing a recent Gallop poll, journalist Robert Sheer reports that "a majority of Americans ages 18–29 believe sending U.S. troops to Vietnam was not a mistake ... the young now approve of an irrational war in which 3.4 million Indochinese and 58,000 Americans died...." Holding steady across the age divide, "70% of those 50 or older ... with contemporary knowledge..." retain their beliefs in the war's essential wrongness. This leaves Nick Turse addressing an aging choir that already knows the hymnal by rote, while among his own peers, not to mention Sheer's "18–29 year olds," his thunder confronts a formidable headwind.

When *Kill Anything That Moves* was launched in such a promising whirl of enthusiasm from the more respectable corridors of the Left media ghetto, it fleetingly appeared as if Turse might indeed have re-set the historical clock. But the dust stirred by that initial thrust settled quickly. And the sound of silence greeting Turse's book from the elite opinion-making heavyweights, whose reviews and news stories are essential for gaining the kind of national recognition the author and his sponsors had clearly hoped for, has been deafening.

Perhaps because so much of what Turse has reassembled already appeared—if not in every specific, certainly in kind—within its pages while the war was in progress, *The New York Times,* for example, may judge *Kill Anything That Moves* as twice-warmed news. Such thinking would provide the paper's managers all the sanctimonious cover they'd need to help stymie any genuinely healthy re-examination of American crimes against humanity in Vietnam, oft reported, but never officially acknowledged, much less repented. But why would the *Times* and the other great organs and outlets of bounded propaganda, whatever else divides them, want to re-air the real history of Vietnam today? The last thing the elite political class wants is to reconnect Vietnam to the present, certainly not in the direction that Nick Turse has failed to provoke them. They know Vietnam was not a mistake; it's a template.

To jump start a renewed public conversation about Vietnam that aims at eliminating that template as a future military option—presumably Turse's more elusive and essentially unpainted target—apparently demands a bigger boost than one explosive charge dredged from the archives can deliver. This assumes that the Vietnam template isn't already losing favor among national security managers. In which case, asks W.D. Ehrhart, still in the conversation long after that conference at Gettysburg, what particular end is Turse's so-called "hidden history" meant to serve beyond exhibiting "a randomly presented litany of mayhem?"

Bill Ehrhart has spent decades since being wounded during the Battle of Hue bringing to literature, classroom and public forums—in consort with a large community of like-minded veterans—compelling eyewitness accounts of the systematic nature of atrocities committed by the U.S. military throughout Indochina. Having read my essay criticizing Jonathan Shell's breathless review of *Kill Anything That Moves*, Ehrhart expressed the opinion that "Schell's reaction to Turse's book is ridiculous." What Schell gushes over as novelty, Ehrhart calls "old news." And, after examining the book, he dismisses it with a terseness both unsparing and poetic: "disjointed, disorganized, without direction."

But that's hardly the worst of it, and these next sentiments of Ehrhart's deeply echo my own. "If Turse were a true journalist and scholar, he would be shouting, 'Why didn't anyone listen to veterans who told these stories forty years ago?' He ripped off our history shouting—Look what I discovered!—and presented the case as if it's being told for the first time."

Turse's claims to originality are slippery enough, but the "rip off" exceedingly worse. Regarding the former we are told that, as the author's research deepened over the years, he "began to get a sense of the ubiquity of atrocity during the American War," a hip way of showing he knows how the Vietnamese refer to the same conflict. And elsewhere, "...I came to see the indiscriminate killing of South Vietnamese non-combatants ... was neither accidental nor unforeseeable."

We might overlook this silly pretense were it not at the expense of a consciously organized veterans' resistance which arose following the belated revelation of My Lai, and operated within the larger antiwar movement where the narrative of Vietnam genocide had been long evolving. In the very language and political formulations that Turse now appropriates, often literally, a veritable legion of veterans loudly proclaimed those very revelations that the author wishes to showcase as novel insights. Moreover, we based our evidence for the ubiquity of American war crimes on our actual wartime experiences, as we helped sway the public to finally reject the war we ourselves had been fighting in. These are the unique historical episodes that Turse completely ignores.

In his account antiwar veterans appear, not as a movement making history, but as a handful of individual "whistle-blowers within the ranks or recently out of the army..." whose denunciations were "marginalized and ignored." For the rest, Turse buries our unprecedented story in a thicket of footnotes, devoid of their original contexts, and where only a disciplined scholar might be able to reassemble them into anything approximating what actually occurred. A reader may judge for herself, if the public testimonies on U.S. war crimes policies in Vietnam delivered by antiwar veterans during the final years of the conflict were, as Turse suggests, "marginalized and ignored." She might discover that the veterans were being heard at the time, if not listened to, much more than Turse is today. [See the Clipping File which follows this review].

Nick Turse's decision to airbrush from the record the provenance of the Vietnam war-crimes narrative, and the roles of veterans within it, defies explanation. As already noted, the scope of research under display in his copious list of sources makes evident that he knew this story well. My own emails with the author, who had seen my pre-published version of this history while still in dissertation form—thick and unwieldy as he rightly chided me—date from 2007. And while it touches me less personally, though only slightly, Turse's use of similar methods for downgrading the stature and significance of the American antiwar movement is equally perplexing.

No old Movement hand intimately familiar with those times could fail to notice how Turse prunes the most powerful unarmed, overwhelmingly non-violent, forces of domestic resistance to governing authority in U.S. history to the status of a sideshow. Here's one particularly ham fisted sample of his distorting style. He characterizes as pitiful Movement efforts to reveal the true nature of the war through "pamphlets, small press books and underground newspapers," that, if even glancingly noticed by empowered insiders, were dismissed as "leftist kookery."

When one turns to the footnote for this passage to scan the names of these presumably obscure "pamphlets, small press books and underground newspapers," one finds instead that the printed matter antiwar forces produced to advance their war crimes accusations was packaged by the very titans of American trade and newspaper publishing: Random House, Simon and Schuster, Holt Rinehart, Vintage—the quality paperback imprint, Avon—the mass paperback imprint of the Hearst Corporation, a couple of smaller but respected houses like Beacon and Pilgrim Press, two or three international publishers, their reputations unknown to me, and *The New York Times*.

I understand that many of the interested parties who may see this essay will simply react to the issues I have raised here with a resounding, "So what?" Maybe Turse got some of the story wrong, they might admit, even in ways that make him appear amateurish, if not perverse. But he nails the big picture bearing on the carnage and destruction, to a large degree intentionally orchestrated by the U.S. during its aggressive war against Vietnam. But I would take issue even with that. On the thin narrative thru-line where Turse strings the graphically descriptive details of one atrocity after another, he seems to weigh the vile handiwork of individual GIs operating in the field on a par with the far more deadly toll that sprang from cold hearted policies of mass murder designed by high level commanders, political bureaucrats and academics: the indiscriminate use of artillery and air power to remove and disrupt populations, and which caused the overwhelming number of deaths and casualties among the South Vietnamese.

Turse certainly reports on, and strongly denounces, *pacification*'s deadly harvest of non-combatants. But by placing so much emphasis on the 300 Pentagon investigations that originally ignited his zeal for this subject, the statistical significance of his soldier-initiated atrocities pales before the ranks of two and a half million draft aged men who'd served in Vietnam during the war. Let's assume those 300 cases of substantiated atrocities are actually representative of thousands of unreported heinous incidents committed by thousands of individual soldiers—which I firmly believe was the case. That still would leave a substantial body of other veterans with clean hands, to the degree any soldier at war can make such a claim. Let's just say they weren't involved in rape, torture, mutilation, pre-meditated murder or manslaughter, or willful destruction of livestock or property.

A very large number of veterans therefore might feel unfairly tarred by Turse's sweeping brush, assuming they ever became aware of his book in the first place. I sense this would matter very little to Nick Turse. As he makes no effort to conceal in a recent essay, "Who Did You Rape in the War, Daddy" [TomDispatch.com, March 19, 2013], Turse seems to harbor a truly bizarre resentment toward war veterans, notably the many he has interviewed over the years and now accuses of not coming clean to him about the things they'd seen or done. Reading that, it occurred to me that Turse had learned very little about veterans when his research was initially focused on PTSD. He seemed to have missed the fact that deep issues of trust determine who veterans will talk to about war, and as is commonly understood, that they generally talk only with each other.

But now Turse is pissed, and he engages in a bit of shadow boxing with veterans as ghostly adversaries. "I know a lot about war without fighting in one," he defiantly lectures some unidentified veteran other. And, it has cost him. But he expresses pride because this "just isn't the sort of knowledge that's easy to come by," and who said it was? Anyway, this could be one digression too many, so read his essay cited above and judge for yourself. My own take is that Turse is suffering from the equivalent of penis envy in having been denied firsthand experience with warfare. He has had to find compensation, but his vicarious knowledge of war is made harder to come by because veterans are deceitful, and won't "come clean." Turse's judgment here is clouded by his temper tantrum.

Turse's other signal observation is that accounts of Vietnamese viewpoints and victimhood are largely absent from the 30,000 volumes covering the American representations of the war. This is hardly surprising since the opportunities for serious research and interviewing in Vietnam were not available until decades after the war. By the time mass tourism had blossomed there well into the millennium, returning veterans have typically expressed astonishment that the recovered Vietnam they find today is totally unrecognizable from the country they had once fought in. This is the Vietnam in which the kind of research Turse brags about is finally possible. Long before that, veterans established humanitarian projects in Vietnam and have for decades been in the forefront of campaigns to raise public awareness of the human suffering still afflicting so many Vietnamese who survived the war, not least the toll in human lives from herbicide poisoning and unexploded ordinance, all reaching now into the third and fourth postwar generations.

Neither Bill Ehrhart nor I, among thousands of others—veterans and non-veterans alike—have ever abandoned through our writing and political action, and in classrooms where we have taught or been invited to speak, our commitments to keep the flame of truth about *the real American war in Vietnam* from being extinguished. To that protracted struggle, Nick Turse has added his flawed and impassioned contribution. But the impulse that will lead, if ever, to the cleansing of our butchery in Vietnam from the national conscience, is unlikely to come from collective, much less individual, efforts of the progressive camp.

It is an odd fact of our culture that, when controversial topics are avoided or suppressed, they can sneak back in as entertainment. Who knows if Vietnam won't slip into the popular media slot that's been vacated by the Greatest Generation? It's a fair bet. But when, and in what form, it's impossible to predict. Will the space be dynamic enough to air the most damning facts, and here Turse's indictment could be included when the papers are served. How much energy remains in the aging antiwar crowd to re-fight these old battles? Is the Old Lifer bound to win, or will the young break the propaganda spell? And, if our side won, what would that look like? It's something to think about. I'm not waiting for the Rapture, but I'm preparing for the opening, if and when it comes.

InTheMindField, April 5, 2013
Counterpunch, April 9, 2015

Veteran War Crimes Testimony, 1969–1971: An Annotated Clipping File

I have listed below more than ninety articles dating from the revelation of the My Lai massacre in late 1969 until the fall of 1971 in which American war veterans presented compelling, eyewitness testimony on the "true nature of the Vietnam War." Over and over in these accounts the veterans charged that Vietnamese civilians were routinely subjected to atrocities that resulted from policies designed and executed at the highest levels of American civilian and military wartime leadership.

While accusations that the U.S. was engaged in "genocide" against the population of South Vietnam were expressed early and often by the antiwar movement from the war's outset, the overwhelming majority of the articles cited here appeared in big city mass circulation daily newspapers. They are contained in a clipping file I maintained while working with the Citizens Commission of Inquiry which organized public forums for veterans to testify about war crimes they had witnessed or participated in while serving in Vietnam.

We conscientiously gathered the press accounts of CCI's organizing track record, fortunate to have had access to an out-of-town newspaper stand available in Times Square, New York City. At the same time CCI never engaged a clipping service, which I am certain would have increased many fold the citations I have presented here. In some cases there are multiple accounts generated by a single press event, cited here to demonstrate how widely we were able to get the war crimes message out within the U.S. media during the course of CCI's brief existence.

Some of the most respected reporters and war correspondents of their generation covered these stories to include Richard Dudman, Neil Sheehan, Nat Hentoff, Nicholas von Hoffman, Homer Bigart, and Jules Witcover. Some annotation has been added where I felt it would be useful.

1. "New Antiwar Group Writes GIs," William Serrin. *Detroit Free Press*, May 21, 1967. A veterans group in Detroit, Veterans Against War, held war crimes hearings at Wayne State University. The reporter describes them as "carbons of the Bertrand Russell International War Crimes Tribunal."

2. "Letter From a Vietnam Veteran," Major Gordon Livingston, M.D. *Saturday Review*, September 20, 1969. A West Point graduate and regimental surgeon with the 11th Armored Cavalry under Col. George S. Patton, III. One of the most eloquent antiwar statements ever written by a veteran of the war, Livingston with considerable understatement concludes "that Americans simply do not care about the Vietnamese."

3. "Vietnam Genocide," a special supplement published by the *Guardian*, a weekly tabloid of the American Left, December 8, 1969. Among several articles on the massacre at Song My (My Lai), including one titled, "One tragic village among thousands," is an article by Ralph Schoenman, "War crimes follow 'Standard Operating Procedures.'" Schoenman had recently completed several years of work with the Russell Tribunal, which had been publicizing the accounts of war crimes provided by the North Vietnamese, which had been dismissed as propaganda in the western media. There's also an article by former Green Beret Don Duncan, "What makes an atrocity," and an article on chemical defoliation in Vietnam.

4. "Peace Group to Set Up Panels on Atrocity Charges," *New York Times*, November 30, 1969. The article reports "the formation of citizen's commissions ... where former soldiers would provide first-hand evidence of war crimes ... including electric torture and killing of prisoners [as] part of an American policy in South Vietnam ... carried out on orders from those higher up."

5. "Viet Atrocities Hearings Set for 11 Cities," Timothy Ferris. *New York Post*, February 14, 1970. Jeremy Rifkin of CCI announces hearing in the U.S. for Annapolis, MD, saying that "the committee will examine whether specific U.S. military policy in Vietnam now in effect are in fact war crimes." CCI quickly abandoned this posture of an open-ended inquiry.

6. "Viet Cong scalps were GI souvenirs US deserters say," *Toronto Daily Star*. March 5, 1970. CCI's first press event actually took place in Toronto. Dr. Gordon Livingston participated, as did two American military resisters who had deserted their units for Canadian exile. Thereafter, CCI would only permit vets with honorable discharges to testify, not from lack of solidarity with the exiled GI resisters, but to enhance the credibility of the veterans' eye witness testimony in the eyes of the U.S. media. Within two years, Tod Ensign and I would form the Safe Return committee to work

specifically on the campaign to win amnesty for military resisters living in exile and underground in the U.S.

7. "Antiwar Group Plans Meeting in Annapolis," *The Evening Star* [Washington, D.C.], Mar. 6, 1970. While Tod was in Toronto, Jeremy was in D.C. to drum up media interest in our next event.

8. "War crimes unit stages Vietnam horror showing," by Don Frese. *Evening Capital* [Annapolis, MD], March 12, 1970. Photographs, motion pictures and slides of dead and maimed children were used to convey the horror of the Vietnamese War.... The inquiry ... is intended to show how war crimes fit into our overall war policy." And in one paragraph, the reporter writes that an "ex-soldier told of his involvement in widespread bombing of villages and defoliation of the land. **'We were told to kill everything that moved'** [emphasis added]."

9. "Eyewitness report on U.S.-Viet horrors." *The Baltimore Afro-American*, March 17, 1970.

10. "Rebel Officer Cites My Lai," Cy Egan. *New York Post*, March 17, 1970. Lt. Louis Font, a West Point graduate attending Harvard grad school, announces he will refuse orders to Vietnam, in an act of 'selective' conscientious objection. Font will go on to help found the Concerned Officers Movement, and to work closely with CCI.

11. "War Crimes in Vietnam," a flyer announcing a Teach-in at New York University, March 17, 1970. The meeting, featuring the Citizens Commission of Inquiry, "will document the truth about genocidal massacre of the civilian population of South Vietnam." This was a big moment for me personally; I met Jan (Barry) Crumb and joined VVAW, which he had co-founded; and soon thereafter I began to work full time with CCI.

12. "U.S. Army Veteran Alleges Vietnamese Civilians Slain," *Springfield Union* [Springfield, MA], April 7, 1970. West Point graduate and former Infantry Captain, Robert Bowie Johnson, quoted in the article, said, "'irrational acts' of servicemen in Vietnam are traceable to the 'irrational policy of the United States in Vietnam.'"

13. "Group Tells 'True Nature' of War: New massacre claim probed," Adam Fisher. *Springfield Daily News*, April 6, 1970.

14. "U.S. Army Veteran Alleges Vietnamese Civilians Slain." *The Springfield Union*, April 7, 1970.

15. "Ex-Pilot Alleges Civilian Slayings," Douglas Robinson. *The New York Times*, April 7, 1970.

16. "Army Opens Probe of New 'Atrocity." *The Miami Herald*, April 8, 1970. This, and a similar article by UPI, reported that the Army intended to investigate the charges we had made at the Springfield press conference.

17. "Army Probes New Charge of Viet Deaths." *The Evening Star* [UPI], April 8, 1970.

18. "3 Viet Vets Charge 'Routine' Use of Torture by U.S. Troops," by Timothy Ferris. *New York Post*, April 13, 1970. Here CCI is quoted on precisely what Jonathan Schell says he learned from Nick Turse's book only in 2013, that "The U.S. military machine was [a] … system in which torture was standard procedure and extrajudicial executions common."

19. "They'd Probe Pentagon on 'Atrocities,'" New York *Daily News*, April 14, 1970. At this press conference, where I gave an account of torture I had witnessed personally, CCI called for an "investigation of the Pentagon by some independent agency. It's absurd for the Pentagon to investigate itself for war crimes."

20. "Ex-GIs Charge Viet Prisoners Were Tortured," Jim Stinglet. *Los Angeles Times*, April 15, 1970. CCI had held simultaneous press conferences in LA and NY, featuring the eyewitness testimony on torture by six war veterans.

21. "GIs reveal new atrocities," *Guardian*, April 18, 1970. By this time coverage of CCI's work in left newspapers was rare.

22. "Two ex–GIs say troops torture prisoners in Vietnam," by Douglas Crocket. *The Boston Globe*, May 8, 1970." Larry Rottmann and I were joined in this press conference by Noam Chomsky, who revealed information on the secret war in Laos, which the media essentially ignored.

23. "'67 Yank forays in Cambodia," *Chicago Sun Times*. May 8, 1970. This UPI story did, however, pick up on Rottmann's testimony on having participated in covert operations in Cambodia, the other "secret" war that had just become widely known with the official U.S. invasion of that country.

24. "Ex-Intelligence Officers List War Crimes Witnessed," Dave O'Brien. *Boston Record American,* May 8, 1970.

25. "Torture Techniques Reported," *The Militant*, May 8, 1970. The only coverage we ever received in the SWP organ as far as I can recall.

26. "'Unofficial' atrocities attributed to Pentagon," Richard W. McManus. *The Christian Science Monitor*, May 8, 1970. Jeremy Rifkin is quoted saying, "Individual soldiers should not be made scapegoats for Defense Department policy."

27. "Parallel News," Nat Hentoff. *The Village Voice*, May 14, 1970. Hentoff got hold of and reprinted here the article by a *New York Times* reporter about CCI's April 14th news conference on torture that the paper had apparently killed. The *Times*' failure to run this story was also the subject of a letter to the paper's editor, April 21, 1970, signed by the Princeton International Law expert, Richard Falk and several other sponsors of CCI.

28. "Badges Given by U.S. Unit for Killing Enemy: Ears Accepted As Evidence," Tom Nugent. *Detroit Free Press*, June 10, 1970.

29. "Pacifists Offer My Lai Defense," Timothy Ferris. *New York Post*, July 7, 1970. CCI charged that only enlisted men and low ranking officers were being tried for their roles in the My Lai massacre, "scapegoating a handful of GIs for military strategies and policies conceived at the highest levels of government."

30. "Ex-GIs Tell of Torturing Prisoners," by William Greider. *The Washington Post*, July 19, 1970. The big news for me in this article was that Bill Greider was able to corroborate my allegations of torture through an interview with the Interrogation Officer in my 11th Infantry unit.

31. "Ex-GIs Describe Electric Torture of Viet Civilians," William Greider. *The Des Moines Register*, July 20, 1970.

32. "Ex-GIs Recall U.S. Brutality," *The Providence Journal*, July 20, 1970.

33. "Viet Veterans Hit 'Torture' by U.S. Units," *The Evening Star* [UPI], July 20, 1970.

34. "Vietnam Veterans story: GI Torture of Prisoners," *San Francisco Chronicle*, July 20, 1970.

35. "LIer Charges US Tortured Vietnamese," *Long Island Press*, July 20, 1970.

36. "Atrocities in Vietnam Said, 'a Way of Life,'" Carl Shires. *The Richmond News Leader*, August 18, 1970. "We were told the only good gook was a dead gook," testified former marine and admiral's son, T. Griffits Ellison.

37. "Veterans Say They Saw U.S. Atrocities in War," *The Washington Post*, August 18, 1970.

38. "Torture of Viet Cong described by ex-GI," *The Detroit News*, August 18, 1970.

39. "Veterans Tell of War Crimes," *St. Louis Post Dispatch* [UPI], August, 18, 1970.

40. "Ex-Officer says Cong tortured on his orders," *The Minneapolis Star*, August 18, 1970.

41. "Tales of War Cruelty," *S.F. Examiner*, August 18, 1970.

42. "Electric Shocks Get Viet Cong to Talk," *Wheeling News Register*, August 18, 1970.

43. "Veterans Describe U.S. War Crimes," *Winston-Salem Journal*, August 19, 1970.

44. "Vets Report on Brutality," *The Richmond Evening News*, August 19, 1970.

45. "Vietnam Vets: Yanks Commit Atrocities Daily," *St. Paul Pioneer Press*, September 26, 1970. A CCI hearing in Minneapolis followed that in Richmond. Our purpose, we explained, was to place "responsibility for the

war crimes ... on the joint chiefs, the administration and board members and stockholders of large defense corporations." And, "to explain the real nature of the war and put pressure on them to stop."

46. "5 Vets Charge Murder," Joseph H. Trachman. *The Philadelphia Inquirer*, October 20, 1970. I told the assembled media that CCI's purpose was to "enlist public sentiment for the convening of an international tribunal, similar to Nuremberg...."

47. There is an article in the Swedish newspaper, *Afton Bladet*, October 25, 1970, reporting on the testimony I had given before a meeting of the International Enquiry on U.S. War Crimes in Vietnam, in Stockholm several days later.

48. "War Atrocities Termed Commonplace," by James Long. *Oregon Journal*, October 28, 1970. A CCI coordinator is quoted saying, "The My Lai massacre is a logical outgrowth of policies set at the highest level—individual soldiers do not account for genocide."

49. "Jane Fonda's newest cause: probing US 'war crimes,'" by Evelyn Keene. *Boston Sunday Globe*, November 1, 1970. There was definitely a put-down tone in this article toward Jane, but it announced our plans for the Winter Soldier Investigation.

50. "City to Hear of Vietnam 'Crimes,'" Peter Benjaminson. *Detroit Free Press*, November 3, 1970. Jeremy Rifkin announces the upcoming Winter Soldier Investigation to the Detroit media.

51. Detroit Police Department Inter-office Memorandum. November 7, 1970. This 4 page memo was generated after the cops received a phone call from Lee I. Schulte, manager of the Detroit Veterans Memorial Building, which had been engaged by Tod Ensign, "Coordinator-Counsel" for the Winter Soldier Investigation. It reports on "a discreet confidential check with forces at Wayne State University regarding a Tod Ensign who ... was a student" there in 1965. The memo noted that "Detroit and Windsor will be the scene of an unusual early December denunciation of 'American War Crimes' in Vietnam, if the ambitious plans of two national antiwar groups [CCI and VVAW] bear fruit."

52. Articles began to appear prominently throughout the U.S. from the beginning of the trial of 1Lt. William L. (Rusty) Calley for his role in the My Lai massacre. For example, "U.S. Details Case Against Calley," Homer Bigart. *The New York Times*, November 18, 1970; "Witnesses Back My Lai Sergeant," Douglas Robinson. *The New York Times*, November 18, 1970.

53. "War Foes Blame U.S. Commanders for Viet Atrocities," Richard Maynard. *The Washington Post*, November 24, 1970. This announced CCI's National Veterans Inquiry, to begin in Washington the following week.

54. "Nuremberg III," Nat Hentoff. *The Village Voice*, November 26,

1970. Hentoff here essentially challenges the rest of the media to pay attention to CCI's upcoming National Veterans Inquiry.

55. "Slaughter not unusual: ex–GI," William McGaffin. *Chicago Daily News*, Nov. 28–19, 1970.

56. "Viet Vets Telling of Atrocities," *New York Post*, December 1, 1970. The article begins, "Twenty honorably discharged Vietnam war veterans presented eye-witness accounts today of incidents in which Viet-women and children were tortured, mutilated and even massacred by U.S. and allied ground forces."

57. "Antiwar Group Hears of 'Crimes,'" *The New York Times*, December 1, 1970.

58. "Vietnam atrocities told: Military intelligence involves systematic use of electric torture and beatings," Jerry Oppenheimer. *The Washington Daily News*, December 2, 1970.

59. "Ex-CIA man speaks of Vietnam killings," *The Times* [London], December 2, 1970.

60. "Veterans Tell of Atrocities," Richard Dudman. *St. Louis Post-Dispatch*, December 2, 1970.

61. "Viet Veterans Tell of GI Atrocities," Powell Lindsay. *The Pittsburgh Press*, December 2, 1970.

62. "City Ex-GI Tells of Shelling Peasants," *The Philadelphia Evening Bulletin*, December 2, 1970.

63. "Billings Veteran to Testify At 'War Crimes' Inquiry," *Billings Gazette* [Montana], December 3, 1970.

64. "We could hear them screaming," Jerry Oppenheimer. *The Washington Daily News*, December 3, 1970.

65. "A Tale of Torture and Murder," *The Daily Freeman* (Kingston, N.Y.), December 3, 1970.

66. "Viet Veterans Recall War Crimes," *The Charlotte Observer*, December 3, 1970.

67. "Ex-GI Says He Saw Americans Commit Executions, Atrocities," *The Florida Times-Union*, December 3, 1970. 68. "Yanks tortured Red prisoners, two GIs testify," *Chicago Daily News*, December 3, 1970.

69. "Torture was policy, Viet war vets say," *The Cleveland Press*. December 3, 1970.

70. "Red POWs Pushed Off Copter, Witness Says," *Los Angeles Times*, December 3, 1970.

71. "GI's threw 2 Viets to death, agent says," *The Detroit News*, December 3, 1970.

72. "Psychological Slavery: A Commentary," Nicholas von Hoffman. *The Washington Post*, December 4, 1970.

73. "'War Crimes' Inquiry Hears of Bombing," *San Francisco Chronicle*, December 4, 1970.

74. "Veterans Ask Inquiry Into Alleged Atrocities," Jules Witcover. *Los Angeles Times*, December 4, 1970.

75. "War Veterans at Inquiry Feel 'Atrocities' Are Result of Policy," *The New York Times*, December 4, 1970. The *Times* wrap-up on the three-day National Veteran Inquiry.

76. "New Vietnam Atrocity Charges Little Noticed; War Veterans Make Allegations of Bizarre Tortures, Crucifixion of Enemy Soldiers," Jules Witcover. *Los Angeles Times*, December 8, 1970. Witcover commented: "One of the major handicaps facing both Congress and reporters through the years in trying to learn what has happened in the Vietnam War has been that too often there has been only one source of information—the U.S. government."

77. "'We can't sleep man,' Veterans Inquiry into War Crimes," Lucien K. Truscott IV. *The Village Voice*, December 10, 1970.

78. "Why doesn't somebody do something?" Nat Hentoff. *The Village Voice*, December 31, 1970.

79. "Taylor Says by Nuremberg Rules Westmoreland May Be Guilty," by Neil Sheehan. *The New York Times*, January 9, 1971. This may have been the CCI's biggest publicity coup. No military commander was more closely identified with the Vietnam War than General William C. Westmoreland.

80. "Five Officers Say They Seek Formal War Crimes Inquiries," by Neil Sheehan. *The New York Times*, January 13, 1971. This was the second article that week by Neil Sheehan on CCI's work. Shortly thereafter, Sheehan broke the Pentagon Papers story in the *Times*. He already had them from Ellsberg well before the articles ran on CCI, or so I was told by the late John Simon, former editor of the *Times Book Review* who had commissioned the omnibus review of the mounting literature coving topics specifically or generally related to the war crimes issue, which would run in March 1971.

81. "4 Officers Challenge Top Brass on Policies in South Vietnam," Lee Dye. *Los Angeles Times,* January 21, 1971. This was the second of back-to-back press conferences that CCI organized for member of the Concerned Officers Movement, who sought to bring war crimes charges against their commanders under provisions of the Uniform Code of Military Justice.

82. "For a War Crimes Inquiry," Editorial. *Newsday* [Long Island, and New York City], March 22, 1971. *Newsday*, under the helm of Bill Moyers then as Publisher, may have been the only mainstream newspaper in the country to editorialize on behalf of a war crimes inquiry.

83. "Should We Have War Crimes Trials?" by Neil Sheehan. *The New*

York Times Book Review, March 28, 1971. An omnibus review of the contemporary literature on the war crimes issue, in which Sheehan comes down hardest on the American air war in Vietnam.

84. Between the National Veterans Inquiry and the Dellums Hearings on War Crimes, both of which were organized by CCI, the Winter Soldier Investigation was held in Detroit from January 31 to February 2, 1970. The event, as Jeremy Rifkin had predicted, did not receive much attention in the mainstream media, owing to its location in Detroit. But WSI was covered extensively in the antiwar press at the time, and received a major publicity boost a year later when the film *Winter Soldier* premiered at Cannes and at the Whitney Museum in New York. The rest is history.

A funding proposal circulated in March 1971 by Winter Film, which would produce the documentary, tells the story: "'The Winter Soldier Investigation' received no national radio or television coverage. Outside of minimal Detroit coverage the only media has been WBAI (New York)." To the extent the war crimes organizing effort among Vietnam veterans is remembered today, however, it is because of the Winter Soldier Investigation.

News of Lt. Calley's conviction on March 29, 1971, engendered a divergence of opinion in the liberal and antiwar communities, where some found themselves uncomfortably in agreement with the hawks, but for very different reasons.

85. "My Lai Verdict is Denounced; Calley Lawyer, Congressman Agree," *The Providence Journal*, March 30, 1971. The Congressman was California antiwar Democrat Ron Dellums, who was quoted saying, "I think it's a mistake to make one man the scapegoat for national policy." The Calley verdict, he said, "makes imperative congressional action on the war crimes issue." Dellums then promised that if the House failed to take action, he would hold hearings on his own.

86. "Liberals Seek War Crimes Inquiry," John W. Finny. *The New York Times*, March 31, 1971. Dellums' threat to hold hearings was vehemently opposed by the then chair of the House Armed Services Committee, Representative Edward Hibert, Democrat of Alabama.

The Dellums Hearings, organized by CCI, took place at the end of April, and were widely covered; citations for some of that coverage follows here:

87. "House Panel to hear Of Alleged Torture-Murder Policy in Viet," *The Baltimore Sun*, April 28, 1971.

88. "Ex-GI Alleges 30 Slayings Near Mylai," by Richard Halloran. *The New York Times*, April 28, 1971. CCI witness Danny Notley made public the Truong Khanh massacre at the Dellums Hearings. The massacre was soon confirmed.

89. "5 S. Viets Back Ex-GI on Atrocity," *Chicago Tribune*, May 8, 1971. An enterprising UPI reporter, based in Saigon, tracked down residents of the village where the massacre had taken place, and was able to provide corroboration of Notley's testimony.

90. "Charges U.S. Coverup on New My Lai," Emile Milne. *New York Post*, May 10, 1971.

91. "Another My Lai; U.S. Command Drags Heels," Lynn Newland. *New York Post*, May 10, 1971.

92. "Notley Urges Inquiry on War Tactics," Michael Gelter. *The Washington Post*, May 11, 1971. As in so many cases when similar allegations were made by veterans in this period, the Pentagon attempted to shift attention from the atrocity with the counter-charge that the veterans were remiss in not reporting the incident at the time of its occurrence, or that they refused—as Notley did—to provide the names of those who had been responsible. It was CCI policy to never "name names," not even those of the officers (except those of high rank) who may have been in command at the time the atrocity was committed, because doing so would involve "drawing attention away from civilian and military higher-ups responsible for the overall strategies."

93. "'War crimes' precedents discussed at Harvard forum," Joe Pilati. *Boston Globe*, May 1971. CCI's Tod Ensign, who was also Danny Notley's attorney, attended this forum on behalf of our group.

94. "General, Ex-Aide Accused of Murdering Vietnamese," William Beecher. *The New York Times*, June 3, 1971. I was particularly gratified by this development since I had served in the 11th Light Infantry Brigade under then Colonel John Donaldson, known to many there as a "gook hunter" who flew around dropping fragmentation grenades on unarmed peasants at work in their rice paddies. Even though the accusation had come from his own pilot, the charges were eventually dropped, since Donaldson claimed those he shot were Viet Cong soldiers fleeing from American forces.

95. "House Unit Disclosed Civilian Killings in U.S. Backed Program," Felix Belair, Jr. *The New York Times*, July 16, 1971. An obscure Congressional sub-committee on House Government Operations launched what was perhaps the only official government investigation on U.S. war crimes, focused on a particularly draconian military policy aimed at the assassination of Viet Cong cadres called the Phoenix Program.

96. "U.S. Aide Defends Pacification Program in Vietnam Despite Killings of Civilians," Felix Belair, Jr. *The New York Times*, July 20, 1971. The "aide" in question, William E. Colby, an intelligence operative who supervised the Phoenix Program in Vietnam, was soon to be appointed Director of the CIA. During his appearance before the House Government Operation sub-committee, "Two Republican representatives ... charged that Operation

Phoenix had been responsible for 'indiscriminate killings of civilians ... in violation of the Geneva Conventions.'"

97. "Phoenix Program Details: 'Sterile, Depersonalized Murder' Plan," Mary McGrory. *The Washington Post*, August 3, 1971. The article reports on the testimony two veteran witnesses, Bart Osborne and I, presented under oath before the same House Government Operations Committee, to refute the testimony of William Colby. As far as I have been able to determine, this was the first testimony by veterans under oath before an officially constituted committee in Congress on war crimes committed by American troops in Vietnam. My testimony was analytical and dry, and the transcript is appended to this volume; Bart's was sensational and got all the press, and can be seen here: http://homepage.ntlworld.com/jksonc/docs/phoenix-hcgo-19710802.html.

98. A similar article also appeared in *The New York Times*, "Ex-Soldiers Report Vietnam Slayings," August 3, 1971.

99. "Pacification's Deadly Price," Kevin Buckley. *Newsweek*, June 19, 1972. Buckley, who had spent four years reporting from Indochina, blew the whistle on Operation Speedy Express, the 1968 American offensive which claimed thousands of Vietcong killed, and produced an insignificant number of weapons, leading Buckley to conclude that majority of the casualties were civilians. Buckley's principal contention was that the so-called Pacification program had depended on heavy bombardment of rural villages and led to the indiscriminate killing of an essentially non-combatant population.

Meeting the Enemy: A Marine Goes Home

Meeting the Enemy: A Marine Goes Home, by Suel Jones, is a first rate memoir of the Vietnam War. I resisted reading it. I'd grown weary of the subject to which, for decades, I've devoted more than my share of professional and emotional attention. I'd once hoped that the harsh lessons of Vietnam would make a repetition of that fiasco, if not impossible, then at least very difficult. They haven't. Vietnam is no longer a war for most people; it has become a country, a fascinating destination. As a touchstone for resisting U.S. military adventures, Vietnam seems outdated. For those of us who fought there, however, the war battles on in our thoughts, conscious and unconscious, worse for some than others. I wasn't sure I needed to add someone else's head trip about that war to my own.

But Suel Jones' memoir possesses the best bait there is to draw a reader into his narrative. Somewhere along the trail, despite the handicap of a course in undergraduate journalism, Brother Jones has learned to write extremely well. And what you get is Suel Jones, combat marine, unadorned and tightly framed, not just as actor in his fractured, but totally convincing, representation of combat which I return to below, but the complex inner-landscape of an introspective and highly developed thinker who has spent years, often under solitary—almost monkish—condition, fighting his demons and mapping the man who went to and survived Vietnam.

Our protagonist's operative persona was acquired in rural East Texas, his family working poor and church-going Southern Baptists. This is redneck country. It seems to toughen people in some enviable ways—Suel's language is hard-edged, but appealingly direct—but also keep them in their place through the usual social controls to which we sometimes give the name *community*, including deep provincial attachments to clan and place that those with upward economic mobility are often lacking. It's a double-edged sword, and Suel's life has been cut by both sides. For years after Vietnam, even after he rejected the straight behaviors and values of his hometown familiars in favor of the long-haired, dope-smoking counterculture, an inability to break with his family's non-negotiable red, white and blue patriotism prevented Suel from politicizing his rebellion and becoming an antiwar vet, a decision he seems to regret even more than going to war. Expressing a commonplace that many vets would readily endorse, Suel claims that Vietnam made him who he is today, not just the bad stuff, but especially the good.

Suel's unit in Vietnam operated in a virtually depopulated area around the DMZ, engaging in conventional combat against a uniformed enemy from the North, there to infiltrate the border and secure the supply lines going south. Constant patrolling over the same rough terrain, loaded with eighty pounds of gear, ammunition and water, filthy or wet for days on end, eating out of a can, walking point and the gut twisting job of manning a listening post with the rest of your platoon dug-in to your rear, their claymores and M-30 machines guns pointing right up your backside until, assuming there was no attack, daylight freed you to rejoin your unit. Over eleven months, Suel received two purple hearts for relatively minor wounds (which, a centimeter one way or the other, could have been fatal), suffered a bout of malaria and was bitten by a rat. Toward the end of his tour, he went on R&R to Sydney, and kept largely to himself for five days. His description of the interlude in Australia, the depth of conflict in his thoughts and feelings, charged by fantasies of desertion, all intensified by the dangers and horrors he'd been exposed to in the preceding year, is a stunning and thoroughly original piece of wartime prose.

After the war as the years rushed by, Suel Jones found himself living in a cabin near an Arctic oil field in Alaska, 60 miles from the nearest town, growing uncomfortable in his isolation, and still filled with deep regret over whatever small role he had played as a U.S. invader in the devastation wreaked on the Vietnamese and their environment. He came to imagine that, by returning to Vietnam, "meeting the enemy" face to face, he might outdistance those inner demons and put the war to rest.

Suddenly, in 1998, he decamped from the remote Alaskan wilderness and traveled to Hanoi, an act he describes as "coming home." That might sound like a catch phrase, but the theme is deeply embedded in Jones' ultra-existential tale, and we are shown at least that he certainly inhabits Hanoi as a denizen, not a transient veteran on a battlefield pilgrimage or delegation of friendship. His home is in an alley in Hanoi's Old Quarter. He wanders all over the city, communes with his neighbors, and volunteers at the Vietnam Friendship Village, working with disabled children and Vietnamese war veterans identified as victims of Agent Orange. His descriptions of these routines, and of his life and living in Hanoi, his probing ruminations

Meeting the Enemy: A Marine Goes Home 95

on the puzzling dialectic of foreignness, his own and *theirs*, are entertaining and thought provoking, and perhaps threads for more detailed future writing.

At one point, the author connects with a former comrade from his unit, and convinces him to come for a short visit. For two weeks they meet every morning in a Hanoi coffee shop, and Seul distributes throughout his narrative bits of discussion between these two sixty-something war vets who trade faded memories of combat, and reflect on how those experiences shaped and complicated their lives ever since. The friend is a tourist. His return to Vietnam has been salutary. He may even come back again with his two sons. Suel Jones abides, and ponders still one insoluble conundrum. It never ceases to amaze and humble him that the Vietnamese, despite the suffering we caused them, find it so convenient to forgive us. You know that if the shoe were on the other foot, and this was East Texas, or Staten Island, or French Lick, Indiana, forgiveness might not be so quick in coming.

Veterans For Peace *Newsletter*, **Fall 2010**

Combat and Reconciliation: A Vietnam Vet Returns to Heal Old Wounds

Black Virgin Mountain: A Return to Vietnam
(by Larry Heinemann)

Larry Heinemann, whose war novel *Paco's Story* won a National Book Award in 1987, spent his combat tour in Vietnam mounted on an armored personnel carrier behind a .50-caliber machine gun. His 25th Infantry Division operated over terrain that concealed a vast and largely undetected Viet Cong tunnel complex near Cu Chi, today one of Vietnam's hottest tourist attractions. Heinemann has returned several times to Vietnam as a visiting writer. Most recently he rode the train south from Hanoi, indulging in the antics at Cu Chi, nursing a rush of anticipation as he neared Nui Ba Den, or Black Virgin Mountain, the immutable landmark of his former battleground, and title for this journal of postwar lamentations.

Certainly, *Black Virgin Mountain* is no classic of travel literature. By his own admission, the author is an indifferent traveler, not much at ease beyond the streets of his native Chicago. And while Heinemann positions himself squarely in the antiwar camp since his return from war, his rants—and the book offers many—are not burdened by the consistency of a political line. The true subjects of *Black Virgin Mountain* are neither period nor place, but class bias and soul baring. Heinemann's narrative scores a bitter dirge for working stiffs everywhere who feel they were bred for cannon fodder, and maps a soldier's heart for the wounds he carries long after his war has ended.

When draft notices arrived for Heinemann and his brother on the same spring day in 1966, there was no drama about the outcome. "No one told us we could hightail it to Canada ... declare ourselves conscientious objectors." A healthy blue-collar prole with a "straight-arrow upbringing" like theirs, he writes, either served or went to jail. Three Heinemann brothers would eventually go into the military, two to Vietnam. Among them only Larry remains. One brother was a postwar suicide; the other left his family never to be heard from again. Heinemann mines his text with enough dyspeptic comments to underscore just how upset he remains that working-class families like his were sacrificed in a draft suspiciously skewed toward social privilege (an iniquity that some believe remains unattended in today's all-volunteer force).

That is not to say Heinemann had regrets about leaving home. His old man had a "fierce and violent temper" inflamed by the stresses of driving an inner-city bus, "the bedrock," Heinemann now guesses, "of all those belt-whippings." Being an unwilling conscript on a short track to the front lines did not improve the author's circumstances or his attitude. At Fort Knox Heinemann's mechanized infantry unit "trained with silly, pointlessly extravagant thoroughness for service in 'Europe.'" And if, on looking back, Heinemann now judges the Army "a monumental waste of time," well, at least, he says, it wised him up to the world's slippery ways. And in its unexpected bounty, the Army quartered Heinemann outside the town where he would meet his future wife.

But when it comes to Vietnam, Heinemann sloughs the details of his gruesome wartime memories, and simply deadpans that GIs "were not pleasant people ... and ... what happened there is not pleasant to recall." Today those "unpleasantries" remain permanently bonded to his postwar conscience after nearly 40 years of "long nights, still; extraordinary nightmares, vivid and precise, still; and otherwise, yet and still, a severe unease." Heinemann unequivocally associates these disturbances with the mayhem GIs routinely dispensed in Vietnam to which he "was not simply a witness, but an integral, even dedicated, party."

If Heinemann is purposefully evasive about his private war-primed agonies, there's nothing vague in his retrospective explanation for why Vietnam was always "unwinnable.... To say we could have won the war is ... saying that we didn't fill our hearts with enough hate; didn't shoot enough Vietnamese down like dogs ... didn't napalm or strafe them hard enough; didn't poison enough ... of their ... farmland with Agent Orange."

When Heinemann came home from the warscape he describes, he hoped to seamlessly reclaim his civilian self. He didn't know he would coexist for life with the sorrows of war. Perhaps this is post-traumatic stress disorder, a psychic burden that afflicts a minority of returning veterans who, in a sense, become their wars. *Black Virgin Mountain*, a hard and honest work, reads like the troubled interior monologue of such a veteran who cunningly survives, not despite, but because of his wary ambivalence toward the world. It is all the more affecting when Heinemann reveals that he, too, like so many of his vet contemporaries, has dissolved dark demons in sobs before the Wall—the Vietnam Veterans Memorial in Washington.

Return trips to Vietnam have also been "important" for Heinemann to see "the country at peace." He devotes some pages to his conventional touring, mostly in Hanoi, and his prose slouches appropriately in sketches of ceremonial meetings with the "big potatoes" of Vietnam's governing and cultural elites. He intuitively seeks the company of ordinary Vietnamese, often veterans themselves; in small, unspoken acts of reconciliation. But only when he is drawn south to where he was a soldier and finally glimpses the Black Virgin Mountain straddling its familiar horizon does he realize that he's "come home"; not to revisit the war, but "to be rid of it."

The Sunday Boston Globe, **June 26, 2005**

Armed with the Facts

America's Military Today: The Challenge of Militarism, by Tod Ensign with Christian C. Appy, Martin Binkin, Dan Fahey, Linda Birde Francke, George and Meredith Friedman, Charles Sheehan-Miles, and Servicemembers Legal Defense Network.

The conditions of daily life in the military are largely invisible to a majority of U.S. citizens who've never served a day in the armed forces. This is something of a paradox, given the centrality of military imagery in U.S. cultural life, from the ubiquity of honor guards in public parades and ceremonies to the virtual saturation of televised sporting events with glitzy recruitment ads, not to mention the steady flow of films dramatizing the nation's wars and military exploits, past or present, fact or fiction.

Certainly, there is a general level of public acceptance, largely unexamined, of the need for uniformed forces within a highly disciplined and regimented institution to carry out the mission of U.S. defense, and, when necessary, to fight the nation's enemies. But the actual details of military life experienced by the average service person under everyday circumstances—not just in the context of warfare—are seldom a topic of probing journalistic interest or popular concern.

America's Military Today, written by Tod Ensign and several collaborators, provides an antidote to such neglect. In truth, for a general readership, no better primer on this subject exists in print today. But the book will serve most valuably perhaps as a resource and reference for the activist community in which Tod Ensign (and Citizen Soldier, the organization he heads) has played a leading role for decades as watchdog of United States militarism, and advocate for the human rights of GIs and veterans.

Through such activist networks, this work will ideally find its way into the hands of people currently presented with the option of military "employment." This population would reap immediate benefits from a read of at least half the book's chapters, in particular those describing in generally objective language the contemporary recruitment scene, which provide a fascinating account of what basic training looks like in today's all volunteer force, as compared with the draft-based military of the Vietnam era.

From the outside, today's military actually looks like a job with a competitive pay scale (at least if you're single) and living conditions that are closer to a college dorm than a barracks. But, in reading Ensign's book, a potential recruit might also learn—ideally before, not after, signing an enlistment contract—that a recruiter (especially an unscrupulous one) can promise a chosen area of training but not deliver on it for reasons of "military necessity," a Catch-22 that trumps any individual claim or expectation, and from which there is no redress.

Separate chapters treating the special, often disadvantaged, experiences of minorities, women, and gays and lesbians, are warning signs for those within these cohorts who buy the hype about discriminatory cultures and practices being absent in today's military, or whose fantasies about military life are fixated on the outward bound idyll portrayed in those sexy TV recruiting spots. In fact, for anyone joining the military today, in the context of war in Iraq and Afghanistan, the experience is a bit like checking into the Roach Motel. It's easy to get in, but harder and harder to get out (assuming you keep your skin intact).

Stop Loss, a policy much employed of late by the Defense Department, can legally extend a service person's obligation beyond the terms of his or her enlistment contract. And, given how the reserve component of a service person's commitment is interpreted these days, even those returned to civilian life remain vulnerable to recall, a little known, but all the more draconian element of the so-called back-door-draft.

Many enlistees today must be prepared to serve, and possibly fight, in a war zone. From the letters of such fighters currently in Iraq, Ensign has fashioned a chapter that painfully demonstrates how, like their Vietnam counterparts, many of today's U.S. combatants haven't a clue as to what they're supposed to accomplish in Iraq, other than to wreak havoc and destruction.

A chapter on the Gulf War Syndrome reveals a second disturbing parallel between Vietnam and Iraq, presenting a new episode in the impact of a toxic battleground on the long-term health of vast numbers of returning veterans. In Vietnam, it was Agent Orange. Now, it is feared that tens of thousands of Gulf War vets, and no doubt many more Iraq War veterans to come, have, or will have, ingested doses of damaging radiation from shells fabricated with depleted uranium (DU), whose exploded particles are blown helter-skelter about the war zone. It need hardly be said that the numbers of Iraqis victimized from such exposures could, in the years ahead, reach epidemic proportions.

America's Military Today may find its primary use as an anti-recruitment handbook, but the book's other half takes the reader well beyond a nuts and bolts account of the conditions and problems faced by contemporary GIs and into areas of military structure and policy that threaten immediate pan-societal consequences.

In his essay, "Filling the Ranks," Ensign examines the potential for a service-wide "personnel crunch" resulting from spreading U.S. troops too thin in Iraq, and throughout the world, that could replace today's volunteer military with a new draft. Ensign's discussion is comprehensive, but he recognizes that any prediction on the outcome of this debate is still premature.

One thing is for certain: Should a new draft come, it will take women as well as men, and might even go beyond the military to universal service for all individuals of draft age, with few of the exemptions that formerly made military service the disproportional burden of minority and white working class males.

In "Policing America," Ensign, a lawyer, writes knowledgeably on a trend advanced by the PATRIOT Act in our post–9/11 national security environment toward weakening the time honored doctrine of *posse comitatus*, which limits the military's role in domestic law enforcement. At issue here, ever in the minds of generations of U.S. lawmakers from the framers onward, has been the commitment through such traditional safeguards to prevent the military from ever posing a challenge to the institutions of civilian control.

What may be the book's most important essay, "Military Justice," is co-written by Ensign and Louis Font, an experienced courts-martial trial attorney. The two advocates take aim at the Uniform Code of Military Justice (UCMJ), exposing the pattern of systematic violations of civil and human rights that pervade the military justice system by virtue of the arbitrary, often unassailable, powers of judicial authority invested at every level of command. If a reader who has not served in the armed forces reads only this chapter, he or she will grasp the most singular distinction between the rights of civilians and the rights of those in service: When you join the military, your ass belongs to Uncle Sam, and you can basically kiss due process goodbye.

Vermont Guardian, December 2004

A Skillful Chronicle of Kerry's Conflicts

Tour of Duty (by David Brinkley)

How little the John Kerry celebrated in Douglas Brinkley's "Tour of Duty" as the quintessential Vietnam veteran typifies in educational or social status the vast majority of his contemporaries who also fought in that theater of conflict.

Christian Appy has demonstrated persuasively in "Working-Class War" the blue-collar composition of the American fighting forces in Southeast Asia, including the corps of young officers, among whom, even in the military academies, only 10 percent came from the professional class or above. Yet like another senator—the good Republican played by Derek Jacobi in the film "Gladiator"—Kerry might with equal grace proclaim, "I am with, not of, the people."

Therein lies the tale that Brinkley tenders in a lengthy, highly readable, and well-researched biographical history that draws generously from the diaries that Kerry, a young naval lieutenant, kept to document his wartime experiences, and from his extensive correspondence home. We learn that Kerry, a product of St. Paul's prep school and Yale University, chose to fight in Vietnam and did so bravely. He led with distinction the five-man crew of a small craft that patrolled and provoked the Viet Cong enemy in a web of inland waterways throughout the Mekong Delta. Kerry was wounded three times and decorated for valor. And, like many GIs in Vietnam, Kerry found that his conscience began to trouble him in the execution of his duties, especially the incessant, indiscriminate fire directed at apparent noncombatants.

Kerry killed an enemy under circumstances that are not entirely clear, but probably sanctioned by war's ambiguous rules of engagement. The incident, finessed somewhat clumsily in Brinkley's account, surfaced during

Kerry's reelection campaign for the Senate in 1996 when he was questioned about having shot a wounded guerrilla who had already fallen. Kerry rallied several high-profile Vietnam veterans to defend his lightning decision to shoot an adversary who, while down, remained armed and potentially deadly.

Coming home, Kerry, according to his former wife, suffered nightmares and flashbacks. In this sharing of first the dangers and now the lasting regrets of war, Kerry could authentically personify, if never truly represent, the Vietnam veteran community. As for his politics, Kerry had already developed while in-country cogent arguments for opposing the war. His decision to join Vietnam Veterans Against the War was a gesture of solidarity with veterans he called "brothers," as well as a risky tactical move for a man who had begun to plot his career in public service while still in high school.

His personal ambitions notwithstanding, Kerry gave clear public voice to the same position taken by the veterans group. In his appearance before William Fulbright's Senate Foreign Relations Committee in April 1971, Kerry volunteered this straightforward testimony: "I committed the same kinds of atrocities as thousands of others in that I shot in free fire zones, used harassment and interdiction fire, joined in search and destroy missions, and burned villages. All of these acts were established policies from the top down, and the men who ordered this are war criminals."

Brinkley reports that Kerry parted company with the antiwar vets in the months immediately following his moment of celebrity, and over the years he has been called a betrayer of the cause by some former comrades. But Kerry had always taken pains to emphasize that he was "never outside the system." The difference is that those Vietnam veterans who have kept faith with Kerry's antiwar arguments before the Senate still continue to advocate for that historical interpretation of their war, whereas Kerry has never been able to bring that piece of his ideals to the table for serious examination within the system. And yet, the boogeyman of Vietnam still haunts the corridors of power where war policy is forged, and its lessons never seem to fall from fashion.

"Tour of Duty" is a fresh and welcome retelling of these lessons, and of how acutely Kerry once wrestled with them. Brinkley inserts many details to enhance the verisimilitude of his portrait of both the era and the man. Nonetheless, a number of gaffes and bizarre formulations underscore a suspicion that the Vietnam era is not one in which the author is deeply positioned. Jolting references to Kerry's fellow combatants as "colleagues" are one thing. But the potboiler rhetoric used to describe the National Liberation Front—the Viet Cong are "treacherous," they "infest" the Delta—and its struggles for reunification with Hanoi is amateurish.

Brinkley carries the story forward to Kerry's present drive for his party's presidential nomination in which voters, it seems, can't decipher Kerry's stance on our current war with Iraq. And indeed, if Brinkley's skillful profile of his subject is accurate, one can easily imagine the anguished content of Kerry's interior monologue as he struggles to disentangle any scruples about Iraq from his memories of Vietnam. As a young, disaffected warrior, Kerry once dissolved such ambiguities in a rush of insightful empathy, asking himself "what it would be like to be occupied by foreign troops, to have to bend to the desires of a people who could not be sensitive to the things that really count in one's own country?" To what degree Kerry sets his politics today by this internationalist benchmark, no one, not even he, seems to know.

The Boston Globe, January 19, 2004

War and Remembrance

Gregory Vistica examines "the corrosive power of secrets" in his expanded look at Bob Kerrey's Vietnam experience.

The Education of Lieutenant Kerrey (by Greg Vistica)

Nearly two years ago, Greg Vistica broke the story about a massacre of some 20 women and children by a Navy SEAL team commanded by former senator Bob Kerrey that took place over 30 years ago in Vietnam. At the urging of his agent, Vistica has turned the article, which ran originally in The *New York Times Magazine* (April 29, 2001), into a book, *The Education of Lieutenant Kerrey*. Vistica's deeper professional motive for keeping Kerrey in his cross hairs was his desire "to get as close to the truth as possible," closer presumably than in the initial expose.

In the magazine version, Vistica pits one eyewitness recollection of what took place in the hamlet of Thanh Phong on Feb.25, 1969, against another: Kerrey alleges that the unarmed civilians were killed from a distance of a hundred yards in the confusion of a firefight, while a fellow SEAL, Gerhard Klann, is adamant that the victims were rounded up and shot point-blank. In his book, Vistica concludes without ambiguity that "Klann's is the most accurate version," and that "Kerrey is not a truth teller."

In marshaling his prose over the same impressive range of sources that informed his article—not least the many interviews conducted face to face with his subject—Vistica makes clear that his revised judgment rests, not on newly minted research, but on the facts already at hand. When he first reported the massacre, Vistica was hardly alone among the media voices who chose to tread lightly in dealing with Kerrey, even after Kerrey used surplus campaign funds to hire a fast-track public relations firm to trash Klann, the man reported to have saved Kerrey's life in Vietnam, and to spin the news toward Kerrey's version of what took place at Thanh Phong.

Kerrey was, after all, a war amputee and Medal of Honor recipient, and despite having giving up his safe seat in the U.S. Senate to serve as president of the New School University, he remained a viable candidate for national political office. So, what made Vistica vary his tune?

Vistica concedes that he was not as objective at first as he should have been. Overawed by Kerrey's "bright and charming" personality, and his expressions of apparent remorse, Vistica initially undervalued the testimony from survivors of Thanh Phong—dismissed by Kerrey as "dupes of the Communist government"—whose unrehearsed accounts of the massacre so closely parallel Klann's.

In 1970, Richard Nixon, in one of many desperate acts to stem domestic opposition to the war, manufactured a hero; and so Kerrey accepted the nation's highest award for valor, though he believed it undeserved. Ever since, Kerrey's life has followed a fabled trajectory. The angry antiwar vet is suddenly a local war hero who makes a killing as a health club operator. Then he enters politics and defeats a secure incumbent for the governorship of Nebraska. The fairy-tale cycle continues as Kerrey conducts a highly public romance with Hollywood actress Debra Winger, is elected to the Senate, then runs credibly as a candidate in the presidential primaries.

In the meantime, Klann has been living a nightmare. And, unfortunately for Kerrey, Klann relieved his heavy conscience about Thanh Phong by confessing to a naval officer who, only years later, told the story to Vistica, who has discovered since his original article that in the early 1970s many veterans testified publicly throughout the United States about atrocities they and their units committed as standard practice throughout Vietnam. Vistica ultimately shies from making any judgment about the wider conflict, where he now suspects such dark incidents were not uncommon.

What remains the central issue for Vistica is not Thanh Phong, but the fact that Kerrey, whose memory may indeed have failed him, has misplaced the truth. Vistica sees Kerrey's dissembling around Thanh Phong primarily as the character flaw of a particularly slippery politician, even as he dutifully reports the erratic behavior of a man clearly traumatized by war.

And for Kerrey, who has frequently deflected criticism since Vistica's original revelation by claiming, "I'm no hero," add the pressure of having pretended to be one for the past three decades. If you strip away Kerrey's postwar life of storied overachievement, you see a man who all but fits the classic stereotype of the disturbed Vietnam veteran. Documented throughout the Vistica profile are the constant "mood swings," the sudden, unpredictable bouts of temper, and, in his public life, Kerrey's reputation as a chronically unreliable political ally.

As an investigation of "the corrosive power of secrets" in the life of one public figure, "The Education of Lieutenant Kerrey" is a very good read that might have claimed a longer shelf life had the author taken it a few steps further. In the end, Vistica has not just squandered his chances to explore more systematically what U.S. units did routinely in the atrocity-producing atmosphere of Vietnam combat. He has failed to understand what Vietnam did to Kerrey, not to mention the thousands of other veterans whose troubled readjustment to postwar life was not shielded by the bright, shining lie of a Medal of Honor, which, if such an award can ever be said to be deserved, was apparently given to the wrong man.

The Boston Globe, **February 16, 2003**

Warriors' Honor and the Ordeal of Survival

When I Was a Young Man: A Memoir (by Bob Kerrey)

The publication of a Vietnam memoir, like Bob Kerrey's *When I Was a Young Man*, is an occasion for review on several levels: an addition to the literature of war, an American social history in its time and place, and, with this particular exemplar, the painful saga of an individual veteran whose name until a year ago was synonymous with integrity, heroism, and virtual fulfillment of the American Dream. Emblematic of Kerrey's fall from grace was the question the former Nebraska Senator felt compelled to ask a West Point expert on the Laws of War—"Am I a war criminal?"—just days before *The New York Times Magazine* ran an article, "One Awful Night in Thanh Phong" (April 29, 2001), exposing a dark secret from Kerrey's Vietnam War record.

At the core of Kerrey's self-indictment was a botched covert operation that—he now says—has haunted his conscience and dreams since that night on February 25, 1969, when a team of Navy SEALs under his command entered Thanh Phong, a peasant hamlet on the southern coast of Vietnam, to kill or capture a Viet Cong official. The mission ended in disaster, and by the time the seven commandos—dubbed Kerrey's Raiders—withdrew, they had killed as many as twenty non-combatants, mostly women and children.

Kerry has accepted full responsibility for the deaths of those unarmed Vietnamese villagers, while maintaining steadily that they resulted from a tragic accident, though he acknowledges his memory of the details is fogged by time and trauma. For another member of Kerrey's team, Gerhard Klann, the mental picture of what took place that night is snap-shot clear. According to the *Times* story, what Klann remembers is that when the Raiders failed to find their intended quarry, and to ensure the security of their own withdrawal, the women and children were rounded up at Kerrey's command and executed point blank.

This public revelation of what would certainly be a "war crime" if it were true, provoked a wide band of commentators throughout the media to intensely revisit the history and nature of U.S. involvement in the Vietnam War, as Kerry's alleged role in the Thanh Phong atrocities occupied the headlines of print, electronic, and dot.com news outlets for a full two weeks thereafter. While calls for further inquiries and investigations ebbed and flowed in the tide of punditry, few have answered Kerrey's anguished question of criminal culpability in the affirmative.

For one reason, Kerrey's "accident" scenario, though rife with inconsistencies, and widely reported across the political spectrum to lack credibility, was nonetheless endorsed by the other five members of his unit—despite the fact that one of them, Mike Ambrose, modified the recollections he originally provided to the *Times*. To construct this unified consensus, Kerrey, now president of the New School University in New York, gathered his former combat mates, less Gerhard Klann, at his home on April 28, 2001, where, according to news accounts, the vets discussed Thanh Phong until 2 a.m. Afterwards all but the seventh SEAL were now agreed that the shooting began some distance from the victims, as far as one hundred yards, and only after the commandos were fired upon by an unseen adversary, with the civilians tragically caught in the return fire.

It was this message that Kerrey had already begun to voice publicly a week before the *Times* disclosure in an apparent effort to head off, even discredit, the contradictory memories of Gerhard Klann. And it is this version of Thanh Phong, subject to one or two minor refinements, which Kerrey sticks to in his memoir, while continuing to hedge that "even today I wouldn't swear my memory is 100%." In one typical spin on an earlier reported detail, where Gregory Vistika, author of the *Times* article, had designated Gerhard Klann as the "most experienced member of Kerrey's team," Kerrey pointedly anoints Mike Ambrose in the memoir—without reference to Klann—as "my most trusted enlisted man." Both Klann and Ambrose had served prior tours in Vietnam.

As memoir of a life in its historical moment, *When I Was a Young Man* is, at best, a mixed accomplishment. Kerrey's sketch on growing up in the post–World War II heartland lacks nuance, and might apply generically to practically any white middle class American boy born at the dawn of the Cold War. Kerrey had to be one of the best trained junior officers of his generation, getting all the merit badges from Frogman to SEAL schools in the Navy, with cross-training in the Army as an Airborne Ranger. Yet his narrative on these experiences offers the dry read of a field manual. The chapters on Vietnam, adding up to Kerrey's fifty days of in-country service and a Medal of Honor, which he himself admits is probably undeserved, are essentially a brief in support of his account of Thanh Phong. As for Kerrey's opinions on the Vietnam War, he proves time and again the disclaimer from his Preface, "I am not a historian," with unexamined endorsements of official U.S. government interpretations of the war's most controversial events: the Gulf of Tonkin incident, the Tet offensive of 1968, and the status of South Vietnam as an independent state—all of which remain mired in unresolved historical controversy. That many of the hawkish commentators on the Thanh Phong tragedy, who continue to promote Vietnam as a noble cause, characterize Kerrey's views on the war as dovish, even antiwar, is truly astonishing. Like most American politicians, Kerrey comes in one flavor: red, white, and blue.

There are several chapters in *When I Was a Young Man* that almost redeem the book, and give evidence of a more solid character behind Kerrey's somewhat facile public persona. In response to his dad's dying wish, Kerrey has done some homework on his family's history, especially in tracing the fate of his uncle John, the senior Kerrey's older brother who survived the Bataan death march in the Philippines in 1942, but disappeared with no trace toward the end of that war. John, who sometimes visits Kerrey's dreams, appears in cameo throughout the memoir as an oddly comforting link to the ageless chain of human warfare, and as emissary of the fallen to those who make it home only to face with paradoxical ambivalence the mysteries of their own survival. Kerrey survived, but lost the lower part of a leg in a fire fight, and the scenes of his recovery in hospital, and his gradual resumption of civilian and family life are original and extremely affecting.

Since memoir is about—actually *means*—memory, it is not so strange that Kerrey throughout the text expresses his reliance on the powers of memory to compose his work. He describes the football field of his high school playing days as "a place where a man can recall an afternoon or evening of his youth with absolute clarity. Thirty, forty, fifty years later, the memory will still be fresh." Not so the field of combat where, Kerrey cautions, "memory is always a liar." Less absolute on this theme, yet generally supportive, is the observation of a fellow Vietnam veteran, the writer Tobias Wolfe for whom memory, if not always false, "is a storyteller" inclined at least toward mixing truth with omission, even fiction. It would seem therefore that we cannot look to memory to help us judge which of the vastly divergent accounts of Thanh Phong is truthful and which is not. For that task perhaps motivation is a surer guide. Between the high profile public figure Bob Kerrey and the obscure steel worker Gerhard Klann, reported to have a drinking problem, but who nonetheless came forward with great reluctance, which of the two men has the most to lose by the worst version of the truth?

Should it eventually come out that Kerrey's, not Klann's, memory is the liar, what measure of individual responsibility would Kerrey bear for the atrocities at Thanh Phong? Much less, I think, than those who would shift accountability for such horrors, hardly as exceptional as official memory would like us to believe, onto the low ranking individuals who did the fighting over those who led and planned the war. Thanh Phong is repugnant to decent American opinion. Yet, until we can fully face the scope of unwarranted havoc our nation once wrecked upon Indochina and its peoples, one senses we will be doomed to relive this national nightmare, episode by episode, until the last Vietnam veteran goes unquietly to his grave. Isn't the real lesson of Bob Kerrey's personal ordeal that one day all of us will have to face this truth?

PeaceWork, **July/August 2002**

A slightly shorter version of this review appeared in *The Boston Sunday Globe*, July 18, 2002, as, "From the Heartland to the Heart of Darkness."

That's Vietnam, Jake

***Home to War: A History of the Vietnam
Veterans' Movement*** (by Gerald Nicosia)

Three million American soldiers—men for the most part—participated in the U.S. invasion of Vietnam over the decade-long duration of that war for us—roughly 1964 to 1973. Recent events confirm why one might yet debate whether we who did the fighting were, to paraphrase Remarque, "fit" for soldiering; that we proved no more (or less) fit for peace than veterans of any other war cannot be seriously doubted. The road back—*readjustment* in psych-chat—from armed conflict to civil living has never been a smooth one. For topical proof of this, just ask a couple of chaps named Kerrey and Kerry.

Vets come home and the wars come with them, lying doggo sometimes for years, then popping up at the most inconvenient of times. Nonetheless, Vietnam veterans, in at least one particular of our postwar readjustment saga, are indeed "quite different from veterans of earlier wars," as Ralph Nader judged in 1973. No prior war, he argued, had ever "witnessed such moral dissent by soldiers and new veterans." On this singular distinction, progressive vets have proudly dined out for years. Two Vietnam vets who protested the war on their return—but not the system that spawned it—made it all the way to the U.S. Senate only to see their shiny acts of combat heroism tarnish into a basis for war crimes accusations: Bob Kerrey's enemy body count suddenly unmasked as a slaughter, perhaps point blank, of unarmed innocents; and John Kerry, in a much less publicized revelation, described in an interview by one of his in-country teammates as having "finished off" a wounded Vietcong soldier. (The allegations are denied by both men.)

Well, that's Vietnam, Jake. A real historical twister that dumped the onus of war crimes responsibility not on those who planned and directed the U.S. fiasco or who commanded the battlefield but on the shoulders and consciences of their youngest, greenest junior officers, like Bob and John, and on the citizen soldiers who filled the lowest drafted or enlisted ranks of the infantry. In this history, the Vietnam vet is indeed a standout. It is for the uniqueness of his exceptionalism, often absent deeper links of similarity with other generations of ex-combatants, that *Homo vietnamveticus* is the subject of a considerable literature, and now he reappears—as antiwar warrior and in his many other guises—in *Home to War: A History of the Vietnam Veterans' Movement*.

Less by thematic design than sheer magnitude of detail, author Gerald Nicosia doggedly tracks each metamorphosis in activism and image that positioned Vietnam veterans—typically in problematic terms and often as stereotypes of our own creation—on the wavy periphery of public awareness lo these many years. Among the peak manifestations of Viet Vet Cult and Legend to which Nicosia's narrative devotes ample coverage are:

- the "war crimes movement"—the multiplicity of public revelations by veterans throughout 1970–71 of atrocities routinely committed by their units in Vietnam, almost always against civilians;
- Dewey Canyon III, the 1970 encampment on the Mall in Washington of 2,000 vets, many of whom returned medals won in battle by tossing them onto the steps of the Capitol;
- two juridical extravaganzas bracketed by twenty years: the political trial of the Gainesville 8 and the groundbreaking product-liability suit concerned with health effects on soldiers exposed to battlefield defoliants;
- and, in between times, every manner of emotionally charged but well-scripted mayhem in hospital wards, presidential nominating conventions, national monuments and politicians' offices—which vets staged to dramatize less and less our moral dissent but increasingly our grievances over allegedly shoddy reception on the home front and, most urgently, our war-induced maladies of mind, body and spirit that few (least of all those who sponsored and managed our oops-sorry-our-mistake slaughter of 58,000 Americans and 2 million Vietnamese) wished to hear about.

And "what a long strange trip it's been" for most ex–GIs—a blue-collar sort of crowd—leading, ironically, back to where we started from (taking into account accommodations to a post–60s world). By the end of the 1970s, the vet noir as antisocial pariah or rebel politico had been gingerly transmogrified into the unappreciated poster child of the Reagan years who was said only to yearn for the "welcome home" he was denied (and who do you think is blamed for that?!). Now, after thirty years, it should come as no surprise that Vietnam veterans occupy all the perches of conventional vet culture left absent by attrition in the ranks of their dads from the class of '46. Guess who's sitting on that American Legion barstool now, playing old fart and flag-waver at the head of the parade on Memorial Day, not to mention wielding significant influence in policy-making throughout the vast Veterans Administration (VA) bureaucracy. And let's not forget Al Gore, the vet who would be President; a lot of good it did him!

Nicosia seldom synthesizes such points directly, but they can be assembled from the details of his anecdotal and personality-centered style of reporting—based on interviews with more than a hundred veterans—which captures quite faithfully the raucous *Sturm und Drang* that attended the ends Vietnam veterans sought and, in a variety of organizational configurations, ultimately accomplished. But a critical historical question about Vietnam veterans, overlooked in Home to War, remains for some curious scholar to scout and elucidate: Would Vietnam veterans qua Vietnam veterans, in the absence of widespread expressions of moral dissent by a strong minority of our comrades, have become a powerful enough force to out the submerged realities around readjustment difficulties, secure an unprecedented degree of recognition for post combat stress, personify the effects of herbicidal poisoning on human health?

With few exceptions, American veterans of earlier wars endured their homecomings and re-entry pains in virtual obscurity—give or take a parade or two—and there is little in public record or popular expression that registers or examines their scars of war. The Vietnam legacy has clearly altered the ground rules of postwar readjustment for vets, but other dividends of the war's historical memory may be limited. A shifting political climate at some not so distant date may readily permit the Pentagon to commit ground forces in substantial numbers, perhaps under ambiguous circumstances similar to those of Vietnam, without tripping the level of public anxiety that restricts the easy exercise of such an option today. Institutional self-interest being what it is, of course, there will be no escaping an upfront calculation by military planners of the price tag for such heretofore disguised or unacknowledged disabilities as posttraumatic stress disorder (PTSD, suffered, incidentally, by more than 15 percent of all veterans who served in Vietnam) sure to plague that next war's crop of trauma victims.

If the Gulf War vets, and not without a tremendous, ongoing struggle of their own, are beneficiaries of this shift in how our society sees and responds to its postwar veteran culture, it is because Vietnam veterans—cued by unique historical forces—were freed and mobilized to act out our readjustment woes in a highly public manner, often as spectacle. But where our antiwar protests were, at least initially, ideologically disinterested and fueled by the horrors we witnessed in a war fought essentially against a civilian population, our movement's subsequent campaigns around PTSD and Agent Orange have largely traced the paths and objectives of veteran politics long sanctioned in the United States by statute and tradition: the quest and attainment of social entitlements that other disadvantaged members of our society, equally deserving by any reasonable moral measure, are routinely denied.

In *Home to War*, Nicosia lends credence to this point nicely in quoting the late Democratic Senator from California Alan Cranston's axiomatic *raison d'état* for veteran entitlements, one that other needy social castes may never appropriate: "Veterans' programs are an inseparable cost of national defense." Veterans' public clamor for compensation and relief must never be allowed to dampen morale among future recruits when next the empire decides to show its force. Vets are told, and most believe, that their basic complement of entitlements is a reward for patriotic service, for having— at least potentially—reduced their odds of personal safety in relation to civilian counterparts not similarly threatened. Few would impeach any society's humanistic obligation to care for those who actually bear the weight of battle. But veterans' entitlements in terms of social policy are a wash. It's Catch-22: Wars screw people up, thus many vets become totally dependent on their medical and pension entitlements; to merit this range of benefits, most Americans would have to go to war. Well, there are other forms of service or servitude under the benevolent skies of capitalism in the late modern, as Fredric Jameson might say. Rewards for these services are perennially in arrears.

Since World War II, Congress has provided a benefits package of some kind for all its veterans, in peacetime and at war. A portion of that expenditure, following an older tradition dating to post–Civil War social policy, is automatically earmarked for the care of elderly and indigent veterans, who may or may not claim a disability connected to their time in service. By 1910, according to Harvard sociologist Theda Skocpol, in *Protecting Soldiers and Mothers: The Political Origins of Social Policy in the United States*, 90 percent of the surviving veterans of the Union Army received disability and old age pensions. To determine the duration and generosity of their other benefits, like education and medical care, veterans, like any other special interest, must enter the lists of patronage (and sometimes protest) politics and, ultimately, roll their proposals Rube Goldberg–like through the arcane grooves of the legislative process.

It is in his copious scoring of these labyrinthine pleadings for a few fat crumbs from the rich man's table that Nicosia establishes his strongest and recurring theme, his cry of hypocrisy in high places. He seems genuinely outraged to discover that a man like Ronald Reagan, whatever highfalutin' blather he could toggle on command about "honoring those who served their country," found enlightened demands by veterans for readjustment counseling centers tantamount to mollycoddling. Reagan loosed his chief budget piranha, David Stockman, to slow the vets' advance. And still it's the hit man's snooty attitude (not, say, the institutional domination of his adopted class) that's really disturbing, as Nicosia cites the "disdainful curl" of Stockman's "Ivy League lips."

What you won't find in *Home to War* is even the smattering of historical annotation offered in this review to set and analyze veteran status within the American context as an evolutionary phenomenon of our social history. There are, unfortunately, even deeper flaws in *Home to War*, a work that Nicosia has cobbled up in large portion from scores of personal interviews conducted—mostly circa 1988—with those who played key roles in the vet movement during its most dynamic years. But perhaps Nicosia was overwhelmed by the din of disparate, feuding voices he collected, which make his reportage read at times less like history and more like hearsay. When, for example, Nicosia lingers on the minutiae and infighting in the veteran movement's antiwar and radical left-wing phases in the 1970s, his chronicle far too frequently suffers in its respect for accuracy.

I base this charge on my firsthand knowledge as a full-time organizer within the Vietnam veterans' movement from 1970 to 1981. Typical of Nicosia's failure to serve the Vietnam veteran story more reliably, or to approach the standard that writers like Todd Gitlin, Kirkpatrick Sale and Fred Halstead achieved for SDS and the antiwar movement, is the following attempt to recreate an episode from the "war crimes movement" mentioned above:

> Congressman Ron Dellums (D–Calif.) and John Conyers, Jr. (D–Mich.) assembled an ad hoc panel before which COM [Concerned Officers Movement—a formation of antiwar officers still on active duty that emerged publicly in late 1970] members and a few vets could testify. The panel was scheduled to meet four days, beginning Monday April 26, in the House Caucus Room of the Cannon Office Building. An immediate fear arose among the VVAW [Vietnam Veterans Against the War] leadership that if they let themselves be associated with these ad hoc hearings, they would again share the discredit Mark Lane brought with him.

Nicosia has the venue and the scheduling right. But here's how it really was: John Conyers and at least twenty other members of Congress attended some portion of the four days of ad hoc hearings, which were sponsored solely by Ron Dellums and organized by the Citizens' Commission of Inquiry on

U.S. War Crimes (CCI)—where I was veteran coordinator—in cooperation with Dellums's Congressional staff. Mark Lane—with whom CCI had fought bitterly six months earlier about the planning of another war crimes event, the Winter Soldier Investigation—had absolutely nothing to do with the Dellums hearings. COM played no role, nor did any active duty officer appear before the panel. The majority of those veterans who did testify were, like myself, card-carrying members of VVAW, and no one that I ever heard of was discouraged from participation in the Dellums hearings by the leadership of that organization, most of whom I spoke with frequently and knew quite well.

If an author is off by a couple of points, hey, not to worry, writers are only human. But in this case, factual peccadilloes, though often trivial when taken one by one, add up too rapidly to be ignored. Other examples: Nicosia states that in 1970, CCI coordinator Jeremy Rifkin was an investigative reporter recently kicked out of Vista for left-wing activities. Neither characterization is true. My own name appears several times in this book; I confess that I was never interviewed, but still I wonder how I came to be a platoon leader in Vietnam when I was actually a counterintelligence officer. Nicosia's version of the founding of the CCI, the war crimes commission, is even more convoluted than his account of the Dellums hearings. (And let me emphasize that I am not quibbling over matters of interpretation but contesting errors of fact that could have been corrected.)

As for CCI, the New York–based committee was founded by Ralph Schoenman in November 1969, just after the revelation in the U.S. press (twenty months after the fact) of the infamous My Lai massacre. Schoenman had been a principal organizer of the Bertrand Russell War Crimes Tribunal—an unofficial panel of prominent world figures who assembled on two occasions in Europe, heard testimony and judged as "genocidal" the U.S. conduct of the war in Vietnam. By early 1970, CCI had come under the sole direction of two New Left activists, Tod Ensign and Jeremy Rifkin, who refined and implemented the strategy originally conceived by Schoenman, to organize veterans and publicize their firsthand knowledge of the routine and widespread nature of U.S. atrocities in Vietnam, thus arguing that My Lai expressed the logical epitome of such practices and was not merely the isolated, aberrant act of a few deranged GIs.

Reliable accounts of these events are readily available. A colorful appreciation of Ralph Schoenman, onetime kibitzer extraordinaire of the American left, now quite forgotten, is offered by Tariq Ali in his lively antiwar memoir *Street Fighting Years* (Collins). Tod Ensign's retrospectives on CCI's origins and political objectives, in *Big Book: Nobody Gets Off the Bus* (Viet Nam Generation) and in *Against the Vietnam War: Writings by Activists* (Syracuse), are precise and illuminating. A rival to Nicosia's history, covering some of the same subject matter, but more sparingly and with greater finesse, is *The Turning: A History of the Vietnam Veterans Against the War* (NYU) by Andrew Hunt.

Nicosia not only fails to improve the verisimilitude of his story line by consulting publications like those suggested above but inexplicably ignores a work that liberates the ageless condition of war madness from the private obscurity of psychiatric research and places the issue of postwar readjustment for veterans solidly on both the sociological and public agenda: Paul Starr's *The Discarded Army: Veterans After Vietnam*. Also overlooked, perhaps for being too openly progressive, are more recent works of high academic quality, like Hunt's *The Turning*, in which the Vietnam veteran experience is never separated from the war or the other conditions that shaped it. Another such indispensable source would be Christian Appy's *Working-Class War: American Combat Soldiers and Vietnam* (UNC), which correlates lower socioeconomic status with the high risk of dying in combat, thus contextualizing in class terms the apparent contradiction underlying widespread support for the war within blue-collar communities, as distinguished from the more impersonal interests of the war's managers and their corporate backers, whose ambitions and bottom lines could only be fertilized with cannon fodder from the most dispensable stocks. Indeed, there is much evidence in his text to suggest that Nicosia is somewhat spooked by things progressive—say, the presence of the left throughout the early episodes of veteran activism. Many *Nation* readers, I imagine, might find the author of *Home to War* a bit too quick on the draw to identify—with no leavening gloss or commentary—"Communist" and "Trotskyist" influences in the antiwar movement. The fact that Nicosia expresses many liberal sentiments and is a self-described pacifist makes it all the more curious that the red-scare atmospherics of the cold war seem to exercise such influence over his critical capacities.

When Nicosia's text is left unclouded by such under-examined anxieties, it is at its most valuable. The chapter and verse account in *Home to War* of the protracted campaign on the fringes of the American Psychiatric Association (APA) to establish and legitimize the diagnostic criteria for PTSD will be of interest to veterans and specialists alike. The author correctly locates the genesis of this campaign within the antiwar movement. It started when many vets who had already testified publicly about the heinous war crimes they or their units had committed sought relief from tormented memories through some form of group-oriented therapeutic intervention. Through their antiwar activities in 1970–71, the vets came into contact with psychiatrist and postwar trauma expert Robert Lifton, an active opponent of the war who worked to expose its atrocity-producing nature (a characterization understood fully by anyone who'd fought in Vietnam). Joined by his colleague Chaim Shatan, the two psychiatrists helped organize therapy sessions known as "rap groups" in the New York offices of VVAW.

Exploiting this radical initiative, several Vietnam-vets-turned-psychologists laid siege to the psychiatric establishment, energetically guided by Shatan and aided by the collaboration of a small but empathic cadre of mental health professionals working throughout the VA. Only by the end of the decade, when the clinical data had become so overwhelmingly unavoidable, did these advocates for treatment of what was initially termed PVS—Post-Vietnam Syndrome—finally see their unstinting efforts rewarded by the insertion of paragraph 309.89 establishing PTSD as a recognized illness in the revised edition of the APA's diagnostic manual, the DSM III. A subsequent manual would describe as the "essential features" of this disorder "the development of characteristic symptoms following exposure to an extreme traumatic stressor involving direct personal experience of an event that involves actual or threatened death or serious injury ... or witnessing an event that involves death, injury or a threat to the physical integrity of another person."

A most bizarre spin was put on PTSD and the history of its eventual acceptance within the world of establishment psychiatry by Holy Cross College sociologist and Vietnam vet Jerry Lembcke, in *The Spitting Image: Myth, Memory and the Legacy of Vietnam* (NYU). It's an interesting sidebar, and one that Nicosia might have profitably addressed, but doesn't, in *Home to War*. Professor Lembcke holds that the concern of doctors Lifton and Shatan with the postwar emotions of Vietnam veterans was, wittingly or otherwise, aimed at the depoliticization of the radical veterans' movement. The two PTSD advocates are accused of no less than "the construction of a mental health discourse that would displace the political discourse that had, up to that point, framed interpretations of Vietnam veterans' experiences." Apparently Lembcke's sociopolitical vision does not permit the "bad"—politically radical—and the "mad"—clinically neurotic, borderline or psychotic—to coexist within the same human actor. Thus he marks the inevitable demobilization of the radical Vietnam veterans' movement as the outcome of a conscious conspiracy by meddling liberals, rather than as a function of the limited possibilities for expansion provided by an American culture so rapidly turning rightward. A much stripped down but still effective VVAW continues to exist, but then again, so does the IWW.

In drawing his account to a close, Nicosia devotes many pages to— though by no means provides the whole picture of—the legal and political wrangling that drove and energized the product-liability suits against Dow and other manufacturers of Agent Orange well into the mid-1980s. There is much as well on the protracted lobbying and legislative intrigues that endured the 1980s into the 1990s—and that are as yet unsettled—to win care and compensation from Congress through the VA for the many medical conditions that are now at least statistically associated with exposure to herbicides.

Omitted from Nicosia's recasting of the Agent Orange story, among other things, is the political alchemy of a handful of New Left activists, some around Citizen Soldier, the organization founded by Tod Ensign and myself that transformed a local exposé televised in Chicago into a national crusade. The feature distinguishing those players whose efforts are central to Nicosia's reportage from those whose historically critical activities he ignores is the political agenda of the latter, who insisted that responsibility for Agent Orange–related illnesses could not be separated from responsibility for the war itself. Those vets, myself included, were struggling to keep Vietnam alive as the best means of preventing future Vietnams. We were—and continue—fighting for a historical interpretation that applies the word "aggression" to the U.S. intervention in Vietnam, not the word "mistake." But as Nicosia's narrative quite accurately reveals, the potential for the Agent Orange controversy to embody that political objective for long was preempted by a litigation strategy against Dow and the major herbicide manufacturers. When settled, the class action did not come close to providing adequate compensation for those who required care, but the effort was by no means without value for political education on the effects of commercial toxins on human health. Nor did it lack historical significance, for attacking corporate prestige.

Home to War is voluminous and contains at least one version of everything you've ever wanted know about Vietnam veterans, and their/our high-profile exposure over the past thirty years. One would like to think that many of these accounts are more accurately reported than the ones of which I have, and have signaled, firsthand knowledge here. While Nicosia is clearly full of sympathy for his subject (if perhaps a trifle over fascinated), Vietnam veterans in this portrayal only rarely transcend their ambiguous status as tabloid curiosities or hallowed icons of patriotism: vets who act by acting out. As for a deeper probe into the explanatory realms of postwar readjustment and the veteran culture of entitlements in America—and the place of Vietnam veterans therein—the reader will have to look elsewhere.

The Nation, July 9, 2001

The Jaws of Victory: A Historian Argues We Could Have Won— and Nearly Did Win— the Vietnam War

A Better War: The Unexamined Victories and Final Tragedy of America's Last Years in Vietnam
(by Lewis Sorley)

As an alternative title for "A Better War," why not "The Creighton Abrams Story"? General Abrams, who died in 1974, commanded U.S. forces in Vietnam from 1969 into 1972. Certainly this work by historian, career soldier, and retired CIA analyst Lewis Sorley reads as much like ghosted war memoir as history. It is based substantially on 455 taped recordings of two to six hours' duration housed among the still sequestered "Abrams's Special Collection," and rare is the page in this lengthy text where a comment in Abrams's own words does not accompany the author's polemical defense of our Vietnam debacle. Yet Abrams—appealingly earthy and at times humane—is revealed by Sorley's editing as a man seldom capable of completing either thought or sentence. It is not Abrams's military brilliance but his spirit of true belief that Sorley wishes to invoke as motivational guidance for the dubious conclusions of "A Better War."

Many unreconstructed enthusiasts for U.S. policy in Vietnam, especially former combatants, have alleged that victory was denied them because Washington "tied their hands" militarily. In fact, short of nuclear weapons (whose use was a strategic impossibility), American forces held back little in their arsenal. Despite the use of firepower throughout Indochina that was unprecedented in modern warfare, it is almost universally believed that, after a decade in Vietnam, the United States was beaten and forced to withdraw.

Nay, writes Sorley: "There came a time when the war was won ... in late 1970." A buoyant Abrams, recorded during a staff briefing, announces "Christ, we can all go home and give lectures on how you fight the people's war." Such euphoria rises from two debatable assertions: that the countryside throughout South Vietnam was finally "pacified" and that U.S. air power (notably B-52 bombing raids) had "interdicted" the enemy's resupply line along the Ho Chi Min Trail, "forcing him back to a protracted war strategy." Even if correct, this was what the outgunned but patient North Vietnamese did best: choosing the terrain of battle—whether in combat, diplomacy, or politics—that allowed them to come back and fight another day. South Vietnamese leaders would later wonder whether their U.S. advisers "trained them for the wrong war."

Nonetheless, in the best tradition of the Dolchstoss or "stab in the back" school of history, Sorley argues that our victory on the battlefield, engineered during Abrams's "better war," was lost by Washington at the bargaining table in Paris. One-sided concessions were made, Sorley contends, first by President Johnson's chief negotiator, Averell Harriman, and later by President Nixon's man, Henry Kissinger. While Harriman is reviled by Sorely and his many sources as an arrogant and senile fool, it was Kissinger who delivered the most telling blow to U.S. officials' "nation building" dreams for South Vietnam. The 1973 cease-fire that Kissinger signed in Paris left "thirteen NVA (North Vietnamese Army) divisions ... an estimated 160,000 troops in all—still in place in South Vietnam." This, according to the author, was a determining factor in the fall of Saigon two years later. But Sorley casts important doubt on his own cry of "sellout" by quoting Britain's guru of counterinsurgency, Sir Robert Thompson, who frankly saw that the terms of the Paris accords were "an inevitable acceptance of the battlefield realities."

Old antiwar hands may take some comfort from Sorley's portrait of factional backbiting that persists within the ranks of the war's architects and managers, expressed throughout the narrative in the bitter reflections of military and political contemporaries and co-thinkers who survived Abrams. Coming in for especially heavy weather are Johnson, Harriman, Clark Clifford (who succeeded Robert McNamara as Johnson's secretary of defense), and, with unexpected harshness, General William Westmoreland, who, in the eyes of Sorley and his interlocutors, botched the "early" war in Vietnam between 1965 and 1968. In one truly bizarre observation, and speaking for himself, Sorley suggests that South Vietnam's President Nguyen Van Thieu "was arguably a more honest and decent man than Lyndon Johnson." A contrasting view holds that Johnson, a tortured cold warrior, left a domestic legacy no president since Franklin Delano Roosevelt can touch; while Thieu, a puppet of the Cold War, left a legacy of torture.

Sorley raises many challenges to the postwar cannon, imbedded for the most part within technicalities of military craft. Experts in the field, and historians of the period generally, may or may not be moved to reexamine these arcana, including the impact of the refusal (by both Johnson and Nixon) to call up the reserves, thus denying the green and youthful U.S. forces "access to the experienced small-unit leadership," not to mention Sorley's unqualified praise for the Phoenix Program, designed and implemented by Central Intelligence Agency director William Colby to "neutralize" Viet Cong leadership indigenous to the South. Buttressed by frequent quotes from Abrams, Sorley heaps repeated kudos on the village militias that U.S. "mentors" beefed up in the post Westmoreland era, arming them to the teeth with modern light weaponry. This can only strike many veterans who witnessed the war from below as revisionism approaching the surreal. GIs disparaged these "regional" and "popular" forces as "ruff-puffs," harmless "papasans" at best, too old for conscription by either side, South Vietnamese or Viet Cong.

Sorley makes abundantly clear that he and Abrams alike never doubted the preference of the average Vietnamese residing in the south for the prolonged presence of a foreign invader linked to a fascistic client state in Saigon over the national aim of unification, even under the thumb of a dictatorship in Hanoi. Such a belief flies in the face of everything we know of Vietnam's long effort to free itself from foreign domination. Former Green Beret Don Duncan once cleverly noted that what we brought to Vietnam was only "anticommunism ... a lousy substitute for democracy."

The Sunday Boston Globe, **August 1, 1999**

War and Madness

Hell Healing Resistance: Veterans Speak
(by Daniel Hallock)

Recently, I came across an astounding fact, that the request to the American Psychological Association for new standards in treating patients came in the late 1940s from the Veterans Administration to "assure that service personnel returning ... from World War II received competent mental health care." Just another of history's many metaphors, you might say, for the longstanding alliance between war and madness, which is the true subject, if not so blandly stated, of a valuable new book by Daniel Hallock, *Hell, Healing and Resistance: Veterans Speak* (Plough, 1998, 456 pp., $25).

Tales of war-spawned madness abound in this text, beginning with a charged Preface by Phillip Berrigan, which gave me pause. I oppose those tactics which Berrigan and his comrades employ in bearing witness to the insanity of warfare, most recently, with their attacks on a Naval ship at Bath Iron Works in Maine. It's certainly not about "destruction of property" for me, but something to do with "vanguardism" that I find counter-productive as political education within a democracy.

Berrigan was a combat soldier, a "good killer," he reveals; thus, when he takes a hammer to something even as hateful as a Destroyer, I see, not a reasonable act of moral witness, but the violence—the compulsion to keep fighting—the evil genie which war unbottles in soldiers, so hard to recap when the shooting stops. Having read the personal account of his battlefield, I feel greater sympathy for Phillip Berrigan, and extend the hand of comfort from a fellow vet and victim of war-bred trauma; perhaps he too suffers from the same disease.

Berrigan might react, quite rightly in some respects, that his individual victimization is insignificant in relation to the dangers of human extinction he and others are desperate to bring to our attention, and justify their tactics accordingly. And yet, Hallock's interviews with veterans show nothing if not the patterns of psycho-social dysfunction among a collectivity of *individuals* whose violence in battle washes over so many seemingly *controlled* actions of their postwar lives, often most extremely in acts of violent self-destruction.

Despite the author's inclusion of participants from U.S. military adventures that span World War I through the Persian Gulf, the central focus of Hallock's study remains, unavoidably, the Vietnam experience, since its veterans have been privileged to exhibit so much more systematically and publicly than other groups of former combatants, exactly how the grammar of war shapes the syntax of potential lifelong madness in civilian life. Two manifestations of these phenomena are *suicide* and *post-traumatic stress disorder* (PTSD), which, not surprisingly, are indexed in Hallock's book only with reference to the impact of war on Vietnam veterans.

Through no fault of the author's, these exclusionary juxtapositions represent historical fictions. PTSD is not new with Vietnam; soldiers from time immemorial have suffered this disorder. The record is ample, often most clearly recognized and stated, not in the literature of medical or social science, but in works of the imagination. In a poignant moment from Somerset Maugham's *The Razor's Edge*, a Chicago matron, disappointed in her daughter's fiancé just home from World War I, bitterly recalls how Civil War veterans, too, "were never good for anything" for the rest of their lives. Anecdotally, war stress has been known by a variety of euphemisms, including *nostalgia, homesickness, battle fatigue*, and *shell shock*. Yet *war madness*—to strip PTSD of its clinical camouflage—was not officially entered into the diagnostic manual of mental disorders by the American Psychiatric Association until 1980.

I suspect that the logic of recognizing PTSD as a condition common to soldiers of all wars applies as well to the question of war-related suicides, and I have no doubt that suitable studies would reveal an over representation of self-destruction among, say, World War II veterans every bit as dramatic as that among those who fought in Vietnam. It is a short empathic step, though seldom taken, to then recognize beyond the ranks of former soldiers the wider circles of others traumatized over their lifetimes by war; the most obvious and immediate being the innumerable non-combatant civilians who populate the scenes of battles. And of course *Hell, Healing and Resistance* is well stocked with accounts of how veterans bring the uncorked violence of war back to the home front, where dysfunction breeds dysfunction, overflowing the dockets of domestic law and police blotters throughout the land.

Hollock's is a timeless tale of the tragedies unleashed by war. Yet, even if the accounts of horrors always seem to overshadow healing and resistance, there is much good news in his book as well, among those vets, for example, who've found humanity through their pains, and now contribute to it. Here are lesson learned, as Hollock discovered among many of his interviewees, that a rational society ought to place in wide and continual circulation— the ever urgent task to teach the truth about war and madness. Thic Nhat Hanh expresses this urgency with great simplicity and power in a Foreword to the book: "We cannot imagine the long-term effects of watering so many seeds of war."

PeaceWork, **December 1998/January 1999**

Obsessed by Vietnam

Our War and What It Did to Us (by David Harris)

David Harris left Stanford University in 1967. As a senior baby boomer, he was steeped in the myths and ideologies of the Pax Americana following World War II; he came of age questioning why the Vietnam War seemed so different from his father's war. "The war is a crime," Harris preached in "a thousand speeches" throughout the mid-sixties; then, renouncing his student deferment, he refused the draft and went to prison.

Three decades after confronting the defining predicament of his generation, David Harris, with *Our War*, challenges the Cold War assumptions of the world into which he was born and socialized. And while he never saw Vietnam action in the traditional sense, he remains at war over how History will interpret this American adventure for the generations that follow; he demands a reckoning, long overdue, for the act of aggression committed by the United States and its leaders behind a smokescreen of manufactured altruism.

Harris's narrative is inflamed, a retrospective drenched in undigested passions, though seldom in disproportion to the humiliations he suffered as a price for clinging to the high ground. More perplexing are the matters Harris has chosen not to address. Given his public visibility—magnified by a failed marriage to celebrity Joan Baez—and the drama of his incarceration among hardened criminals, a reader might reasonably wonder why Harris hasn't provided more on the domestic cultures of draft resistance and prison life and less avuncular commentary on the core facts surrounding the war.

Perhaps *Our War* should be treated as Volume One of a work-in-progress, a mantra of right-thinking recitations and reflections on Vietnam that Harris, an apparent Calvinist now seeking the path of Siddhartha, needed to get off his chest before mining more subtle veins beneath the crust where good and evil only seem to lie in absolute distinction. Thus, Harris substitutes narrow moral judgments when evaluating national and individual responsibility for the war which others might examine against a wider band of social, political and historical criteria.

A string of quotes can illustrate Harris' somewhat fuzzy, occasionally New Age, philosophical patter: "When a nation acts, all its citizens are joined insolubly in their responsibility for the consequences of their national behavior." "When the question is asked, who did this?—we must all raise our hands." "Holding on to our denial will never allow us to escape the war ... rather than owning our experience, it will continue to own us." "Evil is not only banal ... it is also participatory, and it only happens if everyone does their little bit to make it possible." Well, not everyone, "I am proud to say," Harris intones with that self-righteousness not unknown among pacifists, "that when my turn came, I declined to do mine." Indeed, his was a noble act, even if he does say so himself.

Fortunately, such boilerplate thins out early in *Our War*, as the author happily contradicts his theology of universal guilt, allowing that "[t]here are those among us more deserving of blame than the rest and they must be held ... responsible." Leading the accused for the Nuremberg Tribunal of Harris's mind are Robert McNamara, Richard Nixon, and that Great Satan of Harvard Yard, Henry Kissinger.

The war, Harris reminds us, lasted "nine years" after McNamara privately decided it was "unwinnable," and "a lot more people died after [he] decided their lives were being wasted than before, and he never once said as much as a word to warn them.... I cannot fathom how he manages to live with himself. Were I he, I suspect, I would have blown my own brains out years ago."

Honorable suicide is not the imaginary option Harris offers the hated Henry K. Meeting up with a friend recently, an old Movement hand who'd become a Senate aide after the war, "we got on the subject of Kissinger one afternoon," Harris recalls. And Nancy, he discovers, still harbors homicidal fantasies: "It's amazing," she says. "All those good people dead, and nobody has managed to kill that son of a bitch yet."

Commenting on the nauseating television spectacle of Richard Nixon's funeral, Harris echoes the verdict of his sometimes colleague at *Rolling Stone*, Hunter S. Thompson "Richard Milhous Nixon was as evil a man as any who has ever partaken of the apex of American political power.... More people died on his watch than on any other, and he took a particular public pleasure in the devastation he wrought."

A substantial portion of Harris's text is devoted to describing the agent of that "devastation," unprecedented American fire power, and its impact on the lives of Vietnamese and Americans alike, most specifically our own veterans, a sprinkling of whom pop up, bearing witness to their sins. Toward these survivors Harris expresses an ambivalence fashioned of familiarity and detachment: he acknowledges the vets' authenticity as a class, "poor boys" marked as fodder for the battlefields; but on a karmic level, they are not of his tribe.

Harris, by his own admission, is a Vietnam junkie, "obsessed" by the war. A precocious student born and raised in Fresno, California among the provincial gentry—western WASPS with DAR roots—by the time Harris was selected "Boy of the Year" in the high school class of '63, he already "knew about the Geneva Accords ... about the obstruction of free elections, about Ho Chi Minh, Bao Dai, and Ngo Dinh Diem ... the napalm and strategic hamlets...."

Few of the sixties generation can touch that claim, which may account for the mature Harris's taxonomic preoccupation with military nomenclature and the war's other raw materials, catalogued throughout his untitled chapters in the form of litanies, glosses, and asides: field tactics, weapons systems, place names, GI pidgin, Vet chat.... A more in-depth and chilling probe of the CIA's Phoenix program is prompted by a revulsion for the widespread use of torture by Americans which, Harris stresses, "touched me in a way nothing else quite did.... Nazis tortured, not Americans."

Harris is a mainstream intellectual who lived through the agony of Vietnam refusing, despite mellowing into middle age, to accommodate apologists for the war on any significant point. A graceful writer, he has written a quirky book; from the few peeks he allows us into his personal saga and jail time, we may hope for an even more interesting sequel.

The Dissident, **June 1997**

How We Bombed in Laos

Back Fire: The CIA'S Secret War in Laos
(by Roger Warner)

If, during the second Indochina War (1960–1975), Vietnam was the main event and Cambodia the sideshow. What did that make Laos? A kind of sinister shadow play where the cadres of Cold War adversaries, well concealed from public observation, battled to achieve an ironically similar objective: the national unity of a former French colony populated by diverse ethnic and tribal peoples who, for many centuries, had lived in virtual isolation from one another. At issue: which ideology, capitalist or socialist, were the Laotians involved in the task of "nation-building" to achieve?

Representing the interests of the West were the American CIA and its local allies, the Laotian royalist elites, and elements of an Iron Age mountain people known to us as Meo tribesmen. In the rival camp were the Pathet Lao, an indigenous revolutionary movement allied closely with the North Vietnamese and benefitting from both the political and material support of China and the U.S.S.R. This, in broad outline, is the story recorded by Roger Warner in *Back Fire,* a useful, if somewhat anecdotal contribution to the literature on the U.S. "secret war" in Laos, which is rooted substantially in the recollections of former CIA operatives who were there.

By agreement of the major powers at Geneva in 1962, Laos was to remain neutral in the East West conflict. But the United States was unreconciled to a solution, favored by Britain and France, whereby Laos would follow the model of Austria or Finland, "leaning economically and culturally toward the West" but allowing the local communists a role in politics and government. For its part, the Pathet Lao, with full backing from Hanoi, never slackened the drive after Geneva to unify Laos under its own banner.

It was behind this pretense of neutrality, according to Warner, that the CIA sponsored its relatively low-level guerrilla and ground combat operations in Laos, providing Montagnard irregulars with arms, logistical support, training and sustenance while effectively blocking, for a time, the Pentagon's efforts to widen the U.S. military commitment in Laos along more conventional lines.

Warner's extensive profiles of many of the agency's old hands in Laos reveal them to have been idealists. The field level spooks often imagined they could beat the communists at their own game by winning hearts and minds, and by rallying the noncommunist locals to fight on their behalf.

Key to the CIA campaign, designated Operation Momentum, were the Meo who already opposed communist expansion, and were the only force that stood between the Plain of Jars (50 miles from the frontier with North Vietnam and occupied by the Pathet Lao), and the Mekong [where the provinces controlled by the Royal Lao Government bordered Thailand]." "The weak part of the proposition," acknowledged Bill Lair, the CIA official who designed and ran Momentum for many years, "was that, in the end, the Meo were probably going to lose if the North Vietnamese kept on pushing."

By the late '60s, the North Vietnamese army was pushing very hard—indeed, within the Pathet Lao border areas—to enlarge and defend its elaborate logistical pipeline to the south, which was known as the Ho Chi Minh Trail. The escalation of the war throughout neighboring Vietnam had by then led to the inevitable expansion of the American military presence in Laos which. Warner's informants recall somewhat bitterly, the CIA had long hoped to avoid.

In fact, as Warner clearly demonstrates, the CIA had itself initially tipped the military balance by introducing air power to support its Meo clients as they steadily lost ground to the advancing insurgents. And so the real dirty little secret of the American war in Laos was not so much the romantic counterinsurgency conducted by an odd lot of CIA misfits on the back lots of the Cold War—though this had dire consequences for the Meo who were pawns in a nation-building fantasy that, as Bill Lair admits, was doomed from the outset by the bombing. Once the full force of the U.S. Air Force was unleashed, reports Warner, the bombing of Laos would become what columnist Anthony Lewis, writing in 1973, called "the most appalling episode of lawless cruelty in American history."

Such judgments do not explain, nor can Warner, how it was exactly that the civilian population became a favorite target for the more than "two million tons" of bombs that the American Air Force would ultimately drop on it throughout Laos. Doing the next best thing, Warner gives considerable space to the experience of Fred Branfman, who spent several years in Laos, first with the International Voluntary Services, then as a freelance journalist, and who almost single-handedly succeeded in documenting and making public the extent of the secret bombing which, even at the time, was widely believed to be of limited military effectiveness.

The Pathet Lao, assuming power in 1975, decided the issue of which side would achieve national unity on behalf of the Laotian people. But the ideological battle has been resolved in favor of the West, whose free-market principles now dominate the Laotian economy. In either case, the peasantry, who bore the brunt of the war's horrors and destructiveness, seem mired, according to recent press reports, in a cycle of poverty, illiteracy and short life expectancy, regardless of whose banner is flying over Vientiane.

The Washington Post Book World, September 19, 1995

On the Lam from Vietnam

Busted: A Vietnam Veteran in Nixon's America
(by W.D. Ehrhart)

Much in the way that Diane Arbus bewitched the eye of an entire generation by equating black-and-white still photography with a sociology of human bizarreness, Michael Herr cut a pattern that literary-minded veterans of the Vietnam War have, in large measure, tended to emulate with their own prose ever since. In his critically acclaimed *Dispatches* (1977), Herr fixed his own brand of voyeurism to what was surreal in Vietnam, and gave short shrift to the war's more tedious—but telling—day-to-day realities. Within the paradigm Herr helped to engineer, we were shown the GI as anti-hero in the whirlpool of his action-packed, private war, but we seldom saw the hand that pulled the plug.

Most vets have never gotten any further than the rest of us in sorting out the relationship between class, race and cannon fodder that characterized military service during the Vietnam era, much less grasped the war's complex link to U.S. geopolitical ambitions. This is the singular achievement of W.D. Ehrhart's autobiographical memoir, *Busted: A Vietnam Veteran in Nixon's America*, which filters the conventional subject matter of Vietnam-influenced literature through the consciousness of a former combatant who was, and remains, radicalized by the war.

For some time, Ehrhart, a consummate outsider, has ridden circuit on the fringes of Vet-Lit, delivering a prolific output of poetry and prose to small press and "niche" publishers who command few reviews, offer spotty distribution, keep no backlist and, ultimately, warehouse their titles on the rear seat of the author's car. By placing *Busted* with a respectable university press, Ehrhart has resolved the dilemmas of backlist and storage. The University of Massachusetts has also reissued two earlier volumes of Ehrhart's memoirs, *Vietnam-Perkasie: A Combat Marine Memoir* and *Passing Time: A Memoir of a Vietnam Veteran Against the War*.[1]

Busted is an American original, a "portrait of the artist as young man," writes H. Bruce Franklin in the book's illuminating foreword. The story is built around one brief escapade in the author's postwar life. As a burned-out antiwar vet in the early seventies, Ehrhart joins the merchant marines and goes to sea; he is then "busted" for possession of marijuana and kicked off his ship. A judicial farce ensues because Ehrhart refuses to surrender his seaman's card voluntarily and challenges a Coast Guard judge to "take it from me." Ehrhart's lawyer, a wily tactician who exploits an inept prosecutor's procedural errors, forces one postponement after another. It is between accounts of each stage of this silly and vindictive "trial" that Ehrhart narrates the compelling tale of how a minister's son from a conservative backwater in rural Pennsylvania, who had campaigned for Goldwater in 1964, joined the Marines at 17 to fight the Commies in Vietnam before they landed on the beaches of Waikiki.

What he found in Vietnam, he tells us, "bore no resemblance to what I had been led to expect by Lyndon Johnson and *Time* magazine." He was not the "liberator" he had hoped to be. Instead, he confronted the classic dilemma of the American G.I. in Vietnam: Nearly every hostile act he engaged in seemed to be aimed at the very population he was supposed to be "liberating." In such a war, survival, not glory, becomes your only goal, so you would "hunker down inside your flak jacket and helmet and hope the big stuff landed on somebody else's head." In the meantime, a larger consciousness about the war emerged out of Ehrhart's feelings of resentment toward corrupt South Vietnamese officials like Premier Nguyen Cao Ky, "who wore tailored purple flight suits and admired Adolf Hitler."

Hatred of the Vietnam War festered like an open wound after Ehrhart's return in 1968. But it was Nixon's 1970 invasion of Cambodia, and the killing of the four Kent State students, that finally spurred him to action. He joined Vietnam Veterans Against the War and started to speak out "mostly at very high decibels." Still, "the war went on like a ballpeen hammer in the hands of a steady workman." And Ehrhart's response to political frustration was to hit the road (at this point, in the form of shipping out), a pattern of behavior he'd established many years before as a restless man.

In fact, when Ehrhart isn't writing about the consequences of his marijuana bust, or his twisted roots in small-town U.S.A., remote dad and long-suffering mom, smartass high school antics and self-indicting flashbacks of his "crimes" in Vietnam, he's describing how he cruised the nation's highways and byways with fitful desperation trying to "outrun America" and its crazy war. If the road offers occasion for temporary flight from the demons who tail him, it is also a gantlet lined with hostile forces. There isn't a cop anywhere who likes the way Ehrhart parts his hair, and an innocent drive around the block can wind up with our hero spread eagled on the hood of his car and staring down the barrel of a service .38. The law knows a real outlaw when it sees one.

A good deal of the narrative in *Busted* is in dialogue, with the author's apparent interlocutor, a straw man, because the conversation is really with himself. A case in point is the deliciously Socratic duel Ehrhart stages between a liberal (his lawyer) and a radical (himself), stretched nearly the length of the book, debating whether or not he should go to law school and challenge the system from within.

Like a lot of former combat soldiers, Ehrhart is haunted by ghosts. Siegfried Sassoon, convalescing from wounds during World War I, thought he was going mad when the corpses of his dead mates appeared to him in London's Piccadilly Square. Ehrhart seems more at ease with the specters of his fallen comrades as he talks with three former squad members who were killed in action. These three form a chorus, a kind or collective Jiminy Cricket.

As a structural device, this use of ghost characters seems, at first, derivative, the one false note in an otherwise remarkable composition. Then it dawns on you that Ehrhart has adapted this convention as a private memorial to the victims of the war, Americans and Vietnamese alike. Not surprisingly he gives these shadowy projections of his conscience some of his best lines, including this ironic indictment of the moral hypocrisy he finds rotting at the core of American ideals:

> Ya kill people, beat 'em up, tie 'em up, lock 'em up, burn down their hootches, shoot their chickens an' their pigs an' their water bo, trash their crops, turn 'em into shoeshine boys and shortime girls, bop their little ones on the head with Ham and Motherfuckers, waste their forests, fuck up anything that moves or grows or stands more than six inches off the ground, an' they give ya a bunch a medals and a bunch a stripes an' a guaranteed VA home mortgage loan. "Nice work. Fine work. You're a credit to the flag" they say. Then you smoke a little a God's contribution to peace, love, and happy days, and they wanna throw you in the slammer.

Another figure haunting Ehrhart's recollections of the period is Richard Nixon, whose legal entanglements happen to coincide with the author's trial. Thus Ehrhart has ample occasion to engage in some eloquent Nixon-bashing as he chronicles his own days in court. Typical of his spicy asides is a reminder that Nixon turned "expletive deleted" into "a household phrase overnight"; then, with somewhat less humor, Ehrhart observes that "even in their sanitized form," Nixon's White House tapes "revealed that the man who had promised Peace With Honor was a mean-spirited emotional hunchback with the vocabulary of a peepshow operator and the morals of a shark."

Such outbursts derive their justification from Ehrhart's desire to distance himself from policies and value he once upheld before learning to think for himself. Yet the dominant tone in *Busted* is neither bitterness nor anger but compassion. The true source of Ehrhart's moral authority as a critic of the Vietnam War rests on his steadfast refusal to traffic in the surreal romance of combat that so characterizes the picaresque school of Vet-Lit, and unwittingly feeds the "warrior dreams" of our young.

The Nation, **September 18, 1995**

Note

1. W.D. Ehrhart's *Vietnam Perkasie: A Combat Memoir* (1983) and *Passing Time: Memoir of a Vietnam Veteran Against the War* (1989) were originally published by McFarland & Company, Inc., Publishers (the publisher of the present work). Both of these original volumes are available in ebook format from McFarland.

Travels with Charlie

Dues: A Novel of War and After (by Michael H. Cooper)

Playing Basketball with the Viet Cong (by Kevin Bowen)

It is often said, and justifiably so, that the premier war novel of the twentieth century is *All Quiet on the Western Front*, Eric Maria Remarque's searing and compassionate account of life and death in the German trenches of the First World War. It is a standard—along with the less frequently read works of Remarque's fellow combatants Siegfried Sassoon, Edmund Blunden, Wilfred Owen, Frederic Manning and a few others—against which subsequent novels, memoirs and poetry of war are measured.

It may still be too soon for final judgement, but most of the writing about the Vietnam War by its veterans seems to fall short of what Remarque and his contemporaries achieved as they plotted, with rare objectivity, both the scope of their mad war and the profound transformations affecting those who fought it. Having read the war stories of many Vietnam vets, I am still waiting for Remarque.

Broadly speaking, from the American side there are two categories of Vietnam War literature written by its veterans. First, the popular branch of the genre, which fails so miserably to embrace the experience that it functions, de facto, as postwar apologia, an extension of hostilities by other means. Typically, such works crown their protagonists with exaggerated honors, as "warrior kings" and "rogue warriors," or they are blatantly revisionist, like the so-called "oral histories" regularly churned out by Al Santoli.

By implication, if not intent, the vets who author these works seek to dull the national memory of our military defeat by glorifying the role of the individual American soldier, marking survivors simultaneously as valiant heroes of an unpopular foreign war and victims of political betrayal at home.

Perhaps it is only slightly grandiose to suggest that another social consequence of such high-test pulp is to abet the recruitment of adventure-prone elements among minority and working class youths, who are most apt to face the nation's combat chores in the endless chain of mini-invasions our government now finds so appealing.

A second, smaller category of Vietnam veteran war literature contains those memoirs and works of fiction for which someone in the world of high culture claims literary merit. My own short list of works that "get the war right" would certainly include Ron Kovic's *Born on the Fourth of July* and Ronald J. Glasser's *365 Days*, plus a sampling of the poetry, some of it quite exceptional. I consider it a possibility that even into the next millennium, *Born on the Fourth of July* will be read generally by those who wish to understand some essential truths about the Vietnam War, especially its psychic impact on the American fighting man. With his memoir, Kovic stands virtually alone in dredging up from the inside out the universal affliction of the Vietnam veteran, that residue of volatile savagery that remains the demon of his inner drama.

One shortcoming common to many of the "literary" works on Vietnam is that, while infinitely better written and more honest than the macho agit-trash, they are only relatively more successful in exploring the contexts of class and convention that led many of their authors to the circumstances where the Vietnam War became their subject in the first place.

For example, the theme of a guilt-ridden conscience at having gone to war against his better inclinations pulsates like a nervous tic throughout the work of Tim O'Brien, whose elegant confessions are often mistaken for deep excavations into the dark side of the veteran's postwar psyche. This fixation with the self prevents O'Brien—the writer—from contemplating his call to war on a higher collective and historical plane where the apparent issues of choice confronting those who entered military service were frequently limited by forces beyond their individual will or control.

This is not the particular flaw of Michael H. Cooper's *Dues: A Novel of War and After*, a highly readable, even compelling first novel, where the social reality confronting a typical blue-collar draftee is deftly portrayed, and the post-traumatic readjustment of the veteran on return from combat, while made extreme, is nonetheless credible; it is Cooper's rendering of the war itself—despite his earnest attempts at realism—that is hopelessly misrepresented.

Dues follows its principal character, David Thorne, through three phases of the wartime experience. Despite some annoying anachronisms (the word "geek" had no currency circa 1968, while the redundancy of "marijuana joint" is indeed geeky), Cooper's best writing occurs in the first third of the book, where life on the American industrial fringe is laid out without sentiment in all its demoralizing starkness. A college dropout, Thorne blows a first shot at upward mobility that his hard working parents (Ozzie and Harriet clones reminiscent of the mom and dad in David Rabe's play, *Sticks and Bones*) have mapped out for him with their hopes and sacrifices.

Thorne returns briefly to the nest but finds no balm there for his weary sense of aimlessness. The sympathy he feels for his parents' resilience in times perpetually hard is overwhelmed by the stasis of their home life, depicted powerfully but with a minimum of flair. As draft-bait, Thorne awaits the fateful "greeting" from his local board by doing grunt work—prefiguring his role in Vietnam—in a factory, a dead-end job, the mindlessness of which he further anesthetizes after-hours with endless rounds of beer and reefer. Thorne's dreary prewar existence is transcended and humanized by the friendship he develops with a black co-worker, another preview of what will be a dominant theme of *Dues*. Throughout the novel, Thorne, who is white, will find all his close companionship among the "brothers." What saves this atypical arrangement from becoming a *deus ex machina* of politically correct race relations imposed on the past from the nineties is the utter lack of self-consciousness Cooper builds into these alliances. There is not guilt-fueled liberal agenda here, not intellectualized color-blindness. Thorne's brand of alienation—never overtly political—simply happens to be of the same substance as that of his black comrades; he too, is seen—and sees himself—as the "other."

Thorne, in his own eyes, is a loser, but in Vietnam he discovers something he is really good at—killing. The trouble is, he's a bit too good at it. Over the course of a hundred pages, the central core of *Dues* covering his actual time at war, Thorne plants *gooks* faster than the marksmen of another Cooper (Fenimore) dispatch their slant-eyes nemeses, the *redskins*, in those tales of the American colonial frontier so wittily savaged by Mark Twain in *How to Tell a Story and Other Essays*. Michael Cooper (in fact, the author's pseudonym) has his faceless and endlessly expendable natives pop up like ducks in a shooting gallery, where Thorne greases the lot like so many extras who take their falls on cue in a B movie commemorating the white man's burden. At one point, Cooper constructs a litany of the slaughter:

> On Wednesday he shot a man running to escape on his small boat.... On Friday he shot a man standing atop a bank near the river. They fired simultaneously, but the man was the one who was hit.... The following Tuesday he shot two men on the river in a small

boat. They shouldn't have fired at him.... On Thursday two more. He was starting to wonder if it would be three someday. Then four.... On the following Monday he finally broke the three mark.

And so it goes. But this portrayal simply runs contrary to the grain of history. While Cooper gets much of the atmosphere right in his sketch of daily life at an Army forward base camp, he has conjured up a soldier whose charmed invulnerability has more in common with Simplicissimus, Grimmelshausen's fabulous marauder of the Thirty Year's War than with some grunt who did his time in Vietnam fighting in the Delta or anywhere else. The only way Thorne could have wiped out as many V.C. as he is credited with, in a war where the enemy never paraded in the open as habitually as Cooper has imagined, is if he had been a bombardier on a B-52.

While *Dues* is indeed a work of fiction, the tradition of Great War Novel, in my view, sets critical limits to how far an author can deviate from the realm of verisimilitude where descriptions of combat are concerned. It's not that Remarque and Sassoon didn't weave myths of their own from their ordeals in the trenches; they selected, rearranged, compressed, omitted from their many experiences as they worked them into readable tales. But they did not alter the observable facts of combat. Since they believed that no one on the home front could possibly imagine the horrors of the unprecedented mass slaughter they had witnessed, and which they desperately wished to communicate, they struggled all the more to evoke faithfully the details and images of the battlefield.

With *Dues*, Michael Cooper seems to be suggesting along with others who have preceded him (O'Brien, *Going After Cacciato*; Coppola, *Apocalypse Now*) that only with a flight from reality—"the horror, the horror"— can the weirdness of the Vietnam War be adequately comprehended within a fictional frame. Such mental acrobatics unwittingly distract our attention from the root causes of the war, whose aura, then, hovers in the ether world of allegory as some bizarre, inexplicable exception to our good intentions gone astray.

When Cooper (himself a Vietnam era veteran) returns his man stateside, Thorne is once again on firmer ground, albeit trapped among the tragic vet minority for whom re-entry into civil life has become impossible. Joined by his combat buddy Stanley, Thorne adapts all too quickly to a life on the street. And when Stanley dies of an overdose, despite an ambiguous ending in which a wine-soaked Thorne vows to reform, we suspect he too is doomed. For, indeed, these characters are both retrotypes in fiction, memorializing G.I.s "killed" in Vietnam who didn't actually die until coming home. But the fact is, it wasn't necessary to invent a cartoon version of combat to justify Thorne's postwar fall from grace. Vietnam made a lot of American vets, even those only modestly traumatized by combat, much less adaptable to the world they had known before going off to war.

If the literary prose of the Vietnam War has so often fallen short of the mark, the poetry has been more successful, perhaps because the power and popularity of rock lyrics provided models that G.I.s found accessible in capturing the true-felt moments of this peculiar war.

As with Sassoon, Owen, and Rupert Brooks in their war, much of the best poetry by Vietnam veterans was written, if not in the actual heat of the battle, then at least chronologically close to it. The extraordinary voices of Herbert Krohn, Michael Casey, Larry Rottmann and many others were emerging by the early 1970s, and retain the eerie power to free the emotions of those distant war scenes from their crypts and speed them into a timeless present.

On coming home from Vietnam, Larry Rottmann, always a poet of few words, dug in like a middleweight to pound us in the solar plexus with one short verse after another. No amount of irony—all of it intended—can hide the bitter truths behind a poem like his "S.O.P.":

> To build a "gook stretcher," all you
>   need is:
> Two helicopters
> Two long ropes,
> And one elastic gook.

But that was then. A quarter-century has passed, and a contemporary collection of Vietnam-inspired poems like Kevin Bowen's *Playing Basketball with the Viet Cong* really belongs more to the present than to those gut-charged moments of a long-ago war. Wisely, Bowen has avoided the pitfall—not uncommon in the ongoing work of many Vietnam veteran poets—of composing as if the war took place yesterday.

The measure of this wisdom is that, by the 1990s, Rottmann's "gook"— that inscrutable little creature whom the American soldier viewed, at best, as an unwelcome nuisance in his own homeland—has become Bowen's (and the latter day Rottmann's) Vietnamese, a person with a culture, a language and a human face. Many veterans have struggled, largely through a process of wrenching self-re-education, toward reconciliation with the former adversary, rejecting the one-sidedness of the national melodrama, where, for too long, the tormented G.I. has occupied center stage alone.

In a scene from this collection's title poem, Bowen not only creates a rich, rhythmic word sketch of an unusual postwar encounter with a Vietnamese veteran but wryly notes how improbable such an encounter would have appeared to him as a soldier in 1968.

> You never thought then
> that this grey-haired man in sandals
> smoking Gauloises on your back
>   porch,
> drinking your beer, his rough, cough
> punctuating tales of how he fooled
> the French in '54,
> would arrive at your backdoor
> to call you out to shoot some baskets,
> friend.

If Bowen's poetry reveals his now deep empathy for the Vietnamese, not to mention a considerable erudition concerning their culture, it is not at the expense of erasing the equally deep chasm separating his experience as a G.I. from that of the people who were our former victims. Bowen may have widened his field of vision, but the war understandably remains as an orienting motif. One memory takes him back to the "Temple of Quan Loi, 1969," where an old woman, dressed in mourning, emerges from a temple, staring from the corner of her eye at a group of soldiers, Bowen observing that

> She must wish our deaths.
> Beneath the white silk band
> breasts ache for a husband.
> She passes in mourning,
> counting each step.
> Her prayers rain down like rockets.

Even from the vantage point of middle age, as "In the Village of Yen So," the vet can never be indifferent to recording and reckoning the depredations of the past. Like many veterans, Bowen has returned to Vietnam several times in recent years. In what is now a familiar scene (at least to other visitors like me), an American couple is briefed, over tea, by a village official:

> Numbers tumble in our heads:
> how many commune members
> comprise how many families

as

> In silence we scribble facts
> into notebooks

yet one senses that the mind of the hostess is "fixed on other numbers," a Christmas day long ago and the

> Two hundred fifty-eight killed that
>   night
> Five hundred who went south to war
> Two hundred and sixteen who didn't return.

The literary and pedagogic merit of Kevin Bowen's poetry cannot be separated. His work reminds us that our relations with Vietnam in the present cannot be divorced from our experience with Vietnam in the past. If, however, our understanding of that past continues to be wrapped in distortions or mired in self-absorption—as is so much of the literature by American veterans—than the optimism of so many over a postwar thaw won't disguise the fact that all's not yet quiet on our Southeast Asian front.

The Nation, **February 27, 1995**

The God That Resigned

Anatomy of a War: Vietnam, the United States, and the Modern Historical Experience
(by Gabriel Kolko)

> *A friend should bear his friend's*
> *infirmities,*
> *But Brutus makes mine greater than*
> *they are...*

Anatomy of a War, published by Pantheon in 1985, has been reissued without apparent revision to the original text, presumably for the sole purpose of showcasing a provocative forty-four page "Postscript." In it, the post-reunification Vietnamese leadership comes in for a rather depressing tongue-lashing at the hands of their former confidant and sometimes champion, the author and historian, Gabriel Kolko.

The charge? That classic provender of the Far Left—a sellout. In his "reassessment" of their "entire experience," Kolko argues that the Vietnamese have been stampeded down the capitalist road when they should have—indeed *could have*—continued along the path of revolutionary socialism.

Even under these somewhat cranky circumstances, a new edition of *Anatomy of a War* is a welcome event. This is, after all, a monumental work, synthesized from a vast quantity of raw data and ordered within a methodological framework that the historian Marvin Gettleman once described as "plain Marxist"—which might suggest to some a blend of zeal and orthodoxy worthy of John Calvin.

Kolko has molded an historical epic from the actions, and the motive forces behind them, of the four principal actors of the "American War—the northern and southern communists, the Americans, and their Vietnamese allies." *Anatomy of a War* remains the definitive scholarly response to the question posed by Lyndon Johnson in 1965—but never satisfactorily answered by any of the war's apologists, even at this late date: "Why Vietnam?"

Despite a tendency toward repetitiveness, extending to certain key points and a few stock metaphors (more "vacuums" are created and filled in Kolko's prose than in a high school physics class), there is a relentless, penetrating intelligence guiding this work from start to finish. And naturally, for those of us who, with Kolko, recognize the justice of Vietnam's victory, the reading is bound to produce a certain grim satisfaction as we relive the glory days of that grand check to imperial power and world capitalist expansion, whose every step Kolko documents and analyzes with precision.

But now, twenty years after that dramatic setback to U.S. designs for hegemony over Vietnam, the capitalist fox—if I may turn Hubert Humphrey's anticommunist barnyard homily on its head—has found economics to be a more effective means for wheedling its way back into the Little Red Hen House. This, at least, is the tenor of Kolko's "Postscript," where he charges, unequivocally, that the struggle in Vietnam for "a more rational and humane form of socialism" is being "sacrificed" in favor of what he repeatedly characterizes as a scheme to restore capitalism inspired by the International Monetary Fund and the World Bank. A "market system under state management," the Vietnamese call it.

For Kolko, the turnabout represents a grotesque irony because such a system in his view might have been "attained, albeit under different rulers, had the Americans been allowed to run South Vietnam as they did other Asian 'tigers' [Taiwan and South Korea, for example] ... models that Hanoi's leaders openly aspire to emulate."

This is a low blow, but its sardonic intent underscores Kolko's deep dissatisfaction with a majority of the Politburo members who have governed Vietnam since 1975, leaders he portrays as "lackluster ... apparatchiks" and "mediocre" old men. Not only does he accuse these cadres of betraying the interests of their own "poor peasant" masses, but also of breaking faith with "far flung antiwar activists," who, like Kolko, didn't just oppose the war but supported "the Revolution's social goals."

This "promised ... destroyed" is for Kolko very much a personal affair. A preface for the new edition might have smoothed the transition between the two narratives—that of the 1985 Kolko, full of critical admiration for the Revolution, the Party, and its leadership, and that of the 1994 Kolko. But the emotion of disillusionment so dominant in the "Postscript" gives the book a schizophrenic quality, though the substance of Kolko's criticisms cannot be ignored simply because they are packaged in the charged rhetoric of a "prophet betrayed."

The background giving rise to these criticisms can be summed up as follows. In 1975, the Vietnamese leadership, flush with victory and optimism, faced the daunting task of rebuilding a country that had been ideologically divided and subjected to thirty years of savage warfare. An extension of North Vietnam's socialist orientation to the South, more or less in tune with the Soviet model, was a foregone conclusion.

The many efforts over the next decade to speed Vietnam's newly unified economy toward a socialist transformation were slowed dramatically, however, following a Party Congress in December 1986, when *doi moi*, the "new thinking," ushered in a series of reforms to combat runaway inflation and widespread corruption among government officials.

The ultimate subordination of the Vietnamese economy to "market principles," however, did not really accelerate until 1989 following the steady disintegration of the U.S.S.R. and the Eastern Bloc countries. Vietnam lost virtually all the foreign aid and protected markets of fraternal communist nations. But also its general failure to increase productivity and wealth through a system of state-owned industry and collectivized agriculture was interpreted to mean that the Party had moved too quickly in its desire to create a classless society.

"It is an illusion," the leadership would later conclude, "to wish to advance directly to socialism without going through the stage of capitalist development."

Thus, the Soviet-style command economy has been rapidly dismantled, bringing an end to state subsidies in many forms, including significant amounts spent on education and health care. Large tracts of land have been returned to the private sector, where it can now be legally concentrated into fewer and fewer hands, leading—in the short run at least—to popular transfers from the countryside to the cities and a swelling of unemployment and homelessness.

The goal of achieving socialism has been shelved until more propitious times, but *not* abandoned, its pulse—however weak—being kept alive by the very existence of the Leninist Party. Such, at least, is the new line of the Politburo. The basic idea is: Party + Capitalism = Socialism, a formula Kolko rejects as an intrinsic impossibility.

Vietnam's economy has indeed been struggling since 1975. The cause of its weakness, however, was not, Kolko insists, the Party's premature drive toward socialism, but rather its protracted hostilities involving its neighbors—hostilities which, in turn, depleted Vietnam's human and financial resources and subjected the nation to an international trade embargo.

"No economic policy," Kolko writes, "could have transcended the Cambodian war's [1978–1989] huge material effects, and without this tragic affair Vietnam's subsequent economic performance would have been far better, whatever its premises."

Besides, Kolko argues, based on technical data he cites from a variety of sources, Vietnam's economy was showing steady growth by 1986 under socialist premises, even as the *doi moi* reforms were being introduced and the embargo lifted by most countries of the world, excluding, of course, the recalcitrant United States.

As Kolko sees it, Bolshevik authoritarianism and not overreaching utopian policies finally led the Politburo to curtail the social gains of the Revolution. Fearing a Vietnamese equivalent of Poland's Solidarity or China's Tiananmen Square, the Party, he contends, reduced mass organizations to ceremonial shells and stifled democratic impulses among low-level cadres, veterans, and free thinking intellectuals. Then, bending to pressures from the IMF and the World Bank, Vietnam's "ruling elite" adopted the "capitalist line" as the most certain means of preserving its own power. This last is a charge Kolko repeats frequently.

What seems to rankle Kolko above all else is the appearance among the old Leninist faithful of a species of voodoo economics, Marxist-style. By March 1989, Party ideologues had concluded that "the private individual, small owner, and private capitalist economic forms are still necessary ... in the structure of the commodity-based economy for the advance toward socialism." A "re-reading of "Leninist thought" had led to the discovery of "universal laws of commodity production," which, according to then Prime Minister (now Party Secretary) Do Muoi, justified operating the economy on "market principles" that would "help invent new forms of transitions" to socialism.

"Such a hybrid—'market-oriented socialism'"—rejoins Kolko, "has never existed anywhere." Not only that—had the Vietnamese communists after 1945 "organized the economy and society in the manner Western economists later convinced the Party's leaders was superior" to their socialist alternatives, it "would have led to Vietnam's defeat."

Such a prediction after the fact is more easily asserted than proved. For Kolko to be correct we must conclude, as he does, that the peasants were moved to make those extraordinary sacrifices, without which victory was unthinkable, almost exclusively because of the material advantages offered them through socialist land policies.

It seems equally plausible to suggest that the impulse to defend the homeland—even where the national idea begins and ends at the commune gate—was as firmly rooted in less material forms of self-interest, a traditional hatred of "foreign oppressors," and a yearning for independence. One may legitimately wonder whether Kolko's orthodoxy concerning what socialism *can* and *cannot* be applies with equal force to the present and future as it does to the past.

To test this thesis, Kolko asks whether the same masses can be mobilized to perform similar efforts of a super-human scope on behalf of a form of development under "market principles" that may not only leave them in poverty but also deprive them of the few benefits they had achieved under the conditions prevailing prior to the *doi moi* reforms.

It is a good question. Vietnam's leaders claim to have dismantled their socialist economy from necessity, to avoid descent into the political chaos that beset their former allies. Kolko's prediction is that just the opposite will occur: that Vietnam's new line, based on a tolerance of capitalism's built-in inequalities, will lead to far more damaging social and political turmoil, and, ultimately, to the fall of the Party. And the Party, in his view, is the only force—when properly reformed—capable of restoring the egalitarian society that Hanoi, under Ho Chi Minh's leadership, was beginning to establish after 1945.

One could wish that the tone of Kolko's polemic had leaned more toward empathy than accusation. Beyond that, it's hard to judge whether, or to what degree, his position is right or wrong. If even "pure" science has its theological dimensions, then politics all the more so. Matters of faith are involved.

Are we presented here, for example, with a choice between principle and opportunism, as Kolko would have us believe? Or is Vietnam's pragmatism in accepting the market merely another case of that notable flexibility on the part of its leadership that Kolko has so admired under other circumstances? Assuming the latter, one might still be struck by, to borrow the phrase Daniel Singer applies to the European scene, "the weakness of the ideological resistance" in Vietnam's capitulation to capitalism.

Wherever one's individual needle comes to rest on the gauge of political correctness on these questions, it is nonetheless crucial to see Kolko's "Postscript" as something more than a despairing obituary for the demise of socialism in Vietnam. As a theoretical statement, the "Postscript" also contains Kolko's short list of those irreducible principles that distinguish socialism from capitalism, the Left from the Right.

As such, the eminent historian aims his polemic well beyond the immediate subject, the dilemmas facing contemporary Vietnam. He provides an important working paper for the ongoing debate around socialism's shape and future in a larger world.

From *The Progressive*, vol. 59, no. 2, 1995.
Reprinted by permission of The Progressive, Inc.

Letters Home

Dear America: Letters Home from Vietnam (edited by Bernard Edelman)

At a time when mainstream writing on Vietnam is dominated by wishy-washy analysis, if not outright falsification of the war's factual history, *Dear America: Letters Home from Vietnam* restores some firmness to the documentary foundation from which more disinterested interpretation, not to mention good combat fiction, must ultimately come.

For example, there has yet to emerge from the Vietnam experience a novel that conveys the unsettling immediacy of the fiction produced by eyewitnesses and surviving combatants of World War I. Vietnam veterans-turned-novelists have remained one-sided observers, confining their efforts to genre war stories or fantasy. One reason this absence of a "great war novel" from Vietnam seems paradoxical is that wars can compel a kind of truthfulness, a crucial exercise for literary-minded veterans for whom writing becomes a ritual of sorts to cleanse the soul of its lingering homicidal torments. The literature of World War I has become the standard by which war fiction is measured in our time, but World War I was only a nightmare, not dishonorable, while there was something about Vietnam that was shameful, perhaps still too shameful to be faced either as history or as art.

Dear America returns us to the scene of the crime. For the most part, these letters home were written by young men in their late teens and early twenties. The letters cover most of the war period, though they tend to bunch around the key years, 1968 to 1970. And, in a sense, these soldier-correspondents represent a minority among those who fought, self-selected by a need to express themselves and an ability to write coherently.

Against the background of every conceivable cliché and sentiment, and generally within a historical void, these writers report faithfully the previously unimagined realities of war, detailed with those peculiarities of Vietnam—like the body count mania—that spotlight an alienation and hostility to life that history will someday record as a trademark of Pax Americana in this, our imperial era.

Much of *Dear America* is a record of frustration at never being able to engage the enemy, yet having your buddies drop like flies around you while endlessly patrolling terrain saturated with trip wires linked to devastating booby traps. One platoon reader writes:

> In the months I have been with the company, we have lost four killed and about thirty wounded. We have not seen a single verified dink the whole time, nor have we shot a round at anything. I've developed a hate for the Vietnamese because they come around selling Cokes and beer to us and then run back to tell the VC how many we are, where our positions are, and where the leaders position themselves. The people in the village that my platoon sergeant went through were laughing at him because they knew we had been hit. I felt like turning my machine gun on the village to kill every man, woman and child in it.

Even the most uncompromising opponent of U.S. involvement in Vietnam cannot fail to be moved by the many accounts of genuine heroism, acts that transcend their tainted contexts. Without the slightest embellishment, one medic writes to the mother of a fellow medic who died in his arms:

> The enemy opened up.... Richard was shot in the leg. I told him to lay there until I could drag him back. But he saw an officer had been hit, and he rolled over several times until he was by the man's side and began to treat him as best he could. Richard was hit several more times, twice in the chest. I went to his side and he said, "Doc, I'm a mess." He then said, "Oh God.... Mother I don't want to die." We called a helicopter to take him to the hospital, but he died before the ship arrived.

Indeed it is disturbing, though hardly surprising, to read with such frequency in these letters from virtual adolescents so much preoccupation with dying. In more than one letter, immediately following the description of a comrade's death or wounding, a soldier will speculate on the unmentionable: his own potential violent end. And no one in *Dear America* approached this sobering subject with more objectivity than a GI from Brooklyn named George Olsen, a portion of whose remarkable correspondence with a female friend from college appears in this collection.

"The point man," Olsen writes, "is now on his way home. He was the luckiest one out there, going home to his wife in one piece, while we'll be going back out again until either our time or our luck runs out. He's home safe—we're not. In that distinction lies the difference between those who have luck and those who aren't yet sure if they have it or not."

At twenty-three years of age, George Olsen was one of those whose luck ran out.

In contrast to the unselfconsciousness of the text is the verbose wrapping in which the book is packaged for the marketplace. Editor Bernard

Edelman's deft ordering of the letters thematically (arrived in-country, combat patrols, the death or wounding of comrades, last letters, and so on), along with his restrained commentary at the beginning of each chapter are, by themselves, sufficient introduction and clarification for letters that otherwise speak for themselves. But because the book clearly owes its publication to the agendas of certain New York City officials (Mayor Ed Koch, park commissioners) who aided a committee of Vietnam veterans in construction of a war memorial in Manhattan, *Dear America* is freighted with a lot of pulpy pseudo-literary baggage in the form of a preface (Koch again), a foreword, and introduction, three pages of acknowledgments and hype aplenty on both covers.

The reader would be well advised to skip all this preliminary hogwash and get right into the letters. While few of the contributors write with the elegance of good fiction or with the clarity of good history, each has a distinctive way of revealing something insightful about the war and about the values and attitudes of the Americans who fought in it—the very information that has been so transparently absent from most contemporary writing on Vietnam. And maybe all that tawdry hype will cause *Dear America* to become fashionable, increasing its distribution within high schools where it will do the most good.

From *The Progressive*, vol. 50, no. 9, 1986.
Reprinted by permission of The Progressive, Inc.

Gung Ho

National Defense (by James Fallows)

The new book by James Fallows, *National Defense*, is destined to be popular among liberals and conservatives alike. Fallows is no fan of Reaganomics, with its demand that Defense increase its share of the national budget. Yet with the precocious talent of a Steven Spielberg for exploiting our psychic insecurities, he turns a mundane appeal for austerity into a vision of renewed American military strength. Fallows is a pathfinder for the new patriotism—a *nouveau philosophe* American style—marking the transition from years of defeat to the trails of future national glory.

The main problem with the military budget, Fallows agrees, is its susceptibility to "threat inflation," a process through which "the public is stampeded into an embrace of expensive, complicated projects" that bear little relationship to the realities of combat. This, in turn, creates a "culture of procurement" which "draws the military toward new weapons because of their great cost, not in spite of it." It is a "culture" in which the top brass and the arms manufacturers conspire to design weapons based on abstract "paper" models rather than on "human elements that have often determined the outcome of combat."

Here Fallows, who "came of age during the war in Vietnam," becomes a spokesman for the Vietnam-trained, middle level officers who are weary of the "war of attrition" model which their managerial superiors have foisted upon them. "This managerial logic" not only "contributes to the growth of ineffective weapons," but it favors procurement skills over time-honored soldierly virtues as the prime criteria for officer advancement.

Moreover, "attrition" emphasized fire power and technologically complex weapons systems that, Fallows insists, don't always work on the battlefield. To cite an example, the state-of-the-art XM1 tank could never operate in the deserts of the Middle East: the dust would clog its delicate mechanisms. There is also the problem that the XM1 might not get delivered to the front because the tank is too wide to fit through the doors of the standard Air Force combat transport. But the generals apparently like its fancy computers and all the gadgetry on the console. The trend of the "culture of procurement" to produce high-tech, low-performance weaponry led the Pentagon to plot the state of our defense as a "curve of unilateral disarmament."

Fallows wants our forces to have more bullets and fuel and more frequent realistic training exercises. He advocates a stand-by conventional military capability for deployment in global trouble spots where American "interests" are believed to be under attack. The thirty-two-year-old author, like the current generation of majors and lieutenant colonels for whom Vietnam is a vivid memory, doesn't want to lose the next ground war. The brute force of massive fire power or "attrition" is out. The new catch word is "maneuver." As described by Fallows, the concept is suspiciously reminiscent of the successful "hit and run" tactics employed by the Chinese and Vietnamese. In the tradition of the Kennedy brothers, this former Carter speech-writer longs for the elusive panacea of a counterinsurgent force capable of making common-sense tactical decisions beyond the operational reach of an out-of-touch centralized command.

However, the "careerist" mentality of the professional officer corps has corrupted the proper military spirit necessary to achieve such reforms. Fallows wistfully quotes from the writing of General George S. Patton that "volumes are devoted to armament; pages to inspiration." Yet Fallows himself never seriously addresses the question of what Americans will or should fight for. He seems to believe that the American malaise can be cured by policy decisions, like those he suggests are internal to the military.

One antidote Fallows suggests to military careerism and its spiritual defects is to scrap the "all volunteer force" and to reinstate the draft. He quotes extensively from earnest-sounding cadres who lament the lack of "quality" soldiers in the volunteer army. There are not enough "middle-class" white youths, and all those "high school dropouts" lack the "technical skills required to run and maintain a computerized tank." Apparently the same MX1 tank that demonstrates the corruption of the "culture of procurement" is less offensive if it if being ground into the desert sand by a white suburbanite.

The draft is also more "democratic," Fallows assures us. Didn't it do the job for us in World War II? Fallows fails to grasp that that war was the great exception of modern American military history, when the entire country was mobilized, with twenty million men and women in uniform. The idea of a peacetime draft to field a large standing army is of recent origin, and it is related to the growth of American power. It is the use of that power which should be examined, not the manner in which military manpower is secured. Let the poor have the military jobs in peacetime; they need them. If there is a war worth fighting, there won't be any difficulty in raising a more democratically representative army.

In his chapter on U.S. strategic policy Fallows convincingly debunks the fashionable "counterforce" strategic doctrine which holds that the Soviet Union could launch a successful "first strike" against the U.S. land-based missiles from which we could not retaliate. Since the American nuclear arsenal is basically untested in war time (as is that of the Russians), no one, Fallows concludes correctly, knows for sure what would happen if the existing strategic forces were set in motion. Are the missiles guidance systems even accurate enough to deliver warheads to their intended targets? This "mutual uncertainty" already provides sufficient deterrence, Fallows believes. To insure the status quo of uncertainty, Fallows calls for a ban on ICBM tests so that accuracy in targeting is not improved. In lieu of a more sweeping disarmament, this isn't a bad idea.

National Defense should be read. It may be a voice of the not so distant future. That sound you may hear while you're reading it is James Fallows sharpening his teeth for the next U.S. military donnybrook. It is possible that Fallows and the far more dangerously placed Casper Weinberger still believe that conventional and strategic war can be kept separate in a military confrontation with the Soviet Union.

From *The Progressive*, vol. 45, no. 10, 1981.
Reprinted by permission of The Progressive, Inc.

The Chosen: An Essay

Some Notes on Being a Veteran in America

Growing up in the fifties after the Big War my imagination often turned on the prospects of soldiering. All the boys I knew expected they'd be soldiers one day. But I doubt any of us gave much thought to what it meant to be a veteran. Those were the old guys wearing piss cutters,[1] limping along behind the color guard at the 4th of July parade. Their club house, the American Legion hall, had the off-limit's look of a seedy shot-and-beer tavern, not the kind of image a boy's fancy would associate with tales of war time glory.

These warrior dreams of tenderfoot baby boomers were blissfully decontextualized. Yet, to be a veteran of military service in the United States during the nineteen fifties was hardly a negative or insignificant thing. The surplus from an emergent American post-war prosperity was distributed first among those who'd been in uniform. A generous GI Bill bootstrapped millions of young middle–American families whose economic mobility had been stalled since the Great Depression. Veteran entitlements provided training and college degrees, mostly for the bread winning men, along with that sine-qua-non of the American Dream, private home ownership through a mortgage backed by the government. And, of course, throughout the decade and beyond, the presence of veterans on the political landscape was virtually iconic; you could hardly hope to hold public office in those years without the pedigree of wartime service.

Now three generations after World War II and several wars later, the census of veterans in the U.S. population approaches twenty-seven million men and women. Given the widespread recognition this honorific enjoys in our society, not to mention its enduring symbolic powers, one would think that the prestige of the military veteran was as old as war itself. There is little basis in fact to support such a thesis. The genealogy of the veteran as a fixed social category is a recent historical construction, and, essentially, of American origin. Not until well after the Civil War did all those who'd served in the U.S. military, whether able bodied or maimed, in the fray or on the sidelines, become, not merely emblems of dutiful patriotism, but socially entitled "veterans."

From the late Middle Ages, England and France also extended special recognition to those who had given valued military service. Both countries provided some State-mandated care or pensions (about which, more below), but only to their severely disabled warriors or retired military cadres, officers for the most part. Generally, soldiers organized for the battlefield when demobilized have been viewed by their societies, even the disabled, not as veterans in the broad American definition as beneficiaries of State policy, but as *ex-servicemen* whose economic and social reintegration on the home front was a communal matter, or the concern of charitable institutions.

I first saw that term "ex-serviceman" when it was applied to me in February 1971 while addressing a group of railways workers in Sydney, Australia. They had wildcatted for the day because, as one improvised placard announced, "Railway commissioner refuses our right to hear M. Uhl American Ex-Serviceman." This is not how I referred to myself. I was a Vietnam veteran, and I had been invited to tour Australia and New Zealand to speak against the war still raging throughout Vietnam and all of Indochina. Since my return from Vietnam two years earlier, I'd been uniting fellow vets in the antiwar movement around the issue of American war crimes.[2] Our contingent of Vietnam veterans within that movement was growing rapidly. And what we called the GI Resistance among those still on active duty had become so widespread that, by 1973, the Nixon administration could no longer deploy effective American ground forces in Indochina.[3] While Australia and New Zealand both sent token forces to fight in Vietnam, and both experienced celebrated cases of draft resistance on the home front, protest movements in their respective militaries or among their ex-servicemen had not developed.[4]

Movement organizers "down under" apparently believed that an American veteran, speaking to these unprecedented GI and veteran antiwar movements in the United States, and describing their impact on American public opinion and policy, would help to strengthen their own spring antiwar mobilizations. In other words, they had plenty of ex-servicemen who'd been to Vietnam, but not one who had stepped forward in public opposition to the war. For that they needed an American veteran. Indeed in validation of this choice the publicity generated by my tour was as great, or greater, than that given to the antiwar events themselves.

I'd had a similar though less public experience the previous year in England. The organization I worked with, the Citizen's Commission of Inquiry on U.S. War Crimes in Vietnam (CCI), was an outgrowth of the International War Crimes Tribunal, created by Bertrand Russell, which had held highly publicized sessions featuring international jurists and intellectuals like Noam Chomsky, Jean Paul Sartre and Simone de Beauvoir in Copenhagen and Oslo in 1967, and concluded that the U.S. government was guilty of genocide in Indochina. In that charged atmosphere I'd traveled to Europe in the summer of 1970 performing solidarity work on behalf of CCI with antiwar forces of the European Left, visiting with active duty GIs stationed in Germany and with communities of exiled American deserters in Sweden and France.

My first stop had been London, where I made contact with the actress Vanessa Redgrave. I hadn't known just how radical Redgrave was; the idea that a world class movie idol might be joined to a disciplined Trotskyist party (the British Socialist Workers Party) was too remote from my experience. I was only beginning my political education; the mysteries of Marxism and Leninism just starting to preoccupy my curiosity. Redgrave invited me to a 4th of July reception she had organized for American airmen who were being bused in from a U.S. airbase outside the city to meet with members of the English antiwar movement. I quote selections from the somewhat jaundiced account of that evening which appears in *Vietnam Awakening*, my memoir and documentary history of the CCI:

> Some grand ballroom in a fancy London hotel had been done up for the affair, and the groaning board was loaded with the best delights money and good taste could provide. A full complement swing band played pop tunes as I stood next to Vanessa and her pal Mia Farrow waiting for the bus load of American GIs to arrive. As they trickled through the door dressed in leisure polyester straight off the racks of the PX, faces shy as sheep, I began to feel ridiculous and out of place myself. When CCI talked with vets and soldiers we tried to be in their element, not our own.
>
> The night was a bust. I avoided the GIs from a combination of inexperience and mixed emotions, out and out embarrassment over the inappropriate setting and insensitivity of bringing these guys to such a place. When the airmen soon began to trickle out again, Vanessa stunned me with a crack as if somehow I bore the blame for her faux pas. "Later for that," I must have thought, while straining to keep my cool. If I'd been better seasoned to the sparing style of the Left I might have rejoined that "the revolution is not a dinner party." I guess Chairman Mao said that.[5]

The particular relevance of that vexing experience to this discussion is one that I had failed to observe at the time. There had been no movement of antiwar English ex-servicemen to mix with the American GIs; no organized resistance in the British armed forces, itself a professional force which had abolished conscription in 1953. I would encounter similar conditions elsewhere in my European travels over the next decade while serving as co-director of Citizen Soldier, a New York–based non-profit GI and veterans' advocacy organization. In France, West Germany, the Netherlands, Italy, and throughout Scandinavia, the countries with which I had the most extensive first-hand experiences, the military draft was still in effect. Typically the duration of service in Western Europe, obligating young men only, was a year to eighteen months. In some cases conscripted soldiers served near their home towns, and, after basic training, might even live at home.

The one exception to this pattern of quiescence was the Netherlands during the late 1970s. At the time Citizen Soldier was cooperating with the American Federation of Government Employees, the largest labor union in the United States, in their initiative to unionize the American armed forces—an effort, needless to say, that was not successful. Inspirationally our military union model was based in part on the work of active duty Dutch conscripts who had successfully created a legal union within their own military. As for the failure of an explicitly antiwar movement of any scale to develop within the respective militaries or communities of ex-servicemen of even these democratic western European allies, the logical explanation, I suspect, is that none of them was the world's dominant power constantly at war.

After 1982, I ceased for some years to play a direct role in the veterans' and GI resistance movements. My radical politics remained constant, but I was no longer an activist on a day-to-day basis. Times had changed. The antiwar movement had fulfilled its historical role, and many folks returned to pick up lives and careers that had been interrupted by Vietnam. For the next two decades the lessons of that war held fast. Despite the bellicose rhetoric of the Reagan administration, a still palpable public disgust with the arrogance of the imperial presidency under Nixon and with the butchery committed throughout Indochina in the name of American values and democracy continued to restrain those in government who advocated overt military intervention in Central America. As it was, murderous U.S. clandestine actions in El Salvador and Nicaragua, largely "invisible" to the American people, left another sorry stain on our nation's history in that region. But on a grander global canvas, Reagan's overt interventionist fantasies would be confined to the invasion of tiny, defenseless Granada.[6]

All those troops and nowhere to go. Nowhere, that is, until Saddam Hussein invaded Kuwait in 1991. That event, declared the elder President George Bush with great exuberance, if scant justification, had finally marked "an end to the Vietnam syndrome," the public's reluctance to project American military power globally through the use of force. And yet, the First Gulf War proved, if anything, that the lessons of Vietnam remained firm. The American public would support the expulsion of Iraqi forces from Kuwait, but only in the context of broad international support to include widespread approval from the world of Islam. American troops, completing their mission literally in hours, stopped just beyond the borders of Iraq and came home. The same general principle applied to the military actions in the Balkans, where the U.S. limited its role to covert action and to air and naval power, declining to involve itself directly in a land war. It would be another decade and more before the real invasion of Iraq, and even then the public's memory of the Vietnam debacle had not been superseded; it was simply ignored.

By 2003 I was once again active in the ranks of the veteran's peace movement. An invitation had come from antiwar activists in Greece for a Vietnam veteran to tour their country in the days leading up to the U.S. invasion of Iraq. On February 18, 2003, I spoke from a platform in Athens during a massive demonstration that was mirrored in cities around the world. An estimated twenty million people had taken to the streets of London, Rome, Madrid, New York, and in hundreds of other national capitals and smaller locales elsewhere to voice their unambiguous opposition to the American invasion.

For me the experience in Athens was singular, and when framed in the vast and unprecedented worldwide mobilization of popular opposition, offered grounds to reexamine the conventional wisdom of a mass movement's efficacy to influence the balance of forces. The vast majority of governments on the planet likewise condemned or criticized this unprovoked aggression on the part of the U.S. Nonetheless, President George W. Bush invaded Iraq as if no force on earth existed that could stop him. Here was a new calculus of world hegemony for which, to my knowledge, no adequate explanation has yet to emerge, unless to attribute every anomaly of recent history with small distinction to the events of 9/11.

What is germane to the topic at hand, however, is a far more mundane observation. Once again I was traveling and speaking in a country where a short stretch of military service was mandatory for all able bodied young men, yet there was no radical grouping among Greek "ex-servicemen" from which a representative spokesperson could be recruited. There were several individuals on the Left currently on active duty who demonstrated in uniform, but who were not perceived by the authorities or the media as being deeply connected with the Greek military.

Among the many comrades who had already fulfilled their service obligations, the concept of a veterans' community or movement was completely foreign. If the idea of a military veteran, *per se*, existed in Greece one got the sense that it could only apply to those who had retired from a full career in one branch or another of the Greek armed forces, and whose views were likely inimical to the goals of the antiwar movement. Of course there was also a certain voodoo attached to the presence of an American who had fought at an earlier time in a war equally condemned by the international community, and who could not only speak to the horrors and crimes of Vietnam, but make cogent comparisons to the conditions of the present. As had been the case in Australia and New Zealand three decades earlier, my tour through several Greek cities attracted considerable media attention.

The latest episode in this chronicle of solidarity travels occurred in early May of 2006. I toured several Italian cities as the Vietnam veteran representative of an anti–Iraq War campaign called Bring Them Home Now. BTHN was comprised mostly of old hands from Vietnam days who had formed a network to distribute information and coordinate actions within contemporary movements of antiwar veterans, GI resisters, and family members of those in the military who actively opposed the conflicts in Iraq and Afghanistan. Through its popular website BTHN was also in daily dialogue with many soldiers and marines serving in the war zones where the view from the bottom, among our interlocutors at least, often contradicted that put out nightly at Pentagon briefings in Washington.

The comrade who organized my itinerary in Italy, an English expatriate living in Naples, had translated various writings and letters from the BTHN website to which he added a commentary, and then published as a book in Italian.[7] This work was the basis of his one-man crusade to spur fellow *militanti* throughout Italy to adopt a strategy for organizing Italian soldiers, veterans and military family members into movements similar to those that had become so dynamic in the United States. The logic of his position was indisputable. After all, wasn't Italy under the Berlusconi government at that time, with Britain, one of two major European allies of the U.S. who had sent elite, if numerically modest numbers of troops to fight in and occupy Iraq? Arguably there might be scores of disaffected Italian combat soldiers, some of whom already returned to civilian life, who would join with the antiwar opposition. For a variety of reasons, however, this initiative was problematic, not least because class structure in Italy, as in most of Europe, is more rigidly stratified than in America.

Beginning in 2002, military conscription in Italy had been gradually replaced with a volunteer force, a process completed by January 1, 2005.[8] Those who enter the Italian army today are, according to Gordon Poole, a professor at Orientale University in Naples, "mostly young men, and some women, from the economically disadvantaged South and small towns or rural areas, with objectively reduced job expectations thanks to liberalistic economic policies."[9] While similar conditions apply here, including the essentially working class character of the U.S. military, there is at least one critical distinction. Educational tracking occurs in both societies, but in general, students pursuing academic and trade or business curricula in the U.S. remain in the same high schools, their extracurricular activities, especially sports, and, to some degree, their social lives, are remarkably integrated. In Italy after grade and middle school, students headed for the university go to one set of high schools, while those bound for the trades, when they don't enter the workforce immediately, attend completely separate vocational institutions. While this single fact may not explain why social mobility is far less fluid in Italy than in the United States, it is certainly one manifestation of that reality.

Having resided in Sicily for parts of each year since the late 1990s through 2010, I have formed a strong impression that Italy's left wing professionals and intellectuals don't have an accessible medium, or idiom for that matter, with which to engage the Italian working class in political dialogue. Whereas during both the Vietnam and the Iraq war periods in the U.S. it has been essentially middle class, college educated activists with their allies in the professions who have played catalytic roles in organizing what would eventually evolve into self-led mass working class movements of veterans and GIs.[10]

Italian workers have a strong tradition on the Left, notably within a trade union movement that is much more dynamic and powerful than its contemporary American counterpart. In Italy the wildcat strike, for example, with its feisty anarchic impulses, serves to level the playing field, not only in dealings with management, but with union officialdom as well. On the larger political landscape beyond trade union activities, Italian workers lack any independent field of action. When they haven't migrated toward the right in an electoral politics of resentment similar to blue collar Republicans in the States, their interests are more narrowly represented by the forces of the center-left in government, as citizens not workers.

There may be active trade unionists and members of Left parties, even radical or revolutionary elements of the Italian working class, who have served in Iraq or Afghanistan. But their capacity to be organized into the Italian antiwar movement in the symbolic roles of former members of Italian armed forces is not only limited by a structural lack of contact with intellectuals and middle class activists across the social spectrum. There remains the historical absence in Italian culture of any tradition of voluntary associations like that which has elevated the public profile of the American veteran, and which, in the U.S., cuts across the nation's social contours.[11] There is no Italian equivalent to an American veterans' peace movement because, in Italy, there are no veterans, only ex-servicemen.

Only over many centuries of recorded time has the concept of the military veteran evolved from the enduring bloody pageant of warriors surviving battles to return home. Sagas glorifying human warfare overflow the shelves at libraries and book sellers. But the historical veteran as a subject in his own right, his post-conflict social reintegration and, in many cases, war-induced psychic transformation, have not until recently been topics for which an expanding curiosity among public scholars can be demonstrated. Even the disabled veteran as a social category worthy of recognition, much less recompense, is itself of relatively modern coinage.

Many details of combat in the Hellenic age are well logged in timeless annals and works of literature. And yet from our knowledge of the warring Greeks we find "no custom of valorizing men wounded in battle." Hoplites maimed in combat who became indigents in, say, Athens, were not treated separately from other impoverished citizens, because, in ancient Greece, there was "no concept of the injured war veteran."[12] Former Roman legionaries were often exiled in colonies along the borders of the empire where they could farm, or fight when required. They were not welcome in Rome, where, along with armed troops, battle hardened ex-soldiers were considered dangerous to civil order, a tradition violated by Julius Caesar which led to his downfall and that of the Republic, the latter albeit given its oligarchic nature a dubious loss.

By the early modern era armies were no longer mobilized among free citizens as in the City States of ancient Greece where even a philosopher might find himself in the ranks of the spear-carrying foot soldiers.[13] The vast Roman Empire required a professional army, which, for much of its history, was comprised of countrymen and urban plebeians and their patrician officers. During Europe's long feudal night with its fragmentation of territorial sovereignties, there were literally multitudes of knights and nobles who raised the king's armies from among their bondsmen and yeoman tenants. As the ruling dynasties strengthened with the emergence of the nation state, armies were gathered, not piecemeal, but on a national level. Under these condition it became necessary to consider "relief measures for the demobilized" that were heretofore the concern of each soldier's place of origin. England in 1593 was the first European state to offer "benefits for rank and file disabled veterans … a nationwide pension scheme."[14]

No doubt humanist values arising at the dawn of the Age of Reason, which transformed acts of charity toward the poor into a civic as well as religious virtue, contributed to the new sense of responsibility that the English State expressed for the welfare of its disabled combatants. There arose simultaneously a perception that the expression of the nation's gratitude for honorable service was not only morally correct, but ideologically useful in boosting morale among recruits called upon to fight the next war. At the same time issues of social control and security were of equal, if not greater, concern to the powers-that-be than were the enlightened ideals exhibited by the creation of the pension system.

Those increasingly displaced from the world of agricultural subsistence on the old estates and driven into the English cities to join the swelling ranks of the unemployed, along with large numbers of convicts overcrowding the urban *gaols*, provided much of the manpower now being dragooned into England's national army. These men were viewed from above as troubling social elements that might represent an even greater threat to the established order after they'd returned from battle. The pension system, while it endured willy-nilly for over a century, could not organize the regime that modern states required to allay fears of popular unrest spurred by disgruntled former soldiers.

Moreover, the distribution of pensions became too vulnerable to persistent conflicts over criteria for eligibility, not to mention disputes over the size and sources of their funding. By the early 1700s, those disabled in service of the English Crown would be confined to military hospitals, where they were issued uniforms and could be governed by means of strict rules and disciplinary measures. Impoverished officers would continue to receive State assistance on the justification that they had "fallen from a certain station."[15] An enclosure for disabled and aged soldiers in need was anticipated by Louis XIV who, in 1671, founded what would become the monumental Hotel Royal des Invalides in Paris. A rule of paternalism similar to that of the English military hospitals prevailed at Invalides for a century, and then evolved into a frontier of social policy" as the hierarchical values of the *ancien regime* were briefly supplanted by revolutionary egalitarianism. With a citizen's army mobilized in the tens of thousands to defend the Revolution, the Jacobin National Convention "embraced a straightforward notion of entitlement and recompense—a breakthrough of sorts toward a new mind-set."

The guiding ideal of that "new mind-set" was embodied in Napoleon's grand declaration that France owed its fighting heroes a "sacred debt." For the brief span of the French Revolution's radically democratic phase, this "debt" was to be redeemed more handsomely than ever before in the history of warfare. The Jacobin Convention moved quickly to provide fair compensation to its many disabled soldiers and to care for their dependents and widows. Class distinctions between resident officers and common soldiers at Invalides were narrowed considerably. Veterans who qualified could choose "between residence in the Hotel and a generous pension...," the latter providing the unprecedented possibility for indigent veterans to reintegrate themselves into civilian life with dignity. But when some men at Invalides became "politically active as a group," their movement was repressed as the power of their Jacobin allies declined, and they were dispersed from Paris into the provinces.[16]

Gradually, the militarized pecking order was restored at Invalides, and owing to runaway inflation, veteran pensions could no longer stretch to cover the costs of subsistence. In the end, "the revolutionary state ... failed to sustain this remarkable policy as provisions for war veterans ... slipped back to more traditional and inadequate levels." The emerging status of the veteran as one "who'd sacrificed everything" and could be counted among the "deserving poor," competed once more with the "traditional image of soldiers and ex-soldiers as antisocial types, if not potential brigands."[17]

These early experiences in France and England foreshadowed the broad-minded view that assistance for the demobilized, and in particular the disabled, ex-soldier could be defended on practical and moral grounds as a reward for valued service, that is to say as a legitimate State policy of entitlement. Historically, the principal obstacle to the implementation of such an initiative in warring nations everywhere was (and remains for most countries today) either one of economic scarcity or of a political raison d'etre to commit the resources. Not until the aftermath of the American Civil War would the necessary conditions be present in one country, the U.S., to transform the ideal of veteran entitlements into an institutional reality. Developing industrial might in a robust and growing internal market would provide the treasure, while the unique system of patronage built into the American political system would help convert the problematic former warriors from troublesome pariahs to valued potential voters.

At the beginning of the Civil War, distribution of pensions to the disabled among the eighty thousand surviving veterans of military actions from the Revolution through the Mexican War remained haphazard. The Civil War would create an additional two million veterans from Union forces alone, of whom more than 210,000 received disability discharges. Requests from the disabled for federal pension benefits or prosthetic devices were streamlined, going first to the Pension Bureau, then on for evaluation to the Surgeon General's office where "evidence of the long term and debilitating nature of wartime injuries was required." When claims were denied, "claimants [could] exert political pressure." By 1875, 6.3% of Union vets were receiving benefits. Thanks to lobbying efforts by their principal advancement organization, the Grand Army of the Republic in support of the 1879 Arrears Act, many beneficiaries were "provided lump sums payments ... that were roughly 2.5 times the average income of American citizens."[18] Confederate veterans received nothing from the federal government; the fate of returning soldiers from defeated armies is another story entirely.[19]

Shortly thereafter, the American veteran, as we define that status today, makes his first appearance on the national stage. As the following description demonstrates, he has become a synthesis of his competing, even contradictory, component roles: State-sanctioned client, patriotic role model, political player and perennial near-do-well: "With the increased physical needs posed by the aging of all Civil War veterans and the mounting evidence that their votes could prove influential in political elections, momentum to change the requirements of the pension system gained adherents in the 1880s. The 1890 Dependent Pension Act led to a benefit system based on military service of at least 90 days, as opposed to injury, and by 1910, over 90 percent of all veterans, or their legatees, were receiving federal checks.... Notwithstanding the benefits provided by the government, the pension applications of veterans illustrate that their lives often remained harsh and difficult."[20]

The relative entitlement of the American military veteran is, from this point on, tied to a minimal service obligation, not to disability alone. Vets wounded in battle would still receive the lion's share of State-sponsored compensation and medical care. But for the aged and the indigent, service itself would qualify many for pensions or care in Old Soldiers and Sailor's homes, while for others preference in federal jobs provided the path to lifetime employment.[21]

The next great leap in service entitlement came after the Great War when Congress enacted a bonus of from $500 to $600 to be paid World War I veterans, but only on the bond's maturity in 1945. By 1932, in the depth of the Depression, veterans lobbied for the immediate payment of what they had come to characterize as their "tombstone bonus." Their legendary march on Washington, although brutally repressed by President Herbert Hoover on the advice of General Douglas MacArthur, who believed the veterans were a communist conspiracy out to overthrow the government, ultimately achieved their objective. Three years later, President

Franklin D. Roosevelt's veto was overridden by Congress, and the veterans were granted their bonus. "The entire epic left a lasting impression on America, paving the way for the GI Bill, a promise of immediate money and education to soldiers returning from World War II."[22]

The slow historical awakening in those countries I have cited to the link between wartime military service and society's obligation to provide disabled soldiers with the means for post-war rehabilitation was always stalked by an underlying resistance, bordering on taboo and virtually universal, against recognizing that, for some veterans, wars might never end, and that, for them, a future of "harsh and difficult lives" was inevitable. Given that the effects of physical wounds were undeniable, it was the ambivalence toward the tangibly disabled that social policies of entitlement initially sought to address and resolve as a means for returning maimed warriors to "normal" and productive lives.[23]

Only in the wake of World War I was the "balance" between mental and physical war-related wounds systematically parsed and the two spheres of disability treated discretely for the first time in history. English neurologist William H.R. Rivers and others began to document the "devastating psychoneurotic effects of war on the character of those who do the fighting...." In the past, the mental disorders created by war "were mixed with the physical problems all soldiers faced from deprivation, disease and exposure." Twentieth century armies, however, "were healthier..., thus the physical [could be] factored out ... and we [were] left with war's destruction of the mind." For specialists like Dr. Rivers, there was suddenly a space for understanding that the hidden psychological wounds of war were commonplace, persistent and often the least susceptible to treatment.[24]

In his groundbreaking memoir, *Goodbye to All That*, Robert Graves wrote of the effects of the horrific trench warfare of the First World War on his own post-battlefield psyche and behavior:

> I was still mentally and nervously organized for war. Shells used to come bursting on my bed at midnight ... strangers in daytime would assume the faces of friends who had been killed.... I could not help seeing [my favorite country side] as a prospective battlefield. I would find myself working out tactical problems and what would be the best cover for my rifle grenade section. I still had the Army habit of commandeering anything of uncertain ownership that I found lying about; also a difficulty in telling the truth—it was always easier for me now, when charged with any fault, to lie my was out of it, Army-style.

Similar references to what we would clearly describe today as post-traumatic stress disorder (PTSD) are not uncommon in other early modern literary works. To cite another example, there is a telling scene in *The Razor's Edge*, a World War I era novel by Somerset Maugham. One character, a Chicago "matron," has this to say about a young aviator recently returned from the front:

> He must see that in the current state of the world, a man has to work. He's perfectly strong and well now. We all know how after the war between the States, there were men who never did a stroke after they came back from it. They were a burden to their families, and useless to their communities.
>
> The young man's guardian responds: The war did something to Larry. He didn't come back the same person he went. It's not only that he's older. Something happened that changed his personality.

It was only with my generation of Vietnam veterans that the post-combat malaise labeled anecdotally through the ages (soldier's heart, shell shock, combat fatigue, and so on), formally codified as PTSD in 1980, was officially recognized by the psychiatric establishment as a war-related disability, a psychological disorder that would go a long way in explaining why so many war veterans, whether or not they received physical wounds, might be subject to post-war lives that "remained harsh and difficult." This acknowledgment of PTSD has been the world historical event in the centuries-old struggle of former soldiers whose lives were shattered by warfare to gain recognition that they too "didn't come back the same person [they] went." And now, as veterans return home to the U.S. and elsewhere from Iraq and Afghanistan, the ranks of those who have been given, and, in future years will receive, the diagnosis that they too suffer from combat PTSD will add thousands more to the roll call of those who will require care and compensation, often for the remainder of their lives. This is bad news for everyone, but not least for those who advocate the projection of force to resolve world conflicts and to maintain U.S. global hegemony. In the public eye, PTSD, more than any other battlefield-induced disability, gives war a very bad name.[25]

As for actually "being" a military veteran in the United States, in the sense of choosing to what degree one embraces that identity depends in large part on the individual. Overwhelmingly, the American veteran's public identity remains a creature of traditional advancement organizations like the American Legion and the Veterans of Foreign War (VFW), whose membership nonetheless represents only a modest percentage of all eligible veterans. Known to those of us in the veteran's peace movement as the "hat" vets, these mainstream groups concerned with promoting the welfare of veterans in general also seek to "preserve the solidarity of the military experience."[26] It is this ideological function, toeing the pro-war interventionist line in the name of patriotic duty, combined, as noted, with the vote-gathering patronage of conventional political forms that provide the true material explanation for the sweep and generosity of our veteran entitlements. For many, if not perhaps the majority, the veteran experience in the U.S. is the extension of militarism and warfare by other means.

Had I served in the military, but not in Vietnam, it is unlikely that I would have embraced the veteran identity at all. Indeed, for whatever their own private reasons, I suspect that millions of Americans who have fulfilled their service obligations and shared to one degree or another in the benefits to which they are entitled, don't get up each morning, look in the mirror and think, "I'm a veteran." Under no circumstance would I have been a candidate to actively participate in the reactionary politics of the American Legion or the VFW. What made the veteran identity available to me was my inclination to become active against the war in Vietnam upon my discharge from an Army hospital in 1969, and the fortuitous rise at that moment of a mass movement of antiwar veterans. Given my experiences in Vietnam, where I came to view American forces as an invading army involved in a war of aggression, I could only project myself publicly as a veteran in opposition to war and militarism.

If history has bestowed on the American veteran a unique social standing and relative cornucopia of entitlements in relation to returning soldiers elsewhere, both now and in the past, the American veteran is also unmatched for an historical accomplishment of his own making. Beginning with the Vietnam generation, a substantial cohort of former U.S. military service members has created the only sustained peace movement among veterans to exist in human history.[27] What began as a small number of individuals in the late 1960s marching identifiably as veterans in antiwar protests grew with amazing speed into a mass movement involving thousands of former service members across the nation, the majority of whom had experienced the Vietnam War firsthand. Over the past forty years, elements of that movement have undergone a variety of organizational and ideological transformations. Depending on topical developments, participants have come and gone, levels of activism have risen and fallen, but the chain of this movement's existence during those four decades remains unbroken.

It is ironic, though hardly paradoxical, that peace movements swell in times of war. Our veteran component of that movement is no exception. Thus, in an atmosphere of perpetual military interventionism that is the cornerstone of contemporary American foreign policy, antiwar veterans in the U.S. have never been more active, nor played a more visible or constructive role among the nation's other forces for peace in organizing public opposition to the wars in Iraq and Afghanistan, and to all such expressions of U.S. inspired hegemonic injustice everywhere.[28] Represented in the ranks of the veteran's peace movement today are veterans from all America's wars, dating from The Spanish Civil War to the present, with young comrades

170   The Chosen

of the current conflicts beginning to join in ever increasing numbers. This is our privilege, and, with our brothers and sisters among all twenty-seven million American veterans, whatever their political orientations or subjective embrace of the veteran identity, is a singular manifestation of our collective uniqueness.

America's military veterans, none more than those of the Vietnam generation, and, now, Iraq and Afghanistan, are a global story line. Their narratives among the fallen and the wounded, as foreign invaders and witting or unwitting executioners of atrocities and torture, their postwar ailments and syndromes, their episodes of dramatic maladjustment to civilian life, are the stuff of literary works, blockbuster movies, and the tabloid news.[29] Of the ex-servicemen and women, or veterans, of other cultures, the world hears little or nothing at all; many are called but few are chosen.

> This essay appeared originally in *Peace Not Terror: Leaders of the Antiwar Movement Speak Out Against U.S. Foreign Policy Post 9/11.* Edited by Mary Susannah Robbins (Lanham, MD: Lexington Books, 2008)

Notes

1. "Piss cutter" is one of several graphic nicknames for the military service or overseas cloth cap.
2. An account of that work appears in *Vietnam Awakening: My Journey from Combat to the Citizens Commission of Inquiry on U.S. War Crimes in Vietnam.* Jefferson, NC: McFarland, 2007.
3. Col. Robert D. Heinl. "The Collapse of the American Armed Forces," *Armed Forces Journal*, June 1971. At the time Heinl observed that, "By every conceivable indicator, our army that now remains in Vietnam is in a state approaching collapse...." For the only extensive accounts or analyses of the Vietnam era G.I. movement, see David Cortright, *Soldiers In Revolt: The American Military Today*, Doubleday, 1975 and Haymarket, 2005; and Matthew Rinaldi, "The Olive-Drab Rebels: Military Organizing During the Vietnam War," *Radical America*, Vol. 8 no. 3, 1974. The subsequent history of the antiwar veterans in the U.S., and of the essentially working and underclass character of those who did the fighting, are well covered in such postwar sources as Andrew Hunt, *The Turning: A History of the Vietnam Veterans Against the War*, New York University Press, 1999; and Christian Appy *Working Class War: American Combat Soldiers and Vietnam*, University of North Carolina Press, 1993.
4. Under the strong cultural influence of the high public profile attained by American Vietnam veterans in their struggles for dignified social readjustment, Australian and New Zealand ex-servicemen who served in Vietnam have now come to refer to themselves as "veterans" as well. The Vietnam Veterans Association of Australia, formed in 1979, has lobbied its government to establish programs for veteran counseling, and around issues of PTSD and Agent Orange exposure. In June 1998, New Zealand Vietnam vets were given a "Vietnam Parade ... a national reunion and march of veterans in Wellington ... Vietnam veterans were gratified by the generally favourable public reception of this event, though some relatively low-key protests by antiwar activists illustrated the continuing controversy generated by the war."
5. Uhl, op. cit.
6. For a cogent summary of these events see, for example, Noam Chomsky, *Hegemony or Survival: America's Quest For Global Dominance*, Henry Holt & Company, 2004.
7. Philip Rushton. *Riportiamoli a casa*. Edizioni Alegre (Italy), 2005.
8. "The Right to Conscientious Objection in Europe," Quaker Council for European Affairs, 2005.

9. Personal correspondence, September 2006; Gordon Poole is author of *Nazione Guerriera: Il militarismo nella cultura degli Stati Uniti* [Warrior nation: militarism in the culture of the United States] (Naples: Colonnese Editore, 2nd edition 2002).
10. Efforts by Lotta Continua, an Italian equivalent in the early 1970s of New Left activist groups in the U.S., organized a working class entity in the Italian military called *Proletari in divisa* (Workers in Uniform), which, however, never functioned independently nor developed on a scale comparable to its counterparts among American GIs and veterans; in fact, Lotta Continua on more than one occasion in the early 1970s showcased American Vietnam veterans at its antiwar rallies. See Uhl, op. cit.
11. The key distinction between the veteran advancement groups in the U.S., the American Legion, Disabled American Veterans, Veterans of Foreign War and the like, and their counterparts in other countries which seek to perform similar roles for their own former service members, is not just the social power of the voluntary association as it has developed in the American context, but the relationship of these advancement groups to the coffers and policies of the State through the American political system.
12. Martha Edwards. "Philoctetes in Historical Context," in *Disabled Veterans in History*, David Gerber, editor. Ann Arbor: University of Michigan Press, 2000. Henceforth, Gerber.
13. See, for example, I.F. Stone, *The Trial of Socrates*, Anchor Books, 1989.
14. Geoffrey L. Hudson. "Disabled Veterans and the State in Early Modern England," in Gerber.
15. Ibid.
16. Isser Woloch. "A Sacred Debt: Veterans and the State in Revolutionary and Napoleonic France," in Gerber.
17. *Ibid.* That this characterization persists even today can be demonstrated by the public remarks in June 2005 of Anthony J. Principi, a former Secretary of Veterans Affairs, who observed that: "History is littered with governments destabilized by masses of veterans who believed that they had been taken for fools by a society that grew rich at the expense of their hardship and suffering." From the website www.vawatchdog.com
18. Robert J. Goler and Michael G. Rhode, "From Individual Trauma to National Policy: Tracking the Uses of Civil War Veteran Medical Record," in Gerber.
19. My colleague Dr. Gordon Poole, whose book is cited above, is an American living in Naples since 1957, where he teaches at the Università di Napoli l'Orientale. He has provided me with the following illuminating comments on the fate of veterans of the defeated Italian Army after World War II:

> As for Italy, a major difference with the US is that Italy lost the Second World War and suffered enormously under German and, to a far lesser degree, US occupation. What we Americans call veterans were *reduci,* those who returned, survivors, lucky to be alive." My Italian-English dictionary gives the following definition for *reduce*: "ex-serviceman* (m.); ex-servicewoman* (f.); (war) veteran (USA); (superstite) survivor. * (fam.) reduce dalle patrie galere, ex-convict." This definition can give you good information for your notation on the difference between US and Italian visions of ex-military personnel. Hoodwinked by propaganda, the Italian troops had fought, often bravely, in a lost cause, in the name of Fascism, patriotism, anti–Judaism, and racist colonialism. Those who managed to return, escaping the Nazis after the 1943 amnesty, often found their cities, countryside, and homes ravaged. Eighty thousand people died under Allied bombs in Naples alone. Then the Neapolitans mounted a popular uprising against the Germans, who had become a brutal army of occupation. No wonder, then, that pacifism was a universal sentiment in Italy after the war, that militarism was seen as wrong, that uniforms were a symbol of insufferable regimentation, and that the Italian Constitution should establish in its fourth Article that Italy "repudiates war as an instrument for the resolution of international conflict." The Italian veterans considered themselves and were considered by most to be unfortunates. Few came back to boast about their exploits; if at all, to tell their woes.

20. Goler and Rhode, in Gerber.
21. Today all veterans discharged under honorable conditions are eligible to receive some degree of health and hospital care from the VA system. Whether these services are cost free or require co-payment is determined by a variety of factors, including service connected disability or need based on income. Veterans whose disabilities are service connected may also be eligible for other benefits, like compensation and vocational rehabilitation.
22. From an online review of *The Bonus Army: An American Epic.* Paul Dickson and Thomas B. Allen (Walker & Company, 2005), by Kevin M. Hymel, on the website ProQuest of the Association of the United States Army, March 2005.

23. David A. Gerber, "Introduction: Finding Disabled Veterans in History," in Gerber.
24. *Ibid.*
25. The cost-of-war implications of PTSD, both budgetary and in the realm of military policy are well understood by the National Security apparatus. Recent news articles have reported that nearly 216,000 veterans diagnosed with PTSD—post-traumatic stress disorder—receive benefits from the Veterans Administration. Most of these veterans are from the Vietnam period, and many, including myself, were granted their disability ratings only during the last decade. Since 1999, the VA's PTSD benefit payments have jumped 150% from $1.7 to $4.3 billion annually. Now, with reports that the percentages, if not the absolute numbers, of returning Iraq and Afghanistan war veterans suffering from PTSD may exceed that of their Vietnam era counterparts, VA budgetary outlays for care and treatment of this malady are likely to skyrocket even further. This fact has led to the introduction within the current policy debate of an expectation that combat trauma, existing scientific evidence notwithstanding, can not only be managed, but cured or even prevented. An ill-conceived plan on the part of the VA in 2005 to review the cases of thousands of veterans compensated for PTSD since the mid-1990s was scuttled, owing to negative political fallout in Congress. But Congress, the Pentagon and VA all seem committed to the pursuit of a strategy that will set limits to PTSD cases in the years ahead. See, for example, "The Politics of PTSD, by Michael Uhl, *Bangor Daily News*. March 9, 2006, elsewhere in this volume.
26. Gerber op. cit., in Gerber.
27. A sizable movement emerged among active duty soldiers and sailors at the end of World War II to demand immediate repatriation and demobilization. While encouraged, and to some degree organized by the Left, it was not explicitly antiwar. The veterans of this movement for the most part celebrated their war and their sacrifices as a necessary evil to defeat fascism in Europe. An earlier version of Veterans for Peace also emerged at the end of World War II, but this never recruited sizeable numbers of participants outside the circles of the Old Left.
28. Veterans for Peace has over 120 chapters from all over the United States. Each chapter can work on their own projects and goals, as long as they stay within the VFP guidelines.
29. See, for example, Michael Uhl and Tod Ensign, *GI Guinea Pigs: How the Pentagon Exposed Our Troops to Dangers More Deadly Than War*, Playboy, 1980.

PTSD

The Politics of PTSD

Recent news articles have reported that nearly 216,000 veterans diagnosed with PTSD—post-traumatic stress disorder—receive benefits from the Department of Veterans Affairs. Most of these veterans are from the Vietnam period, and many including myself, were granted their disability ratings only during the last decade. Since 1999, the VA's PTSD benefit payments have jumped 150 percent from $1.7 billion to $4.3 billion annually.

Clearly since the disorder's recognition in 1980 by the American Psychiatric Association (APA), PTSD—with its long silent history under other names from soldier's heart to combat neurosis—had finally become a cost of war to be reckoned with.

Now with reports that the percentages, if not the absolute numbers, of returning Iraq and Afghanistan war veterans suffering from PTSD may exceed that of their Vietnam-era counterparts, VA budgetary outlays for care and treatment of this malady are likely to skyrocket even further.

Naturally the merits of a given veteran's case for PTSD care and treatment should be judged on the best scientific evidence and screening methodologies available. It is the need based on science that should dictate the size of the VA's budget to accommodate veterans traumatized by war, and not the size of the budget that shapes or manipulates diagnostic criteria to reduce the PTSD population among returning war veterans.

Concern has mounted in recent months among veterans and their advocates that it is money, and not science, that may set the VA's PTSD-related mental health agenda in the years ahead. Not only could this revised agenda have a potentially disastrous impact on the well-being and readjustment of today's returning veterans, but it has already caused considerable anxiety among veterans who have been rated with PTSD in recent years, and who fear their benefits may be unjustly curtailed.

Apparently the VA's ill-conceived plan to review the cases of thousands of veterans compensated for PTSD since the mid–1990s has been scuttled, owing to negative political fallout in Congress. But now the VA seems bent on pursuing its plan to limit future PTSD cases through a new strategy that will pit one prestigious scientific body against another, and which even Congress may have less influence to monitor or challenge.

The VA has contracted with the Institute of Medicine, a component of the National Academy of Sciences, to conduct a sweeping re-examination, not only of all medical and scientific literature on PTSD to date, but on issues related to PTSD's "treatment, prognosis and compensation." Such an initiative, given how much remains to be learned about PTSD, may be timely as long as objective science holds sway over politically motivated cost-cutting.

At the same time, the VA initiative threatens to second-guess, and potentially delegitimize, the long-standing authority of the APA under whose aegis PTSD research and treatment has been studied and advanced for more than a quarter century.

Anyone familiar with PTSD as researcher, clinician or long-term client is well aware of the competing hypothesis around the exact nature of the disorder, not to mention the rival claims of relative efficacy for one therapeutic method vs. another in the treatment of PTSD's persistent and aggressive symptomatology.

Psychiatrist and noted author Robert Jay Lifton, a pioneer in the early efforts to gain recognition for a condition initially observed in Vietnam veterans as post–Vietnam syndrome, and later defined systematically by the APA as PTSD, has long recognized the powers of human resilience among some individuals to survive horrifying episodes of war-related trauma. That's the good news. Where such individual hardiness is not present, many are not so fortunate, and the psychic damage incurred by such victims can lead to social dysfunction, social pathology or even suicide.

Most veterans I know who are rated with PTSD, including myself, will tell you that after living with this condition, often for decades, their symptoms never go away but that with self-vigilance, proper care and the support of loved ones and friends, their symptoms can be managed and kept at bay. Given this well-documented collective experience, the most troubling aspect of the VA-mandated Institute of Medicine's PTSD review is not just the hidden assumption that something is wrong with the existing PTSD science or benefit adjudication criteria, but the introduction within the policy debate of an expectation that combat trauma can be prevented.

Concepts like "survivability" and "resilience" offer hope of coping mechanisms to returning veterans who undergo disturbing changes of behavior because of their wartime experiences. Whereas the idea that an individual's response to trauma in warfare can be "prevented" prior to or immediately following the traumatic event seems suspiciously convenient for those who would bend science to a conservative vision of social policy. Ironically in this scenario, support for the troops in the field does not translate into support for veterans at home.

In July 2000, I had occasion to interview Daniel King, Ph.D., head of the Behavioral Science Division of the VA's National Center for PTSD. Dr King is a quantitative psychologist. He and his team performed statistical analysis on data furnished by clinicians working with PTSD clients throughout the VA system.

One unexpected finding Dr. King had begun to notice around the time we were talking was a quantum leap in cases of "late-onset" PTSD. These were veterans, in their 50s like me, who were entering the VA system for the first time in the mid- to late 1990s.

In fact, the VA's own surveys show that, of the vast majority of Vietnam veterans known to suffer from PTSD, less than one-fourth have ever benefited from VA-related services. Under the circumstances, it seems as if the increased burden in compensation payments that the VA is experiencing should have come as no surprise. Prior to its official recognition, moreover, PTSD was frequently referred to as "delayed stress," while the prefix "post" in the current usage would seem to suggest, logically at least, that the syndrome's appearance can't be tied to a fixed time line.

In my own experience, PTSD is an insidious disease, one which I went to great lengths to deny in my own life for decades. Denial, in fact, was my biggest enemy in the sense that I failed to grasp for years that PTSD, perhaps all mental illness, has a life of its own, and is not subject to conscious regulation like the normal ups and downs most people experience.

When I realized that PTSD often controlled me, and not the other way around, I was able to finally confront my condition, and learn how to better cope with and manage my symptoms. Without the safety net provided by the VA, that would not have been possible.

Bangor Daily News, **March 9, 2006**

PTSD from the Inside Out

In lieu of an editorial for this issue, I wish to share my opening remarks from the 3rd Annual Symposium on PTSD hosted by Maine VFP Chapter 1 in Portland, Maine on June 7th. The preceding introductory comments are by VFP co-founder, Doug Rawlings:

Maine Chapter 001's third annual symposium on PTSD this past June 7th featured four speakers: Michael Uhl, Penny Coleman, Tod Ensign, and Rosemary Masters. Our audience of 85 included health professionals, veterans and their families. The focus this year was on the family: how do those who support PTSD sufferers cope? What can we do to support them? Coleman provided the perspective of a Vietnam veteran widow who has done extensive research on PTSD and veterans' suicides; Ensign gave us a legal perspective on how the current VA system is dis-serving today's active duty soldiers and veterans; and Masters provided us with her experience as a neurobiologist and a psychotherapist who has worked with families trying to cope with PTSD. Michael Uhl set the tone for the conference with his opening remarks—"PTSD from the Inside-Out"—which wove together the politically charged atmosphere of PTSD issues in this country with the impact of PTSD on the personal lives of veterans and active duty soldiers. His own narrative brought the audience into the full meaning of the symposium: we in VFP have empathy and sympathy for those afflicted by PTSD. We have walked the walk, and now we are committed to using our experiences to help others gain perspective on PTSD.

Opening remarks by Michael Uhl, Ph.D.

I've done a fair amount of reading on PTSD, interviewed some of the major researchers and clinicians in the field, read stacks of their journal articles. It was in the mid–1990s while interviewing Dr. Daniel King of the VA's Boston-based National Center for PTSD that I first learned about late-onset PTSD. In those years, there was a sudden spike in the numbers of Vietnam veterans in their 50s seeking treatment in the VA system for war-related emotional issues, many of whom—like me—would subsequently be diagnosed with PTSD. Being something of a classifier by nature, I was happy to discover the late on-set niche as one fragile perch of certainty in my quest for some sign of external validation that this mentally disordering thing weighing me down since my return from Vietnam indeed had a life of its own. It wasn't just a mood swing or a bad day; it had threatened to become a state of being which seemed to literally drive my will toward choices that were irrational and self-defeating. Beyond that my explorations in the clinical, analytical and statistical literature did little to clarify or explain how I experienced PTSD from the inside out, in particular the sense of personal violation that seemed to fuel this raging loss of control. Reading the literature left me with a feeling I can best express, exaggeration intended, through the line of a favorite poem. "AT&T lied. It didn't bring my mother any closer." The literature was missing what for me was a key component.

Let me try to explain. What really struck me most deeply from my encounter with Dr. Dan King, for example, was his own story as a veteran. He was totally blinded from a wound suffered in a conventional fire fight with uniformed combatants while in Vietnam. Returning home, he completed his doctorate in psychology and began working for the VA. Dan told me that he himself does not suffer from PTSD, a fact I found extraordinary given the severity of his physical loss, and the traumatic circumstances under which it occurred. Another Vietnam veteran I know never actually set foot "in-country," as we used to say. He was stationed aboard an aircraft carrier where he loaded bombs on airplanes. His PTSD is rated at 100%. What got to him was a persistent preoccupation with images in his head of those bombs he loaded exploding on the peasant villages where the carrier's jet fighters dropped much of their ordnance.

An ex–Marine I know participated in a village massacre in Vietnam. He's as solid a citizen as you will find on this planet, but he's rated 100% for PTSD as well. I could cite many other cases of a similar nature, including my own as a combat intelligence officer routinely exposed to the abuse and torture of Vietnamese civilians. But in every case the common thread would be that our PTSD seems related, not necessarily to what happened to us— even in the instance of a most horrific wound like that of Dr. King's—but to what we did to others, especially to the unarmed and the innocent.

We say that PTSD is really as old as war itself. But I submit to you that the historical birth of PTSD, its official insertion, bounded by specific criteria, into the DSM—the diagnostic manual—of the American Psychiatric Association circa 1980, also had to do with the way in which this age-old war and trauma related psychic wound had itself evolved in the context of postmodern, non-conventional, counter-insurgency warfare. This is the piece, I believe, that is missing from the scientific studies, the world historical context in which this disorder, within its own military universe, has some of the characteristics of an epidemic.

While my inferences here are admittedly anecdotal, they are not frivolously based. I've had contact with a wide and representative cross section of Vietnam veterans over the past forty years. And most of those I know who operated in the infantry in thickly populated rural zones of Vietnam, or who served as interrogators or bomb loaders, and who suffer from PTDS, are possessed of an empathy that found soldiering in those ambiguous circumstances in direct conflict with the person they believed themselves to be back in their own country, where they were regular Joes, possessed of a sense of fair play, and not inclined to bully anyone. Whereas, in Vietnam, this initial wounding—long before most of us came to define our experiences politically—only deepened depending on the script we would eventually play out day-to-day in encounters with our adversaries who appeared to us most frequently as non-combatant civilians, and we to them as the agents of the horrors of war.

Now it's déjà vu all over again in Iraq and Afghanistan, military occupations where our soldiers once again confront a largely invisible enemy embedded in a very visible civilian population. As a predictable consequence of soldiering under those conditions, we will likely be adding over a hundred thousand new disabled veterans to the VA's PTSD roster in the years ahead—a roster, keep in mind, only begun after 1980, and till now virtually limited to veteran trauma cases of the Vietnam generation. Billions of tax dollars have already been spent, billions more will be needed to treat and stabilize the lives of these PTSD veterans, subsidies which, in many cases, will stretch over the course of a lifetime. What we call PTSD may date from antiquity, but PTSD as an acknowledged cost of war is a modern event. And, it need hardly be said, that every citizen today has the moral and civic responsibility to ask if, and under what circumstances, a given war is worth this particular cost.

In the meantime, leaving aside the thorny larger questions I've touched on only loosely here, and the fact that the essence of PTSD remains mysterious, what we do know about this disorder is very real. We know that those who suffer it are stalked by a particular shadow which darkens their lives, and it is therefore reasonable, as well as compassionate and just, that a good deal of intellectual and professional energies among those acting in good faith around this issue must go into finding from among a wide range of techniques and therapies the means to lighten that shadow, still that hyper-vigilance, quiet the monkey talk, challenge and redirect the antisocial behaviors, ameliorate the pain.

These efforts to heal and manage symptoms, I believe along with Dr. Robert Jay Lifton, a pioneer in this field, benefit from a reserve of resiliency in the human spirit. It is this resiliency that we must emancipate and nurture in our treatment of those with PTSD. Whereas the struggle each individual PTSD sufferer must inevitably—and perhaps perpetually—confront is, who's in control here, me or the demon?

The other obligation assumed by the mental health community, as well as by those of us for whom the PTSD narrative is a matter of humanitarian concern and national policy, is to continue to educate ourselves, and continue to bring what we know and what we don't know to forums such as this to help inform and shape the conversation about PTSD that is taking place all over this country, as the intense, almost daily, media coverage on tragic individual cases can testify. Each of our presenters today is playing a dynamic role in that national conversation. Let us now listen to what they have to share with us.

(Opening comments at the Maine Veterans For Peace 3rd Annual Symposium on PTSD, Portland, Maine, June 7, 2008.)

Veterans For Peace *Newsletter Editorial,* **July 2008**

Surviving PTSD

Forty-two years ago today, I arrived at Valley Forge Army hospital, my tour in Vietnam mercifully cut short by the timely affliction of pulmonary tuberculosis. Having thus survived Vietnam, I have spent the years ever since contending with its aftermath in the form of a wound far more resistant to healing than the disease that once lodged in my lungs.

I wish I could say that my understanding of this unwelcome shadow, this discomforting vulnerability to stress and conflict forever embedded in my scarred memories of war, was in some way proportionate to the number of years I have lived with it. But I can't. All the tests confirm I have it, but PTSD remains almost as much of a mystery to me today as it was when I first became conscious of how frayed my emotions had become during those involuntary episodes of weeping while I was still in the hospital. It wasn't the TB that disconcerted me; that had been my salvation. Something deeper was gnawing at me, and would gnaw at me ever since.

And yet, when I consider those veteran comrades I have known from my own era, and those I hear about almost daily returning from Iraq and Afghanistan, whose postwar lives have disintegrated in acts of tragic self-destruction, I have to count myself among the lucky ones. Did I possess some quality, or benefit from some set of circumstances, that they were lacking? Or was the fault not in themselves, but in their stars? These enigmas surrounding PTSD always cloud my attempts to tease out a more defined perspective on what it is, how it works, and whether my life would have been different or better if not so relentlessly shadowed by its presence.

If I said that PTSD has robbed me of the solid career my background and education had prepared me for, that would be an irrefutable truth. In compensation, my rejection of the premise that Vietnam was a noble cause, leading to years of antiwar activism, emboldened me to challenge orthodoxy wherever it lay in my path, and to forge an independent life that rested strictly on my own talents and enterprise.

While this self-styled independence has cost me greater material rewards, it has carved a space to accommodate my PTSD in a manner perhaps less problematic than had I been more rigidly subjected to the pressures of a conventional career. Even the PTSD-driven tendency to withdraw from society—or in the lexicon of the clinic, to isolate—has been as often as not agreeable to a writer's solitary trade.

I won't deny that I've caused my share of pain to others and stepped on more toes than I'd like to remember. The burden I carry is thus, involuntarily for the most part, parceled out to others, friend and foe alike. But here accumulated familiarity with harmful and repetitive behaviors has paid some dividends. In my long and stubborn coexistence with PTSD I've learned that the symptoms can be managed—not tamed exactly—but kept at bay. Things would have gone much worse for me I firmly believe, had I not committed myself over the past four decades to the old fashioned talking cure—weekly therapy whenever possible—to vent the pressures that beset me from within.

Medication has never performed the benefits for me that I have gotten from an hourly walk each day on a quiet country lane. Intimate relationships? Well that's another matter. But, in the autumn of my days, I have been blessed with a wife of uncommon charity and patience, a weekly date with a granddaughter for toddler gymnastics—and if that doesn't make you smile, nothing will—a son close at hand, some enduring friendships and family ties, and a rescue canine to care for who distracts me from my more self-involved and narcissistic moods. It is moreover this embrace of the small life, with ambition put to rest, that offers true nourishment and peace of mind, even as I cast a wary eye on a past both troubled and fulfilling. And if I've been down so long it seems like up to me, so much the better. This is what surviving PTSD looks like from where I stand today. It isn't perfect, but it sure beats the alternative.

(Comments opening a Maine Veterans for
Peace symposium on PTSD, April 23, 2011)

In My Activist Voice

Heeding the Call

The message of John Grant's article, "The Vietnam War and the Struggle for Truth" (*InTheMindField*, June 22, 2012) should be heard as an alarm bell by all who were blind-sided and unsettled upon learning of the Defense Department initiative announced by the President this past Memorial Day to "commemorate" the Vietnam Era by rewriting its history.

The projected duration of the Pentagon's mandate for this exercise stretches from 2012 to 2025. Let's leave aside for the moment that this actuarial calculation has the macabre feel of a death watch in the countdown of who, in the fading ranks, will one day wear the laurel as the "Last Vietnam War Veteran." What should trouble especially those whose histories and identities are embedded in their opposition and resistance to that war, is what the Pentagon is tasking itself to accomplish during these unpropitious thirteen years: first, to *create*, and then, to *sustain*, a *positive legacy* for the Vietnam War.

That sow's ear can never be transformed into a silk purse. This is a draconian and despicable undertaking, whatever its eventual reach, and a topic I shall return to often as this revisionist plot unfurls, if only to defend my own identity and memories as but one actor among the waves of soldiers and veterans who rose up to oppose our filthy war, even as it was still being fought.

It's hard to imagine that the unpopularity, and eventual rejection, of the Vietnam War by the American public could ever be excised fully from the historical record. But the specific history of the organized opposition to the war is more vulnerable, since it becomes, in the absence of repetition in popular media, more and more abstract and remote to younger generations as it recedes into the past.

The GI Resistance and antiwar Vietnam veterans' movements of the Sixties and Seventies, so unique in the annals of warfare, become prime targets for erasure in this new and approved version of the war the Pentagon hopes to fashion. Even if it were only these unprecedented chapters of the whole anti–Vietnam war saga that the DOD project succeeded in obliterating by 2025, what an immeasurable loss of inspiration this would represent for later generations who must continue to organize and struggle against the plague of American militarism for the ungodly and unforeseeable future.

The first blow to the memory of our antiwar GI and veteran struggles in this revisionist farce was delivered by President Obama himself in his Memorial Day launch of the neutered sounding "Vietnam War Commemoration Project." Obama's myth-driven speech is a testament to his abysmal ignorance of this period of our history; or he was simply pandering to a selected audience of true-believer vets gathered at the Wall, who have succumbed to the pernicious view that the war they could never have defended in youth had become, with the salve of passing years, a noble cause.

By reinforcing the one-dimensional image of returning Vietnam vets universally ill-treated by an ungrateful nation, Obama exploits the repressed feelings of anger, guilt and shame that unbalanced so many of us. We suffered the burden of fighting in a war widely opposed at home, not least among our better informed generational peers. But the deeper wounds resistant to time's cure for thousands of us were rooted in the horrifying awareness of daily acts of violence that we aimed in Vietnam relentlessly, not only at an armed foe, but at a whole people.

Obama glibly conjures, and bathes in glory, the ambiguous battles of Khe Sanh and Hue, but ignores My Lai. In doing so he prepares the ground for sanitizing the judgment once commonplace throughout the world—to include vast numbers in the U.S.—that atrocities in Vietnam, while mostly on a lesser scale, were not in any sense exceptional. "My Lai," as my generation of Winter Soldiers always emphasized in our public testimonies, "was just the tip of the iceberg."

Obama now implies that this brush tars too broadly and prefers the consoling fiction that Vietnam veterans as a whole "were blamed for the misdeeds of a few." But I am too wedded to my own truths about the evils of that war to ever be consoled, and Obama's lies on this particular occasion infuriate me. I went to Vietnam. I lived the war. It horrified me. I came home and actively opposed it. Like tens of thousands of other Vietnam veterans, I witnessed or participated in atrocities. I saw the routine use of torture. These were not the "misdeeds of a few"; they were the essence of that war.

As I wish to make clear, this active dialog, leading to a major pushback against the Pentagon re-write of our history, must emerge rapidly and engage many voices, if, ultimately, it is to blunt the impact of this revisionist assault. I also want to make a tangential observation here concerning a parallel I see between the campaign in contemporary Brazil to defend the historical truths surrounding that country's decades of military dictatorship, and the militant and popular resistance to it, and the similar campaign we must now undertake.

The similarity lies in the shared moment that requires a defense of resistance to illegitimate authority, and of the peoples' right to historical memory itself. But there's also a major difference. In Brazil, the defense of truth is being led by that country's president, while in the U.S. we have a president who is bent on obstructing it. I have included below a short article that I translated from a Brazilian newspaper to demonstrate how an enlightened leader deals with a barbaric practice long outlawed by modern societies, but still glaringly visible throughout the world, and an acknowledged fixture as well of American wars since Vietnam, the widespread use of torture. Although Brazilian President Dilma Rousseff was herself once subjected to such brutality, she now chooses to treat torture not as the "misdeeds of a few," but as a policy of State.

Dilma Never Wants to Know the Identities of her Torturers
(Dateline Rio, June 22, 2012. *O Globo*)

In a restrained voice, choking back her emotions, President Dilma Rousseff told the assembled media during the closing session of Rio+20—an international conference on the environment—that she never wanted to know the identities of her torturers.

Commenting about the recent publication of depositions she gave under torture in the Seventies during her imprisonment by Brazil's military dictatorship, Dilma noted that many of her torturers didn't use their real names, but she nonetheless has suspicions as to their identities.

Dilma chose to emphasize, however, that the critical question isn't the torturer, but the torture, because the torturer was always an agent of policy. "The problem is the conditions under which torture is established and performed. This everyone knows," she said.

"With the passage of time, the best thing that happened for me, personally, was to not become fixated on these identities, and not harbor toward these agents' feelings of hatred, bitterness or revenge ... but not forgiveness either. To want vengeance, or to feel hatred or bitterness, is to remain dependent on those whom we wish to revenge ourselves upon. This is not a healthy state of mind for anyone," said Dilma, struggling to avoid tears.

That's why the [Brazilian] Truth Commission was created, Dilma reminded her audience in conclusion, to turn that page of this country's history, and not permit that it ever happen again.

InTheMindField, **June 27, 2012**

With Paul and Do' at My Lai

A recent visit to My Lai, in the company of Paul Cox, reminds me of why The Fog of War is such a relevant theme for our anniversary convention this year. After our recent VFP Agent Orange delegation had wrapped up its ten days of visits with victims and officials, Paul and I elected to stay in Vietnam for another week, heading south toward areas where we had been stationed in the war. We boarded a mid-day train in Hanoi, and twenty-hours later arrived in Quang Ngai City. We were met at the station (the Vietnamese word for which, Ga, incidentally, is derived from the French Gare) by an interpreter whose services we had arranged for in Hanoi, a man I would place in his mid-fifties, named Do'.

Do's English is unusually good, all the more so since he learned it from GIs as a boy growing up in the vicinity of My Lai. Do's father and older brother were killed in the war, his father under—well—foggy circumstance. The father had been with the resistance during the French War, and later spent time in prison, perhaps under the colonial regime, or under Diem; it wasn't clear. Back in his native village, Do's father later worked for the Saigon government, and, one night, elements of the Liberation Front took him from his house, and shot him in the village soccer field. Because of his father's ambiguous history, neither side trusted this man, Do' said.

Later Do' showed us where the execution occurred. This was after Do', Paul and I had been to the site of the My Lai massacre, and the museum that commemorates the unspeakable horrors that occurred there on March 16, 1968. We were virtually alone in the museum on that weekday afternoon. The grounds are much more formal than when I was first here in 1994—de-historicized from a need to build permanent—but idealized—replicas of the dwellings of that era. The massive stone memorial, where we made our joss stick offerings, is already showing its wear in the harsh tropical climate.

Inside the museum there are shocking exhibits and photographs recreating or documenting scenes from the massacre. Black and white photos, like a rogue's gallery, portray many of those men, already grown to middle age—which I thought very just—who had taken part in the massacre, while other shots honor the few heroes, like Hugh Thompson, who didn't. One large color print caught me off guard, and made me smile: VFP's Billy Kelly bowing over a memorial arrangement of 504 roses, one for each victims, which he had brought to My Lai on the anniversary of the massacre some years back.

On the fringes of the museum grounds, local toilers still worked the surrounding rice fields. It was harvest time, and a small portable gasoline powered thresher, a tool now widely seen in paddies everywhere, was used to remove the grain from the chaff, which is then laid down in bundles as mulch to cover the dry paddy bed.

On the way to his coastal village, Do' asked us to stop at the cemetery where his father is buried. The burial monument was built according to the Catholic tradition with a cross, in observance of his father's religion; the other memorials had symbols typical of Vietnam's dominant Buddhist faith. Again we burned joss sticks, and Do' seemed to feel this gesture of civility on our part would do him honor as well as sooth his father's spirit.

From there we went on to the fishing village at the mouth of an estuary where Do' spent his childhood. His family's ancestral alter is housed in a small well-kept building which sits on a good sized plot of fenced-in land, much of it planted in small vegetable gardens—the only such lot visible among the other densely spaced dwellings and commercial buildings on the narrow lane leading to the water. Clearly, his family had been in the village's upper social tier. Trays of sardines or anchovies lay everywhere drying in the sun. We walked to the dock side, greeted by mirthful fisherman, who used the presence of these two hulking westerners for all the comic relief it was worth. Do' pointed to the shoreline across the river from where we stood, that his brother was swimming toward when he was shot and killed by American soldiers.

If Do' is a bitter man, it doesn't show. His tone is philosophical when he describes his family's tragedies. But he does have an agenda ... one that is similar to other Vietnamese Southerners I met when I first returned to Vietnam in '94. They speak in the language of the vanquished, resentful of the many areas in which they claim discrimination. If they were ARVN soldiers, they get no pensions—even the equivalent of a few bucks a month—that NLF and NVA soldiers often receive, especially the disabled. Members of their families, who may be Agent Orange victims, receive no social welfare. There are no ARVN veterans associations, not even for self-help. Many talk of the hard years in the education camps.

The contexts for such grievances, of course, are found in the years of struggle and sacrifice millions of Vietnamese endured attempting to repel the foreign invaders and to liberate and reunify their country. There was understandably little sympathy for those compatriots who fought against them, even the low level conscripts who had little choice but to serve in the Saigon army. Whereas, on a material level, it was only after the mid-nineties when Vietnam was beginning to recover from, first, the genocidal "American war," and then, the "war in the west" (Cambodia) and the "war in the north" (China), that the combination of economic reforms and the gradual relaxation of the conditions of the crippling U.S. embargo began to create enough wealth to simply keep the population from starvation.

Today, however, Vietnam is a veritable economic tiger. The differences between Vietnam in 1994 and Vietnam today are staggering—virtually two completely different countries. Of course, the country is still predominantly agricultural, and one UNICEF official we met estimates that at least 15% of the population lives below the poverty line. A growing concern among officials we met with is that the gap between the wealthy and the majority who may not be impoverished, but are just getting by, is very great, and ever growing, a fact, I was told, that makes many of the old revolutionaries, and some younger comrades, nostalgic for the better aspects of socialist economics.

But, when it comes to the questions around internal reconciliation that Do's story symbolizes, the fog of war remains dense. It makes me think of what I've read about how veterans were treated after the War Between the States here: the pensions and prosthesis all went to the Union soldiers. The Confederates got nothing. The Union victory meant the abolition of slavery; the communist victory led by the Hanoi government meant American defeat and reunification for Vietnam. For me these outcomes were just. But I also believe that the victims should be equal before the law.

I therefore heartily support the goals of VFP's on-going Agent Orange campaign which will be centered around an omnibus bill soon to be introduced in Congress that mandates (in addition to environmental clean-up of Vietnam's dioxin "hot spots") long overdue care and compensation for all the victims of agent orange throughout Vietnam, those in the north or south and their families, directly or indirectly exposed; members of the Vietnamese overseas community who may have been exposed after spraying began in 1961 and prior to emigrating in 1975; and those U.S. Vietnam veterans and their families who have been thus far overlooked or neglected. In each of these groupings, victims are now reaching into the third and fourth generations.

Veterans For Peace *Newsletter*, **Summer 2010**

VFP Agent Orange Delegation in Vietnam

Following an early April 2010 round of visits in private residences and care facilities with children suffering from a range of debilitating birth anomalies, and classified by the Vietnamese government as "victims of agent orange," a VFP-sponsored delegation of six American veterans was received in Hanoi by Nguyen Tan Dung, the Prime Minister of Vietnam. Mr. Dung used the occasion to insist that, with hostilities between our two countries now nearly forty years behind us, the United States government must finally "take responsibility for the aftermath" of the Vietnam War.

"More than two million Vietnamese people were killed, millions were wounded and more than 300,000 are still missing," Dung said, adding that "three million Vietnamese were exposed to toxic chemicals sprayed by the U.S. military, and that people continue to be injured or killed weekly by bombs and mines left behind after the war." Dung's crisp accounting of this grim "legacy" of the American War retains still, in the scope of its carnage and devastation, the power to chill the soul, not least of one former soldier who unwittingly found himself among the forces of destruction.

Dung expressed his hope that the VFP delegation, through its affiliated project, the Vietnam Agent Orange Responsibility and Relief Campaign (VAORRC), would continue to disseminate information about the aftermath of the war to the people and government of the United States. Dung asked for accelerated cooperation on the part of the U.S. in providing assistance to Vietnamese victims of Agent Orange "to help them overcome the difficulties they face."

Responding for the American veterans, Paul Cox, who'd spent eighteen months in Vietnam as a combat Marine, affirmed that the delegation's intimate contact with victims and their families during our ten-day tour had intensified our understanding of their pain and suffering, and deeply committed us to obtain justice on their behalf. Toward that end, Cox announced, VAORRC will soon introduce a bill in the United States Congress seeking a broad legislative remedy to extend care and medical aid to all veterans and civilians exposed to Agent Orange, and related-compounds, during the Vietnam War, and to underwrite the cost of clean-up in areas of Vietnam where high levels of the herbicide's highly toxic contaminant, dioxin, persist in the environment.

The directness of Mr. Dung's remarks prompted one veteran to ask a staff member of the delegations' host organization, Vietnam Agent Orange Victims Association (VAVA), whether such explicit public language on Mr. Dung's part represented a shift in policy in Vietnam's position on demanding what might be seen as reparations for the staggering and persistent destructiveness caused by the U.S. invasion and decade-long occupation of southern Vietnam? And why only now, forty years after the final spraying mission was flown in January 1971, was Vietnam making such an insistent push to resolve the Agent Orange aftermath?

The response to the latter question was unanticipated, but, ultimately, not surprising. The VAVA staff member, a former colonel in the North Vietnamese army, noted simply that, in the past, every time the Vietnamese sat down with their U.S. counterparts to plot out postwar relations, the Americans let it be known that, if Vietnam put Agent Orange on the table, the session would be terminated. Given that Vietnam's short term needs in the years immediately following reunification in 1975 were most urgently to reform the country's dysfunctional command economy—especially after the collapse of the USSR and the Eastern Bloc—and to convince the U.S. to dismantle its crippling economic embargo, moral restitution linked to what our host characterized as "the most horrific war of the twentieth century" had to take a rear seat to the issues surrounding immediate survival.

As to the suggestion implying that a "policy shift" would put long repressed "moral outrage" back into the center of historical judgement on the Vietnam War, our host revealed how vividly the memory of the U.S. establishment's perfidious disregard for fair play remains in the mind of at least one old revolutionary. The former colonel's response was measured, devoid of obvious emotion, typical, perhaps, of someone schooled in a political culture where taking the long view should never be confused with abandoning the objective. Dung's words, he said, did not represent a policy shift, but were "a matter of emphasis" defined by context, presumably the presence of former soldiers of the enemy's armed forces converted to reliable allies, and fully in agreement with the Prime Minister's message. "In a diplomatic setting," the colonel added, "we would be more polite."

And then came the colonel's stunning explanation that Dung's words traced a continuity in the Democratic Republic of Vietnam's policy toward the U.S. dating from the Paris Peace Accords of January 1973. At the time,

Richard Nixon, in a secret letter to then Premier Pham Van Dong, promised Vietnam $3.3 billion "to contribute to healing the wounds of war and to postwar reconstruction of the DRV." Ever since, in one form or another, Vietnam has never ceased to demand that the U.S. live up to that unfulfilled promise, and to acknowledge its responsibility for the war. A generous resolution of the Agent Orange issue would go a long way toward marking "paid" to that outstanding debt.

The six members of the VFP/VAORRC Agent Orange delegation were Paul Cox, who also represented VVAW and Swords to Ploughshares, Susan Schnall, Ken Mayers, Mike Ferner, Michael Uhl, and Geoff Millard, Board Chair of IVAW.

Veterans For Peace *Newsletter*, Summer 2010

Kerry and the Year of the Veteran

With a John Kerry–George Bush face-off for the presidency now a virtual certainty come November, how might the voting pattern of the nation's veteran population impact the election's outcome? The so-called veteran bloc, calculated at the high end and probably exaggerated, is said to number as many as 50 million voters: an estimated 27 million U.S. veterans (8.5 million from the Vietnam era), 1.4 million service members currently on active duty, a similar number of guard and reservists, to which are added the close family circles of all three groups. It is generally assumed that, by some unspecified and fluid margin, a majority of these voters incline traditionally toward the Republicans, but not necessarily because they cast their ballots as veterans.

Not every working stiff or small-town Rotarian who served in the U.S. armed forces wakes up in the morning thinking "I'm a veteran." It's just a piece of the existential package. But in the context of Bush vs. Kerry veterans' identity and special interest politics may achieve a degree of visibility and significance unprecedented for a presidential campaign. It's arguable that a considerable number of veterans will be drawn into the fray as veterans, and will base their votes substantially on highly subjective responses to one of two broad concerns, which in both instances, not incidentally draw their emotional wattage from contradictory historical interpretations of the Vietnam War.

In this scenario, Kerry would benefit to the degree these veterans take a more kindly view of his combined combat credentials and involvement with the antiwar movement, over Bush's less than gung-ho service record on the home front in the Texas National Guard. Among veterans who see Kerry's antiwar history as "unpatriotic," Bush's avoidance of combat will be less decisive.

Kerry's advantage is that only he, not Bush, can mobilize in-country Vietnam veterans, the most organized and influential group within mainstream veterans' organizations and the peace movement alike, on the basis of a powerful, if mystical, appeal to "brotherhood."

That many of these "brothers" will vote for Kerry simply because he is one of them already seems clear from the rapidly expanding Veterans for Kerry movement picking up momentum in communities all over the country. The small but vocal right-wing vets, whose voices have been temporarily amplified by the national media, for balance or mischief one never knows, have staked their political challenge to Kerry on the imaginary claim that American POWs continue to be held by "communist" governments in Indochina. Seems like a sleeper in today's political market, but who knows? This is America, and Rambo's world view is not without its following.

Ironically Kerry's campaign may play less well in the veteran peace movement than the veteran mainstream. Vet activists who've kept council fires burning for years in Vietnam Veterans Against the War (VVAW) and Veterans for Peace (VFP) somewhat ignored by the media, but with a genuine grassroots presence nationwide, are divided on Kerry. But their reasons are more substantial than symbolic.

There's general agreement that pro–Iraq War, pro–Patriot Act, pro-preemptive-strike, free-trader Kerry will be an instant target of protest the day he takes office. But the "anybody-but-Bush" sentiment seems predominant in the discussion among VFP and VVAW members in interviews and on the Internet. Some will vote for John Kerry from genuine admiration, others holding their noses. The Eugene V. Debs factor, larger than one might think, will again adamantly refuse a vote for what they do not want. I will respectfully depart their ranks on this one, believing that the right is winning the battle in the center.

A veteran voting bloc? Who'd a thunk it? It's the Year of the Veteran, and this bloc may just swing Kerry right into the White House.

Bangor Daily News, March 18, 2004

Warriors for Peace

"There have always been veterans for peace. War makes veterans warriors for peace." With those words, David Cline, wounded and decorated in Vietnam, and national president of Veterans For Peace (VFP), opened the organization's eighteenth annual convention, on August 8, in San Francisco.

Hundreds of veterans who'd served from World War II through the Persian Gulf War gathered here from every corner of the country for two full days of workshops, plenaries and informal conversations, focused largely on ways to express and amplify opposition to the current war with Iraq and to the new patterns of domestic repression that mark the past two years.

One featured speaker, Congressman and presidential candidate Dennis Kucinich, mapped the vets' progressive agenda onto the mainstream of electoral politics before the packed convention. The audience generally took heart that one candidate for the presidential nomination of the Democratic Party would articulate views antagonistic to the broad strokes of the Administration's foreign and domestic policies during the approaching run of primaries.

Breakout sessions, aka workshops, occupied the first day of the convention. Best title goes to a gay and lesbian vet contingent: "We Used to Shower Together." Point taken. At another featured workshop, a new VFP project—Bring Them Home Now (BTHN)—was launched with hopes to stir uncomfortable memories among Pentagon and White House operatives of the "hollow army" brought about by widespread resistance and disaffection within the military during the Vietnam era.

Bring Them Home Now is a coalition of military-family and veterans groups, including Nancy Lessin and Charlie Richardson of Military Families Speak Out, whose Marine Corps son, Joe, just returned from Iraq, and Stan Goff, an organizer from the Fort Bragg area around Fayetteville, North Carolina, a retired Green Beret Master Sergeant, whose son, Jessie, just left for Iraq with the 82nd Airborne. The coalition, which also includes the Central Committee of Conscientious Objectors operating the GI Hotline, Citizen Soldier and Vietnam Veterans Against the War, intends to mobilize the anti–Iraq War sentiment that is growing rapidly among military families and

GIs in order to help convince the American public to pull the plug on Bush's wars.

Veterans For Peace, which has doubled its paying membership to 3,100 veterans—all activists—in a year, "is aligning itself with many like-minded organizations," Korean War vet, Woody Powell, the organization's national administrator, told delegates in San Francisco. United For Peace and Justice, for one, was quick to endorse the BTHN campaign, and veterans and family members are expected to play highly visible roles in the mass demonstration planned for October 26 in Washington.

Like-minded legislators too. Members of the Congressional Black Caucus, planning their fall assault on the Bush agenda, have already asked BTHN and VFP to locate military families and Iraq War veterans who are willing to provide testimony before an ad hoc Congressional panel, reminiscent of the Dellums Hearings on War Crimes in Vietnam in April 1971. Prior to that, however, BTHN will troop military families and their message to bring the troops home directly to Senate and House members at the district level in twenty states before the end of the summer recess in early September.

A press conference to announce the Bring Them Home Now campaign took place in Washington on August 13, and, on the following day, in Fayetteville. The press events, short of capturing headline coverage, were still broadly reported throughout the print, Internet and electronic media. Response to a reporter's question about BTHN during the Pentagon briefing on C-SPAN the evening of August 13 was cautious. "These people," referring to the BTHN families and organizers, "are entitled to their views," said the DOD spokesperson, quickly recasting the issue of troop and family member discontent as a technical problem, a question of resolving the "predictability of rotation."

Will discontent in the ranks and among family members diminish, if combatants know before deploying to Iraq the duration of their tour of duty there? Or will the "unpredictable" nature and length of this war ultimately lead to a kind of malaise in the military that was so costly to troop morale and discipline during Vietnam? It depends on how much Iraq will ultimately become like Vietnam, and on the peace movement's capacity to counter a truly unpredictable element: the fear factor around national security, so expertly manipulated thus far by the Bush team to bolster public support for the war.

The Nation, **August 24, 2003**

Antiwar Veterans Raise Their Voices

In recent weeks, segments of the peace movement earnestly debated throughout cyberspace the pros and cons of the slogan "support our troops"—however it might be modified by an explicit tag line of opposition to the war. Could the public clearly grasp a principled antiwar stance when it appeared to accommodate the welfare or sensibilities of those who were doing the actual fighting?

How could we ensure that the public would distinguish between our support for the troops and that of the war's promoters? Wasn't the call to silence criticism of the war being justified by appeals expressed in those very same words? How might the peace movement coopt that mantra, and provide just enough cover for fellow citizens who occupy uncertain ground—doubting the war's merits, but unwilling to have their own patriotism subjected to challenge—to win them back to the forces of peace?

"Bring more vets to the forefront," proposed Leslie Cagan, an organizer with United for Peace and Justice in New York. "Let's march on the Pentagon," wrote one youth activist, "as long as the vets are in the lead."

Why the vets? "Because we have this credibility," explained Woody Powell, a Korean War veteran and Executive Director of Veterans For Peace (VFP). "Our words are no different from many others', but they seem to carry more weight." Since Vietnam, even for the most committed antiwar audiences, there's a certain comfort zone when a vet steps up to the podium and says, "If showing our support for the troops means silencing our public criticism of the war that is not an option." Those words drew strong applause when David Cline, thrice wounded in Vietnam, and president of VFP, delivered them before an overflow teach-in at American University just days after the U.S.–led coalition invaded Iraq. The teach-in had kicked off Operation Dire Distress, a weekend of protest and lobbying in the nation's capital (March 22–24), attended by hundreds of veterans who, repeatedly, in private comments and public displays, linked support for the troops in Iraq to a demand to stop the war and bring them home.

It is critical that veterans continue to communicate this message from the movement's national stages, even when the Bush Administration declares the war a victory and the occupation begun. But antiwar veterans, like GI resisters and military family members—what Noam Chomsky calls "authentic groups"—are also uniquely effective over the long haul when addressing communities whose social origins are most similar to their own, where empathy, apart from fact-based or moral argument, is often the medium of persuasion. This, you might say, is the "identity politics" of the working class. The love of country and personal courage—core values in many communities—of these vets, in particular those who have tasted the bitter fruit of the battlefield, are seldom called into question. Minimally, veterans who oppose warfare are given a respectful hearing by their Middle American landsmen, and are treated with equanimity in local media, even by the most hidebound provincials of the fourth estate.

More Veterans Becoming Active for Peace

The U.S. march toward war with Iraq certainly stimulated recruitment in the ranks of antiwar veterans. Over the past six months, Veterans for Peace, open to veterans of all service eras, has virtually doubled its membership to 3000 ex-servicemen and servicewomen. The organization has a national office in St. Louis, which tends to its website and some of the national press, and also aids in planning for its yearly convention (August 2003 in San Francisco). But VFP's ninety-six chapters, distributed over thirty states from Maine to California, operate autonomously, and set their own activist agendas, much in the spirit of the movement's overall grassroots orientation.

Veterans For Peace was founded in Maine in 1985 (superseding an earlier post–World War II entity of the same name), and quickly spread to other states at a time "when low intensity warfare was raging in Central America under Reagan," recalled Tom Sturtevant, who served in Korea. The Maine chapter, which Sturtevant heads, is one of the nation's most militant, providing contingents for all the latest national mobilizations, while at home engaging in acts of nonviolent civil disobedience that recently led to the arrests of five members. As part of their community outreach, Maine VFP is frequently asked to visit middle and high school classrooms, where they have distributed thousands of book covers with a nonviolence theme, and have collaborated with the American Friends Service Committee in offering alternatives to military service.

Minneapolis has likewise reported "phenomenal growth," writes Walt Wittman by email, ticking off in comma-less shorthand his chapter's varied and overloaded activist schedule: "What an impossible task: signs speaking engagements forums church meetings letters legislative contacts city council hearings rallies vigils canoe raffles and merchandising plus keeping our sanity." From Washtenaw County, Michigan, Bob Krzewinski reports that he'd "been thinking of starting a chapter, but there didn't seem to be too many of us around." That all changed after February 8, when the Ann Arbor Coalition for Peace "wanted a few veterans up front to lead the march ... and we had an almost constant stream of veterans coming up ... we had 16 people show up at our first meeting."

Roughly 70% of VFP's members served during the Vietnam era, and many, like Dave Cline of Jersey City, have also been active in Vietnam Veterans Against the War since VVAW's heyday during the early nineteen seventies. VVAW "has kept its flag flying," says Cline, maintaining a presence in the progressive communities of the New York metro area—with its original Clarence Fitch chapter—Milwaukee, and Chicago, home of the national office. A VVAW newspaper appears regularly, and reunions have drawn enthusiastic attendance. Many of VVAW's old guard have surfaced from their other lives, and "re-up'd" since the Iraq war began, expanding the group's network to 800 members nationwide.

Veterans from the 1991 Gulf War

For years since their return, Gulf War vets have concerned themselves primarily with a struggle to gain scientific recognition for a weird syndrome of battlefield-induced health problems that has led the Veterans Administration to provide compensation for nearly a third of the 600,000 men and women who fought in the '91 conflict. But some Gulf War vets, like Charles Sheehan-Miles, were politicized by the traumas of combat, and when a rerun of war in the Persian Gulf first threatened, he helped form Veterans for Common Sense (VCS). But he stresses that VCS, which has been contacted by over 2000 veterans, "is not an antiwar organization, per se. A majority of Americans don't identify with that point of view. Our group wants to occupy a middle ground, to address audiences about war's hidden costs, the treatment of casualties and compensation for the disabled. Care for Gulf War vets has already cost the nation $2 billion," he told me. "People should know what a war will cost, before they're called upon to support it."

Sheehan-Miles' group nonetheless joined with Vets For Peace and VVAW, along with Military Families Speak Out (MFSO), a support group for those with family members currently on active duty, in forming a coalition called Veterans Against Iraq War (VAIW) to organize Operation Dire Distress, strongly emphasizing the veteran character of the event. Of course, it's impossible to say what the turn-out would have been had the invasion not yet begun. And perhaps the presence of the several hundred vets who did attend, resplendent in remnants of their old service uniforms and bedecked with medals attesting to youthful valor, though receiving a decent amount of publicity, would have had an even greater impact if wedded to one of the movement's massive national demonstrations. But the reality is that even overtly antiwar veterans covet a degree of independent action from the larger movement. The point, suggests VFP's Woody Powell, is to avoid being "discounted," especially in cases where the protest becomes "strident." It's a fine line, he argues, between "being seduced by our power and having it become diluted."

Coming Home

It is the issue of their postwar entitlements, which Charles Sheehan-Miles recasts conceptually as a hidden cost of war, and which Dave Cline frames in a demand for justice for all the war's victims, that unites all veterans across the spectrum of political views. During our rally in Washington, a number of speakers made bitter reference to the Congressional attacks spearheaded by Republican warmongers to cut billions from Veterans Administration health care over the next decade. The Veterans Against Iraq War website has collected the salty comments of scores of former service members, a surprisingly large number of whom served in World War II, which ridicule these politicians as "chicken hawks," those who demand sacrifice of their fellow citizens, but who have never served, and refuse to put their own lives or those of their children on the line.

It's not quite clear exactly what the dismantlers of government intend with this budget-slashing message for the Department of Veterans Affairs, but something is afoot here in a system that has extended its eligibility since 1996, and increased its enrollment from 2.9 to 6.8 million.

Most veterans I know remain proud of their service, because they feel they owed it to their country. A remarkably candid article in the *New York Times* ("Military Mirrors Working Class," March 30, 2003), reported that the demographics underlying such values place the actual burden of filling the ranks on blue collar communities, with men from backgrounds of affluence or other forms of privilege, routinely getting a pass. Clearly the formation of this belief in service is a social construction of some interest, another tangent of veteran culture worth exploring elsewhere. But the counterweight to reverence for service to one's nation is resistance, which in former days was aimed at conscription, and today at the so-called "poverty" or "economic" draft.

New Recruits

"Economic" is perhaps a better term than poverty since the U.S. armed forces now generally require all recruits to have a high school diploma, thus not only keeping many from the true underclass out of harm's way, as the cliché goes, but denying them access to the potential mobility of a stable military career—admittedly for a minority—with some of the perks that, among blue collar workers today, only civilian government employees and trade unionists typically enjoy. Many service veterans, on the other hand, have found that enticements offered them at the moment of recruitment, opportunities for a college education or skilled training transferable to the civilian job market, had been grossly exaggerated. Youth antiwar activists from communities of color, like Karim Lopez, with Uptown Youth for Peace and Justice in New York City, have found that a tactic of counter-recruitment around this pattern of misrepresentation is ideal, not just for warning potential service entrants of high school age about the inflated sales job by recruiters, but for "making a clear link between the cost of militarization, and an attack on young people's future," with the concomitant cost increases they will face in health care and higher education.

Resistance within the military also has its ineradicable history, and, while only likely to become widespread in wars of long duration, like Vietnam, there have been some well-publicized cases already during this period of militarization. Pacifist hotlines have been ringing off the hook with inquiries by active duty and reserve soldiers seeking information on how to apply for conscientious objector status. As recently as April 7, one such applicant, Gabriel I. Johnson, was shipped out to Iraq from Ft. Hood, Texas, even though his case is pending, "a clear violation of the Army's own rules," said his attorney Tod Ensign, director of Citizen Soldier in New York. There have been other rumblings at the front, with three British troopers reportedly sent home for opposing the indiscriminate killings of Iraqi civilians.

The veterans' peace movement has grown steadily in this time of threatened, and now real, war with Iraq. But can it be sustained with a reasonable level of visibility and consistency when this current episode in the endless series of little wars promised by the Bush Doctrine recedes from public view? Or will the vets' movement ebb and flow in sync with the geopolitical tide? Veterans For Peace was kept afloat following a precipitous decline in membership after 1991, David Cline believes, by its humanitarian work on postwar issues of reconciliation and healing, and projects like Friendship Village, in Vietnam, and the Iraq Water Project, which went beyond a strictly antiwar orientation. VVAW also kept its programmatic hand in by working on readjustment issues and homelessness in the veteran community.

But another idea was broached and discussed by a number of veterans in Washington during Operation Dire Distress. And that was to explore the viability of engineering a certain breadth and volume in the vets' movement by giving it a global profile, forging links as widely as possible with those whose involvement in veterans' and GI resistance issues in their own countries is of long standing. This strategy would create a transnational infrastructure capable of mobilizing an occasionally somnolent membership in every corner of the world to oppose on quick notice the next U.S.-inspired military adventure, and the one after that, and so on. To prevent this apparatus from becoming top-heavy or "think-tanked" within our own sphere, there is no better model than the chapter structure of Veterans For Peace, with its practice of grassroots autonomy. For every doctrine ... an anti-doctrine.

PeaceWork, May 2003

Vets Bite War

"If a war is wrong before it starts, it's wrong after it starts," argued David Cline, president of Veterans For Peace, fixing a theme that played well before an overflow teach-in at American University (AU) in Washington just days after a U.S. led coalition invaded Iraq. Then, to make his meaning unmistakably clear, Cline added that, "If showing support for our troops means silencing our public criticism of the war that is not an option."

The teach-in kicked off Operation Dire Distress, three days of protest and lobbying in the nation's capital (March 22–24, 2003), attended by hundreds of veterans who, repeatedly, in private comments and public display, linked support for the troops in Iraq to a demand to stop the war and bring them home. To build for the event, Cline, who fought and was wounded in Vietnam, joined with old comrades from Vietnam Veterans Against the War to form a broad antiwar veteran front, and then invited Veterans For Common Sense, an organization of Gulf War vets, and Military Families Speak Out, a support group for those with family members currently on active duty, to join the coalition called Veterans Against Iraq War (VAIW).

Thanks to their collective efforts and to Peter Kuznick, a history professor at AU, whose seminar has the intriguing title "Oliver Stone's America," the roster of speakers for the teach-in was deep and talented. For starters, Bobby Muller, whose Vietnam Veterans of America Foundation leads an international campaign to ban land mines, advised the assembly that Iraq, like Vietnam, where he was shot in a firefight and paralyzed for life, is "a propaganda set-up," and that "everything we're being told about it is wrong." Muller urged his activist listeners to understand Iraq within the "framework of hegemony" advanced by the Bush Doctrine of "preemptive and preventive warfare," and to communicate that reality in the least confrontational way possible to the average citizen not privy to elite discussions on foreign policy.

Having a retired "flag officer" voice progressive views before an antiwar gathering that attempts to reach beyond the choir and the cognoscenti always projects a certain aura of legitimacy. Thus the observation was all the more chilling when retired Admiral Gene La Rocque, emeritus director of the Center for Defense Information, warned that "the spirit of militarism is growing" in this land, and that, "regrettably, we in America have become comfortable with war as a spectator sport." With three-quarters of the nation glued to CNN, truer words are seldom heard throughout the homeland of the soon to be less free.

But, with the Bush administration lacking the confidence to trust the war's "information function" to the media, as Dick Cheney once blabbed indelicately to the Freedom Forum, the comments of another speaker, Gulf War veteran Charles Sheehan-Miles, served to remind us that, since Vietnam, the Pentagon has effectively managed to sanitize the martial spectacle they put before the nation's readers and viewers. "Most people don't know that we killed a lot of people in 1991," he said, referring to incidents like the "highway of death," the slaughter of Iraqi soldiers retreating from Kuwait that has never risen above a whisper on the historical soundtrack. Such leads, no doubt, are inconvenient to follow for any war correspondent who wishes to remain in-bed, so to speak, with his or her military sponsors as a price for continued access to the propaganda flow.

One panelist, Joan Duffy, wiped a tear from her eye when former marine Jaime Vasquez, the Jersey City Director of Veteran Affairs, spoke of the battlefield comrades who saved his life after he'd been shot in a firefight, and gave special thanks to the nurses in Vietnam, like Joan and her friend Dotty, who'd come to Washington with other members of the Veterans For Peace from Santa Fe. Other veteran participants traveled from even greater distances, and were represented from Maine to California, and from two dozen heartland and southern states in between.

Straight from the jail cell where he'd chosen to abide after his fellow practitioners of civil disobedience, arrested some nights earlier in front of the White House, had accepted release on bail—because, he said, he did not wish to see the television scenes of "shock and awe" raining missiles on Bagdad—Daniel Ellsberg stepped to the podium. At a teach-in, one may teach. And Ellsberg wove a cogent parallel between the current crisis and the Mexican War, an earlier American adventure in preemptive empire building and bullying of a "weaker nation," as U.S. Grant, who had fought there as a lieutenant, would later express it in his memoir. Ellsberg joked that he's seen a sign at a demo in New York that read, "how did our oil get under their sand," but then uttered a solemn prophesy that "for every marine who dies" in that Iraqi sand, "one hundred innocent civilians will die in the U.S. from wrongful terrorism."

At home that afternoon in Troy, Pennsylvania, veteran Brian Laverty, now a stockbroker, tuned into CSPAN, which broadcast the VAIW teach-in live, and heard writer Jonathan Schell assert that "the policy to stop weapons of mass destruction with force will fail," and that our opposition must now focus on "stopping the next war, and the war after that." Laverty heard that message, and at 5:30 the next morning, he was headed for D.C. to join the demonstration that Operation Dire Distress had planned for its second day.

The lawn off Constitution Avenue, within sight of the Vietnam Memorial, filled gradually until, by noon, roughly five hundred people had assembled, half of them decked out, like militia at a re-enactment, in military regalia hoarded from their time in service. A fresh set of jungle fatigues was delivered in a box of personal items from my unit a month after I'd come to Valley Forge army hospital from Vietnam (not a bullet, but TB). I now donned them for the first time in over thirty years, and joined brother and sister veterans, and supporters, including a sizable delegation of women from Code Pink, behind the lead banner: Support Our Troops: Bring Them Home!—secured at one end by an old vet activist friend, Mike Pahios, a film archivist for the *Today Show* in New York City. I also ran into a guy I hadn't seen since the antiwar veterans movement in late 1970, John Beitzel, a real estate assessor from Chester, Pa., who'd testified publicly about American atrocities in Vietnam, both of us with three decades of life behind us since last we'd met, children grown, retirement years on the near horizon.

We marched around for the better part of the afternoon, laying wreathes at the various service shrines. Since the new World War II monument is still being built, our whole contingent had to approach it by literally descending into the concrete trough of one reflecting pool, drained of water, and then stand at the foot of a construction fence. It was a surreal moment. Just then, three large military helicopters suddenly filled the sky above us, and two mounted D.C. cops galloped to our rear as we stepped from the empty pool, and wheeled left en route to the Korean War monument. From there we could see a pro-war rally roughly the size of ours in front of the Lincoln Memorial listening to the cloying patriotic lyrics of a song reminiscent of the redneck anthem, "I'd rather be an Okie from Muscogee."

We had our sentiments as well, expressed by the skirl of a somber bagpipe, and the slow banging of an Indian drum. But when we finally hit the streets to parade toward the White House, to present a petition signed by more than two thousand veterans who oppose this war—ultimately rejected—we strutted to cadence ditties just like in basic training, only now our verses questioned the military values we had once so blithely parroted: Bush decided to attack, sent the army to Iraq, with guns to shoot and bombs to drop, all this killing has to stop. The punch line of another cadence count, "when you come home, they turn their back," highlighted a traditional concern among veterans for post-service care that had been somewhat muted throughout the weekend by the prevailing message of opposition to the war.

Strangely, it is the idea of service as well as the shared experience in the military that binds veterans to each other. Most veterans I know remain proud of their service, because they feel they owed it to their country. The demographics underlying such values may point to class, placing the actual burden of filling the ranks on blue collar and poor communities, with men from backgrounds of affluence or other forms of privilege routinely getting a pass. Veterans across the ideological spectrum—especially conservatives as Stewart Nusbaumer, a Vietnam War amputee and webmaster of the VAIW site, judges from its thousands of hits—refer to service-avoiders like Dubya, Perle, Wolfowitz, Bill Bennett, and scores of others prominent figures in public life, as chicken hawks—"they'll put your body on the line, but not their own." They, of course, would say they also serve....

   Excerpted from a Veterans For Peace Organizing pamphlet (2003),
   for its additional detail about Dire Distress.

Occupying the Contested Zones of Meaning

The hoisting of the NLF flag over the Presidential Palace of the former southern regime signaled a great victory for the Vietnamese people, which as an American soldier, I had once fought to deny them, and later, as a veteran who had come to oppose the war and everything it stood for, I enthusiastically welcomed.

Throughout the late '60s and early '70s, sympathy for Vietnam had remained steadfast among antiwar vets. But our movement against the war had ended with the defeat and withdrawal of American forces in 1973; by the time Saigon fell in 1975, we had shifted our energies to struggles that were closer to home. Radical vets like myself saw the many post-war issues we would frame around the rights and welfare of veterans and GIs—from amnesty to Agent Orange—not only as a means of gaining humanitarian relief for these constituencies, but as educational and political vehicles for exposing the system which had exploited us all.

My ongoing concern for Vietnam was with fixing American responsibility for the devastation we had caused there, and joining efforts to prevent the U.S. from creating "future Vietnams," rather than with internal conditions that have transformed Vietnam since its reunification. For more than 25 years Vietnam-the-war has never wandered far from my thoughts, whereas Vietnam-the-country virtually vanished from my imagination after 1973.

This anniversary year presents a unique opportunity for me to reunify my own long-divided Vietnams. With my partner Carol Brightman, I am writing a book, part memoir, part reportage, where the political and the emotional involvement of the past provides the bridge for a fresh encounter with contemporary Vietnam.

We have no intention of abandoning our concern over how the Vietnam War is to be remembered by future generations, as we reflect in our work on the many mechanisms our culture has developed over the past two decades for "putting Vietnam behind us." We are well aware that the retreading of official history in the U.S. has conveniently covered over many unpleasant facts about the war, from the true nature of its inception to the roles and responsibilities of those who were its managers.

But we will also try to make sense of the momentous changes underway throughout Vietnam today. This is a Vietnam we are now discovering in peace, and in depth for the first time. Like me, Carol Brightman had only known Vietnam in wartime when, in 1967, she investigated civilian damage under U.S. bombing raids as a member of the Bertrand Russell War Crimes Commission.

We returned once to Vietnam last summer and plan to visit again soon. We do not presume to arrive pointing fingers about what Vietnam's government or economic system should look like. We go with questions, scores of them, some based on our experiences in the past, others of import only to the present and the future.

For reasons of diplomacy, the Vietnamese may disagree with us on the need to "keep the war alive" for purposes of our own domestic political agenda; we might disagree with their choice to embark along the capitalist road, or—God forbid—to reopen Cam Ranh Bay to the U.S. Navy, a plan that is said to be under consideration.

Despite these or other differences, the continuity in our ongoing commitment to Vietnam is expressed by feelings of solidarity around past struggles and by sympathy toward the difficulties of development that confront this complex and heroic nation. We also look forward to rejoining the network of individuals and groups for whom the Vietnam War was and remains the shaping event of their political lives.

PeaceWork, 1995

With Tod Ensign

Introduction

By the late 1970s, Tod Ensign and I were running Citizen Soldier, a GI and veterans' advocacy organization, out of an office in New York City's Flat Iron Building on Madison Square, years before that threadbare stretch of lower Fifth Avenue was designated a "landmark district."

As activists, we had cut our teeth in the movement against the Vietnam War, working with combat veterans who had come home and became vocal in protest of that war. We had also supported active-duty service members who had rebelled, not only against the war, but against the systematic racism that pervaded the armed forces then, as well as a generally repressive command structure intolerant of any individual or collective expressions of legitimate dissent.

After 1973, when universal male conscription was abolished in the U.S., the Army, in particular, underwent a bumpy transition from citizen army to all-volunteer force. Recruitments sagged, and GI grievances mounted, not least around bread and butter issues of pay and benefits.

At that stage, and based on a legal technicality where increases in military compensation were pegged to contracts negotiated by civilian government workers, a major public employees union floated the idea of bringing active-duty GIs into their fold. Considering the fact that many U.S. allies in Europe incorporated GI unions within their armed forces, the undertaking had some basis in reality, unlike so many of the high principled, if utopian, projects of the American Left.

Citizen Soldier became a vocal advocate for the union, and Tod Ensign and I co-authored a number of articles taking up this union drive. I've included a selection of that published material here, which follows the early momentum and enthusiasm for the campaign to its ultimate demise at the hands of both Congress and the Department of Defense. The fact that the union initiative had to be quashed at such institutional heights is some measure of the serious threat this campaign posed to the traditional prerogatives of military authority at the expense of the basic rights to which all Americans are—and should be—entitled.

At about the time the G.I. union drive was being put to rest, two major health controversies arose that were of immediate concern to three generations of American military veterans, men who had served during the eras of World War II, Korea and Vietnam.

Many of the elder vets from those first two periods of conflict had participated in U.S. open air atomic tests in the South Pacific, or in the desert at the Nevada Test Site seventy miles from Las Vegas. High rates of certain types of cancers associated with radioactive fallout were appearing in these populations. At Citizen Solider we organized innumerable media events demanding care and compensation for these Atomic Vets. And Tod and I wrote a series of articles calling the public's attention to the Pentagon's recklessness in exposing these men to unsafe levels of radiation. Our short documentary film, *Nick Mazucco: Biography of an Atomic Vet* (by Richard Schmiechen and Michael Uhl) was produced by PBS, and aired nationally on public television.

But it was the decline in health among Vietnam veterans, reporting a range of illnesses that were disproportionately excessive for men in their age group, which became the focus of Citizen Soldier's activities well into the 1980s. The initial thinking suggested environmental exposure to toxic chemicals as the cause. It was a short leap from there to the defoliation program carried out by the United States in southern Vietnam, using herbicides like Agent Orange to which many GIs had been exposed, that was quickly identified as the most likely culprit behind the veterans' health problems, and the high rates of birth defects among their children.

Citizen Soldier played a key role in winning recognition by the Veterans Administration for disabilities suffered by both the radiation and the Agent Orange veterans and their families, not least though the publication of our book, *GI Guinea Pigs: How the Pentagon Exposed Our Troops to Dangers More Deadly Than War*. The afflictions of the radiation vets have been largely attended to by a suitable government response, and by now time has removed many of these men from the roles. Nor has the Veterans Administration shied away from the Agent Orange controversy, and herbicide exposure is now assumed for a long list of illnesses, to include some types of birth defects. These programs will never be perfect, but they are a far cry from where they were when activists like us built campaigns that brought these issues into the limelight.

When it comes to Agent Orange, the one enormous injustice that has been virtually ignored by the American government, of course, is its responsibility for the human and environmental costs inflicted on a Vietnamese population sprayed by thousands of gallons of deadly herbicides for over a decade.

I therefore wish to provide here a modest historical foundation for supporting the on-going campaign to bring justice to the Vietnamese victims of Agent Orange, who are spreading into the fourth generation since the end of the Vietnam War. I have included here, along with the book's Introduction, two chapters from *GI Guinea Pigs*, the first on the defoliation campaign carried on by the U.S. Air Force Ranch Hand pilots; and the other on the determined efforts of one whistle blower within the Veterans Administration itself, to bring national awareness to the health effects of Agent Orange on American Vietnam War veterans.

Soldiers as Workers

Unionization of the nation's armed forces may be an idea whose time has come.

An American GI jumps from his armored personnel carrier into the rubble-strewn streets of Newark in the midst of a major upheaval. When his squad is ordered to round up "suspicious" persons and shoot at any "threatening motion," he refuses. He cites a section of his union's contract with the Pentagon—which prohibits his deployment against his "own" people. When his commander threatens him with court-martial, he files a grievance with his union's representative.

A fantasy? Perhaps, but unionization of the armed forces might not be as farfetched or as far away as we may think. Today's military is quite different from what it was just a few years ago.

In an Army survey conducted last April, more than 90 percent of all recruits agreed with the statement, "Basic training and army discipline are good for me." Obviously some significant changes have occurred since the end of the draft. Gone are the days when a commander could not be sure how his troops might respond to an order; when drug abuse was rife; when the desertion/AWOL rate increased to one among every thirteen soldiers. The spontaneous activism of thousands of GIs against military racism and the Vietnam War seems to have died out with the end of mass antiwar activity. Last July, the Army announced that it had exceeded its annual recruiting goals for the second time in three years.

To deal with "malcontents" and "troublemakers," the Army has instituted a policy under which it can honorably discharge, at its total discretion, any recruit during his or her first six months of duty. Between 1,200 and 1,700 have been discharged under this program each month since it began. About half of them, according to the Pentagon, have willingly accepted separation. As former Army Secretary Howard Callaway said a few months ago, "I don't want anyone in the Army that doesn't want to be there." As a result of this policy, the Army's AWOL rate has dropped from a high of seventy-three per thousand in 1971 to fewer than twenty per thousand in 1975.

Today's average enlistee is nineteen years old, has a high school diploma and often some college credits, and is twice as likely to mention skills training and retirement benefits as reasons for enlistment as was a 1971 recruit. Unlike the conscripts of the Vietnam era, many young recruits now seem to regard soldiering as just another job in the large and growing public sector of the work force.

The number of public employees has grown from 6,820,000 in 1948 to 16,500,000 today, with most of the increase occurring at the state, county and municipal levels. About half of the public employees perform blue-collar tasks which are indistinguishable from jobs in the private sector. Another large percentage perform routine clerical work.

As their numbers have grown and the types of jobs proliferated, public employees have gradually discarded old ideas of "public service," and "duty to the sovereign" in favor of increasingly militant union organizing, including resort to labor's ultimate weapon, the strike. Such unions as the American Federation of State, County and Municipal Employees (AFSCME) had grown to 350,000 members by the early 1970s. Such organizations as the American Federation of Teachers and the Public Service Employees were transformed from primarily "professional" societies to practitioners of picket-line militance. Such unions as the Teamsters and the Transport Workers, who traditionally represented workers only in the private sector, also became bargaining agents for many public employees.

Against this background, it is hardly surprising that the notion of military unionism should sooner or later attract legitimate interest. In mid–1974, 2,200,000 people were in military uniform, and an additional 1,000,000 civilians were employed by the Defense Department. Added together, they accounted for almost two-thirds of all Federal employees (excluding the 700,000 workers in the semi-public Postal Service.

Labor legislation in the Wagner, Taft-Hartley, and Landrum-Griffin Acts serves to outline and define the rights of workers in private industry to join labor unions and bargain collectively with their employees. The right of Federal employees to organize and bargain, however, is less precisely defined. In 1962, President John F. Kennedy issued Executive Order 10988, which declared as Federal policy the right of employees to organize, and directed Federal supervisors to bargain with bona fide unions "in good faith." Subsequent Executive Orders have refined procedures and policies for such bargaining, but the right of Government workers to organize and bargain with the "sovereign" has remained more tenuous than that of similar workers in private industry.

On November 11, 1974, many observers of the military were startled by an editorial in the pro–Pentagon *Army Times* which warned that "there may be a move toward military unionism [if] Congressional and Administration attitudes toward military benefits [do not improve]." The warning seemed gratuitous. While the possibility of organizing soldiers into rank-and-file unions has long interested many activists who, like ourselves, were part of the GI movement, we could find no indication that such an effort was actually under way.

Seven months later, on June 27, 1975, *The Wall Street Journal* revealed the big secret in an article headlined, "Union Plans '76 Drive to represent Servicemen; Legalities are Explored and Pentagon Shudders." While we had focused our search within the military itself, the American Federation of Government Employees (AFGE) was well along in its planning and research for this massive undertaking. The AFGE, founded in 1932, is a union of public employees which already represents, through binding arbitration, more than 650,000 Federal, State and Municipal white collar workers. Some 392,000 civilian employees of the Defense Department and more than 7,000 uniformed National Guard "technicians" have been represented by AFGE for many years.

AFGE apparently reasons that a "community of interest" exists between civilian and uniformed military workers who often work side by side at the same military installation. The steady erosion of educational, medical, and retirement benefits for soldiers which has been taking place within the armed forces in the past few years, coupled with wholesale job cutbacks and "involuntary retirements," affects uniformed and civilian employees equally, AFGE argues. As AFGE President Clyde Webber recently told a Pentagon manpower panel, "Servicemen need someone to protect them, that's for sure."

AFGE's organizing plan came as a shock to Pentagon officialdom. William K. Brehm, assistant secretary of defense for manpower affairs, declared that, "a military organization cannot be democratic—it must be based on command authority." But Leo Pellerzi, AFGE general counsel, has observed, "It's a volunteer Army now, and that means people are selecting a military career as a means of livelihood—not for patriotic reasons. Servicemen today aren't responding to an attack on the country; they want to be paid."

Whatever the merits of these opposing viewpoints, the Pentagon has conceded that the right of soldiers to join a union is protected by First Amendment guarantees. Decisions of the U.S. Supreme Court establish that neither Congress nor the President can simply prohibit soldiers from joining a union or other voluntary association. A recent ruling affirmed the right of civilian organizers to enter any part of a military base which is normally open to the general public. While commanders are still free to exclude "outsiders" for legitimate "military reasons," any policy of exclusion must be evenly applied; protestors or organizers cannot be singled out.

Nonetheless, the Army has sent a Field Command memo to all installations, reminding them of Army Circular 532-1, which prohibits commanders from recognizing or bargaining with servicemen's unions. The memo further orders that headquarters be immediately notified "if any person, military or civilian, at any Army activity is presented with, or otherwise receives, a petition ... for recognizing active-duty military personnel in other than off-duty employment."

The lines are being drawn, but the battle has yet to be joined. AFGE must convince delegates to its convention next summer to amend the union constitution to allow a significant policy shift. It also must contend with formidable powers within the AFL-CIO, most notably super-patriot George Meany, who will want assurances that an organizing drive within the military will neither upset current labor-management practices nor "endanger national security." AFGE will probably seek to reassure Meany and his cronies in the top AFL-CIO leadership by citing the effectiveness of military unions in the forces of several of America's European allies.

In a memorandum prepared for the AFGE executive council, President Webber describes the character of "military unionism" in Holland, Sweden and West Germany, noting that in these nations, military personnel policy is established either through regular collective bargaining, institutionalized consultation, of some combination of the two. Webber stresses that, regardless of the form of union participation, "unionizing has not revealed any disturbing or negative effects on military morale, combat training, or efficiency." Further, he asserts that "military unionism has not compromised discipline or preparedness."

This claim is backed by GI activist David Cortright who recently interviewed the leader of the Dutch conscripts union, Paul Regouin. When Cortright asked if a soldiers' union was compatible with military discipline, Regouin replied, "Discipline can be achieved in two ways. The old way is to say, 'Behave or be placed in jail.' The other way is for soldiers to see the necessity of the job on their own and to be motivated to do it. Many in NATO ridicule the Dutch soldiers, but last year during [joint NATO] maneuvers, [they] scored the highest."

From the average soldier's point of view, the record of reforms and concessions won by these unions is impressive; many of the traditional GI gripes appear to have been eliminated. In Holland, for example, food, housing, and work conditions are all said to have improved measurably since collective bargaining began. Saluting and other military rituals have been abolished along with such arbitrary punishments as reduction in rank. Individual rights are fully protected, and wage scales have been made competitive with private industry. Of particular importance is the fact that extra duty now must be compensated with leave time, and soldiers can no longer be arbitrarily reassigned from post to post. Assignments now take a soldier's permanent place of residence into consideration.

One might suppose that the prospect of eliminating morale-deadening "gripes" and boosting military "preparedness" would encourage the U.S. military establishment to favor the unionization of the armed forces.

Obviously this is not the case. To conservatives, including the military brass—organized soldiers pose another threat to traditional values, a further "demilitarization" of the social fabric.

For those of us who seek fundamental change in the society, the first steps in organizing the military raise questions of another sort. Mindful of the degeneration into which many union bureaucracies have fallen, we must wonder if the efforts of such an organization as AFGE might, in fact, coopt any possibility of militant self-organizing among GIs. While the AFGE has, for tactical reasons, consistently narrowed the range of issues it subjects to collective bargaining, opponents of militarism might want to broaden bargaining to encompass such matters as the occupational hazards posed by dangerous weapons, the obligation to respect international rules of warfare, and similar questions of far-reaching military policy.

However such problems are resolved, this is certain: antiwar organizers and other activists can influence the direction of military unionism only by entering the work place and understanding soldiers as workers. There is no useful purpose served by moralizing military evil or by calling soldiers "lifer-pigs."

From *The Progressive*, vol. 40, no. 4, 1976.
Reprinted by permission of The Progressive, Inc.

Changes in U.S. Army Mean Soldiers May Unionize

A Stodgy Union Takes On Controversial Campaign

Imagine the possibility: an American GI jumps from his armored personnel carrier into the rubble strewn streets of Newark in the midst of a major upheaval. When his squad is ordered to round up "suspicious persons," shooting any who "threaten resistance," he refuses, citing a section of his union's contract with the Pentagon prohibiting his deployment in a domestic disorder. When threatened with a court martial he files a grievance with his union representative.

Far-fetched? Maybe, but the possibility of a military union may not be so farfetched or as far away as you might think. Today's military has changed from just a few years ago; there are forces already in motion towards unionization.

In September the American Federation of Government Employees, AFL-CIO, in convention voted to change its constitution to allow GI membership, opening the way to organizing active-duty military personnel. The executive council, however, voted to postpone recruiting soldiers for six months. The union leadership, facing implacable opposition from the Pentagon, may be trying to gather and consolidate forces for the tough fight ahead. Or the decision may indicate that the union is balking and that at least a sizeable faction within the leadership is having second thoughts and would prefer to "go slow," perhaps in hopes of wringing other concessions from the federal government by dangling the threat of a GI union in its face.

While other big unions, particularly the Teamsters and National Maritime Union have threatened to sign up GIs, AFGE is the most logical recruiter. It presently represents nearly 680,000 federal civilian workers, making it the tenth largest union in the U.S. Over half of these employees work for the Department of Defense side by side with uniformed personnel.

The union has locals that bargain and negotiate with military commanders on nearly every important defense installation in the U.S. and in Europe. In 1973, the pay rate of service men and women was linked to that of civilian defense workers by a "wage comparability" statute. Since then, AFGE has had some success mobilizing military personnel and their dependents to assist its civilian membership in lobbying efforts for federal wage hikes which would benefit both civilian and military personnel.

It is somewhat paradoxical that a cautious and stodgy union like AFGE, with a very spotty record on contract negotiation and grievance advocacy, should voluntarily become embroiled in such a controversial campaign. AFGE, however, is responding to demands from a military workforce that has undergone marked change since the Vietnam ceasefire.

In 1969, when Nixon took over, the American military had been fought to a standstill in Vietnam and domestic opposition to intervention was growing daily. Nixon's planners modified American strategy abroad by dictating that American troops would be withdrawn in favor of "indigenous" armies. Our "free world allies," were handsomely paid to expand and reequip their military units. With this shift, Nixon was able to eliminate the draft and substantially reduce troop levels (from 3.4 to 2.1 million). The transition to an "all-volunteer" force fundamentally altered the racial, class and sexual composition of the military. The percentage of blacks in all services has grown to 17 percent. In 1976, nearly a third of all army recruits were black, as were 30 percent of those who reenlisted after their first tour. While women still account for only one trooper in 20, their numbers doubled from mid-1973 to the present.

Once in uniform, the average GI finds work conditions within the military not all that changed from the repressive, irksome life that GIs have chafed under for decades. While paychecks are fatter, the hoopla about "exotic duty stations" and "challenging careers" wears thin rather quickly. The Uniform Code of Military Justice (UCMJ) continues to be employed by commanders as a means to "good order and discipline" rather than as an impartial legal code. As former Supreme Court Justice Douglas expressed it some years ago; "military law is basically disciplinary, rather than legal in nature." Rather than reducing the level of dissatisfaction, the introduction of the mercenary concept into the American military seems to have introduced problems long associated with civilian, not military workers.

To complicate matters, the Pentagon chiefs have become alarmed by the steady escalation of personnel costs as a percentage of the defense budget. While the total budget has grown each year, payroll costs—now nearly 60 percent of the budget—have outstripped the Pentagon's ability to buy the hardware it desires. Major defense contractors, predictably, are also unhappy with this state of affairs. An "impartial" panel of blue-chip corporate leaders, the Defense Manpower Commission, has recently added its weight to reversing this trend. In a recent study it concluded, "The Pentagon must determine ways to reduce manpower dollars, without impairing defense needs."

It's becoming clear to even the most gung-ho troopers that the traditional benefits that they have taken for granted (commissary and PX privileges, hospital care for dependents, retirement after 20 years, GI Bill benefits etc.) are to be cut or eliminated. This has spread dissatisfaction up the ladder to the senior NCOs and officers. Because the "grunts"—who comprise 40 percent of the enlisted ranks—never expected much more than "three hots and a cot," their main grievance has been with the archaic system of military justice. The career NCOs and officers, by contrast, regard the withdrawal of benefits as a slap in the face by an ungrateful government.

A year ago, Army Capt. Ron Shaninger, (since dropped from the service), in cooperation with AFGE local 1157 informally surveyed over 5,000 service people of all ranks and all service branches. An overwhelming majority endorsed the concept of one type of GI union or another. The officers and NCOs typically would mention the "protection of economic gains" as a central union goal, while the lower ranks were more concerned with protection from the military's justice system.

Despite anguished shrieks from the likes of Sen. Strom Thurmond (R-SC) and right-wing groups like Americans Against Union Control of Government, the idea of a soldiers' union isn't nearly as outlandish as it may sound. Soldiers' organizations have been a feature of the European social landscape for many years. Today, there are over 60 different unions in the various European militaries. Their authority and jurisdiction vary broadly; from the right to bargain collectively to conducting informal talks with the Defense Ministry. Military unions in Europe play a dual role: they help maintain labor peace (i.e., ensure "productivity' and defense readiness) while at the same time they bring a measure of formal democracy to the ranks, along with meaningful material benefits.

One European union, the Dutch Conscripts Union (VVDM), provides an example of what an American union might look like. According to one of its organizers; "the main point of the union is that [it serves] as a weapon for soldiers to fight for their rights." So far the VVDM has made a good fight. Pay for recruits has increased 1200 percent, duty hours are shorter and less arbitrary and working conditions are safer and more satisfying.

The next move is the union's. AFGE locals on military bases report a steady flow of inquiries about membership from uniformed personnel. Despite the wishes of GIs, the possibility remains that the national leadership will "trade-off" the recruitment of soldiers in exchange for tangible gains for its civilian membership. In fact, much of the rank and file opposition to organizing GIs stems from the fear of present AFGE members that such activity will further dilute an already weak union's strength.

In an interview with *In These Times*, AFGE president Ken Blaylock vigorously denied the likelihood of any such *quid pro quo*, stressing that the union is "serious" about its GI union plans. However, he made it clear that AFGE's commitment is not etched in stone. "Should Carter radically change Pentagon policies that now threaten the welfare of military personnel," he said, "their [the soldier's] interest in the union might dissipate." This, presumably, would absolve AFGE of any responsibility to organize them.

For the present, AFGE's Executive Council has ordered a full-scale study of all economic and legal aspects of such a drive. It has also mandated a plebiscite on the question to be conducted on a local-by-local basis.

Meanwhile, the soldiers and sailors wait.

In These Times, January 12–18, 1977

A Union of Soldiers

The right of American soldiers to join a trade union is emerging as one of the most important issues of post–Vietnam U.S. military policy. Last year, we reported in *The Progressive* ("Soldiers as Workers," April 1976) that the American Federation of Government Employees (AFGE), the largest union of Federal workers, would seek delegate approval at its biennial convention of an amendment to the union constitution extending membership to active-duty military personnel.

Predictably, the suggestion that the AFGE might organize GIs met with an outraged response at the Pentagon. Anti-union forces in Congress and private industry were also quick to voice their disapproval. But no attempt was made to block the AFGE—perhaps because it was felt that the union's "patriotic" rank and file would never allow its leaders to commit such folly.

The pulse of rank and file trade union militancy, however, is beating more rapidly today than many would suspect. We attended AFGE's convention in Las Vegas last September, and found the 2,500 delegates in an insurgent mood. The people we encountered in the huge convention hall challenged our misconceptions about government "bureaucrats," and gave the lie to the prevalent stereotype of overpaid Federal workers feeding at the trough of make-work. Since 1970, government employees have watched inflation spiral by 37 percent, while wages increased by only 22 percent in the same period.

During their week in Las Vegas, the AFGE delegates approved sweeping changes that may signify a dramatic shift away from the union's old "partners with management" way of doing things. They began by electing new leadership, headed by President Ken Blaylock, who pledged an "era of activism"; next, the delegates voted to create a strike fund, though Federal employees are forbidden by law to "vote with their feet." Following an impassioned plea by Blaylock that GIs need representation and that even the threat of enrolling military members would constitute a "weapon in the union's arsenal," the convention repealed the constitutional ban on military membership.

In the months since the convention, however, the AFGE has failed to demonstrate a strong organizational commitment to sign up the thousands of active-duty soldiers who have shown an interest in the union. In an interview last December, President Blaylock indicated that AFGE's talk about GI unions may, in fact, amount to no more than an arm-twisting exercise to add to its bag of lobbying tactics.

"Should the Carter Administration radically redirect Pentagon policies which now threaten the welfare of military personnel," Blaylock wondered, "would the original interest expressed by the majority of military personnel dissipate to the point that it would not be reasonable for us to represent these personnel?" He seemed to be suggesting that the Administration could—and should—head off organizing by providing greater benefits for service members.

It isn't likely to happen, though. In fact, the new Secretary of Defense, Harold Brown, has hinted that GIs face tougher times. Referring to the ratio between funds allocated for military payroll costs and those earmarked for research, weapons procurement, and the like, Brown said, "If there is an imbalance here, it must be redressed." Defense contractors and hardline hawks in Congress have been saying for some time that such an "imbalance" exists. For professional soldiers, the message is clear. They can look forward to continued erosion of their traditional benefits in such areas as commissary and PX subsidies, medical and dental care for dependents, veterans' programs, and retirement compensation.

AFGE, therefore, will probably go ahead with its organizing effort, proceeding cautiously through the thicket of legal, political, and economic complexities that would confront any union attempting to represent soldiers. AFGE clearly faces a dilemma: Pressures from GIs who seek representation of their interests by a national trade union; pressures from Congress and the Pentagon, both totally opposed to unionization as a solution to GIs' problems, yet unable to avoid the "strategic" consequences of increased manpower costs.

The notion of a soldiers' union is a new one in this country, but soldier's organizations of various kinds have been a feature of the European social landscape for many years. There are more than sixty military unions operating in the armed forces of Holland, Belgium, Germany and the Scandinavian countries. In all these instances, the unions have some say in personnel policy, but adhere strictly to political neutrality. However, military unions have attempted to organize around explicitly political programs in France, Portugal and Italy, and in these countries, democratic movements within the military have been sternly repressed.

Nevertheless, the successful European soldiers' unions help bring a

A Union of Soldiers

measure of formal democracy to the ranks, and provide the collective power to win material gains. They may also eventually serve as the basis for deeper, more progressive struggles if favorable conditions emerge.

Here in the Unites States, an important link between civilian defense workers and the uniformed military was forged when Congress established the concept of "pay compatibility" between the two groups in 1972. The next year, AFGE was able to mobilize soldiers and their families to join its own membership in urging Congress to overturn President Nixon's "wage deferrals," and "impoundments." While the AFGE's interest in organizing GIs is largely attributable to the natural affinity between civilian and uniformed personnel, who often work side by side, and to such legal structures as "compatibility," the true roots of GI unionism are to be found in recent changes in the conditions of military service.

The end of the draft in 1973 and the shift to an "all-volunteer force" fundamentally altered the racial and sexual composition of the military. In 1976, nearly one-third of all new recruits were black, as were 30 percent of those who reenlisted after their first tour. While women still constitute only 6 percent of enlisted personnel, their numbers doubled between mid–1973 and the end of 1976.

To bring in the necessary recruits, the Pentagon launched a massive advertising campaign, spending $95 million on television, radio, print and billboards in 1975 alone. Recruiters were placed under intense pressure to meet monthly quotas by resorting to hard-sell techniques and sometimes to outright fraud. Still, there have been indications in recent months that even in a depressed economy, military life is unattractive to a great majority of young Americans. The Marine Corps reported that it was able to sign up only 75 percent of the necessary personnel last October and November, while the Army reported a 10 percent recruiting short fall for the same period.

These recruiting problems, coupled with the rising interest in union representation within the ranks, suggest the service life still falls short. Salaries are substantially higher than they were, but the restrictive and irksome military environment has not been significantly changed. When a GI drags a mortar over hill and dale on perpetual bivouac, after being promised training as a heavy equipment operator, disaffection sets in rather quickly. In fact, statistics show that the bad discharge rate, AWOLs, and non-judicial punishment in most branches of the armed services is alarmingly *higher* today than it was the peak of Vietnam dissidence. In the Navy, for example, non-judicial punishments are twice as common today as they were four years ago. More than 80,000 GIs received less-than-honorable discharges in 1975, and at the current rate, one soldier in eight can expect such a discharge in any year.

Rather than defusing discontent, the "new military" seems to have created new problems previously associated with civilian—not military—labor. When former Army captain Ron Shauninger conducted an informal survey of more than 5,000 soldiers on the West Coast last year, he found that most, regardless of rank, favored some sort of union. "Lower-ranking troops tended to favor more aggressive types of union representation, but I was surprised to find that about a third supported striking under certain conditions," he reported.

The reaction to such findings has not been surprising. Senator Strom Thurmond, South Carolina Republican, has reintroduced a bill which would make it a crime for any active-duty soldier, reservist, or even retiree, to join a labor union. This legislation, which has twenty-four Senator co-sponsors, also provides the penalty of imprisonment for union officials who enroll such persons. "Effective military force is built upon a foundation of discipline, command authority, patriotism, and quick response; unionization would mean the end of an effective defense in this country," Thurmond says.

A network of well-heeled organizations on the Right has launched a propaganda effort under the direction of Americans Against Union Control of Government. It has ties to the National Right to Work Committee, which has waged a long and successful "open shop" campaign.

However, there are apparently some within the Government—even within the Pentagon itself—who understand the potential usefulness of a union in "disciplining" the military workforce and channeling discontent. One position paper prepared by the Army's General Counsel's office argues that the best approach may be to "accept the union and then regulate it." This is, in essence, also the position of the AFGE's executive council. The union's top lawyer has proposed restrictions which would include a voluntary "no-strike" pledge, non union shop, complete political neutrality, and no involvement in "purely military matters," such as command tactics or the "integrity of the chain of command."

Everyone would stand to gain something from such an arrangement, except perhaps the rank and file GI whose pleas for justice might become lost in the shuffle. The Pentagon would gain a "partner" in disciplining its uniformed workforce. The AFGE would gain dues payments and numerical strength from those who believe a weak union better than none. The AFGE might bargain in good faith on behalf of GIs, but if it lacked the clout to enforce its demands, it could expect no more success than it achieved for its civilian members in wage board negotiations last year. Their 4.8 percent average pay gain was well below the rate of inflation.

This dilemma has prompted, among progressives concerned with GI organizing, an important debate over how to respond to an AFGE unionization drive. So far, three distinct viewpoints have emerged. The first holds that since bureaucratic and conservative unions like the AFGE have never offered real leadership on such issues as racism and sexism, much less on militarism or imperialism, their efforts to sign up soldiers should be ignored or flatly opposed. Any such GI union, it is argued, will only co-opt or obstruct political struggles that may arise in the future.

A second group advocated support for the principle of unionization, which attempting at the same time to work with "politically advanced" GIs who will ensure that the union that eventually emerges is the "right one." This approach is quite similar to an old bugaboo of the American labor movement—dual unionism.

A third point of view sees the organization of GIs into a trade union as a potentially progressive step and urges support for the AFGE's drive, whatever its shortcomings. GI organizers who participate in the drive from the outset could introduce issues from below. In this fashion, a militant union could evolve—one capable of fighting for the human needs of its members. This would go a long way toward creating a thinking soldier—one who might ultimately decide that aggression of the sort practiced by the United States in Indochina is not consistent with "national security."

From *The Progressive*, vol. 41, no. 3, 1977.
Reprinted by permission of The Progressive, Inc.

Support Still Strong for Military Union

An April survey of 21,000 active-duty GIs conducted by Citizen Soldier, a military rights organization, once again has indicated that strong pro-union sentiment exists among many GIs today.

The survey, in the form of an eight page tabloid newspaper, was mailed to uniformed members of all service branches at American military installations around the world. The newspaper presented a brief history of the American trade union movement, with particular emphasis on public employee unionism. Along with an analysis of some of the problems and issues facing enlisted GIs today, it contained a questionnaire that solicited each reader's opinion of the controversial issue of unionization.

To date, Citizen Soldier has received questionnaires from 2 percent of those polled, considered a good rate of return. Overall, 43 percent of the respondents states that they favored a soldiers' union. An additional 34 percent checked the "undecided" column, requesting more information. Only 21 percent were flatly opposed.

Of the total number of respondents, 78 percent were from the enlisted ranks, while 17 percent were officers. This corresponds roughly to the proportion of officers to enlisted personnel in the military as a whole. Not surprisingly, the lower ranking enlisted members registered the greatest degree of support for a union (61 percent) but middle and senior level non-commissioned officers also demonstrated considerable pro-union sentiment 41 percent "yes" and 41 percent "undecided." Even among the lower echelons of the officer corps (lieutenants, captains and warrant officers) only half of the respondents were opposed to unionization under any circumstances.

A number of soldiers and sailors attached personal notes and letters to their survey forms:

An Airman Stationed in Germany: *I was a union member (Brewery Workers) before I joined ... due to a layoff and faced with debts. I enlisted—the same old story. I'm disgusted with all this talk of great benefits, job satisfaction and how*

Support Still Strong for Military Union

the chain of command will solve all your gripes. I realize that we can't have a union with the powers the one at the brewery had, however, we need a voice. I don't know where they come up with statistics that only 30 percent of the Air Force favor unionization—it's bull. I firmly believe a union would benefit all military members.

A soldier in Texas: *I have a long career behind me ... be damned sure these grievances don't fall into the wrong hands. A change is long overdue when the Secretary of Defense can deprive the military of their rights. We do as much as anyone to preserve the Constitution ... yet we're not entitled to the rights we fight and die to preserve. Remove from commanders the often abused power of "administrative action" such as "control rosters," and "administrative discharges" which rob the individual of his day in court.... We need a strong and clear signal sent to Congress that we are sick and tired of seeing them strip away our benefits one by one.*

A soldier in Germany: *I agree with you 100 percent that soldiers need a union, especially the lower-ranking enlisted men ... if the people knew half of the story over here, what we have to go through, cramped living conditions, greasy food, undue harassment ... tell me the New Army works and I'll tell you it sucks. Don't get me wrong, we work our asses off—sometimes until nine at night. And for what? About 96 bucks a week by my pay. When I get out, they can find someone else, some other sucker that a recruiter lied to—just like they lied to me. After all, we're just human robots, we don't have any rights ... just a number.*

Air Force Sergeant, Washington State: *How many people share the bathroom where you reside? Your dining room? Your bedroom? Does your salary rise with each cost of living? Do you receive overtime pay? Must you wear a uniform? Do you have an adequate promotion system? These are only a few of the grievances I have. They are sufficient grounds for the AFGE to unionize the armed forces.*

Sailor aboard ship, Atlantic: *If you think I'm bitter, you're right. I just don't care anymore. I have three years left before I can retire and I'll only be an E-5 since I can't pass the written test with a high enough score.... I could write a book about how money and manpower is wasted ... only in the Navy would a man have to wear a coat and tie while he ties up a ship's lines.*

In These Times, July 6–12, 1977

Prospects for a Military Union Setback

Congress Is Out to Prevent Any Form of Military Organizing

The effort to unionize the armed forces suffered a major setback in early September when it was announced that locals of the American Federation of Government Employees (AFGE), the union contemplating the drive, had voted four to one against implementing the controversial unionization plan.

AFGE's decision was apparently influenced by the near unanimous opposition to military unions that had been gathering momentum on Capitol Hill and in the Pentagon. Many AFGE members were also reluctant to undertake a new organizing commitment because they feel the union is not doing an adequate job representing its current membership.

In the two months before AFGE called it quits both the Defense Department and the Senate Armed Services Committee launched comprehensive attacks on unionizing activity by uniformed service members.

On August 15, Defense Secretary Harold Brown issued a new set of regulations designed to severely cripple, if not totally suppress, any organizing attempt. The new regulations prohibit commanders from bargaining with any group representing GIs, and bars individual soldiers from conducting strikes, work stoppages or any concerted activity that "obstructs or interferes with the performance of military assignments."

In the Senate, South Carolina's Strom Thurmond attacked Brown's administrative directive for not going far enough, and introduced a bill to outlaw military unions. The report accompanying his bill (S-274) offers Thurmond's reasoning: The directives, while suggesting the urgency of the problem, cannot provide direct sanctions against the unions themselves.

Brown, however, defended his preference for regulations by arguing that legislative efforts would be more vulnerable to "adverse court decisions" that might lead to greater restrictions on the military's ability to suppress union activity than exists at present.

Thurmond's bill, however, with 50 Senate co-sponsors, has the lead in the race to outlaw GI efforts toward self-organizing and labor's desire to expand its territory. S-274 was unanimously approved by Thurmond's colleagues on the Armed Services Committee, including two erstwhile "doves," Gary Hart (D–Colo.) and Tom Culver (D–Ia).

On September 16, the bill was approved by the full Senate, with only three "no" votes (McGovern, Metcalf, and Abourezk). The AFL/CIO, according to one Senate staffer, made "no effort" to defeat the anti-union measure.

The bill now moves to the House where no significant opposition is anticipated. Jimmy Carter has taken no public position on the legislation.

The implications of the Thurmond legislation are much broader than they appear to be on first reading, say critics, who argue that the bill poses a threat to the rights of GIs, trade unionists and civilian organizers. Specifically, they charge that rights to free speech, assembly, association and petition are seriously undermined by the bill's terms.

The bill, they say, is also an attack on the network of anti-militarist activists and counselors that has grown since the antiwar activities of the '60s. This loosely coordinated network has provided individual service members with support and representation in conflicts with the command structure.

Thurmond's bill strikes at these groups by presenting a sweeping definition of "labor organizations." Under the bill any group that has as one of its objectives, "the participation in the process of resolving individual complaints or grievances in the chain of command," is deemed a "labor organization" and subject to the act's criminal sanctions.

Not only can't unions sign up GIs as members, but the existing right of National Guard and Reserve "technicians" to union representation will also be withdrawn under S-274's provisions. This will affect over 60,000 federal employees who work in "dual status" where membership in a Guard or Reserve unit with part-time duty in uniform is a condition of employment. Warning that this "germ of unionization" might infect the whole military, the bill strips these workers of their union membership and contracts.

The anti-union campaign in Congress has been assisted by the public relations efforts of two far-right organizations: Americans Against Union Control of Government and the Heritage Foundation's American's Against Big Labor. Using mail and polling techniques originally developed by the George Wallace campaigns, these two groups mailed millions of "opinion surveys" that condemn the "unchecked menace" of public employee unionism. Soliciting the addressee's response to heavily biased questions like, "Should soldiers disobey lawful orders due to demands from union officials?," the "survey" includes a strong pitch by Senator Jesse Helms (R-NC) and Jake Garn (R–Utah) for funds to operate a multi-million dollar anti-union crusade.

However the anti-union legislation fares in the months ahead, military union proponents say that it will not alter the underlying conditions of military life that spawn pro-union sentiments. "It will do no good for Congress," says AFGE's President Ken Blaylock, "to ban unionization and proceed headlong, ignoring signals being sent by rank and file military personnel." Such signals, observers say, are flashing brighter than ever, with the frequency of unit-level punishments, volume of AWOLs, and rates of attrition prior to completion of normal duty tours, all at near record levels.

During the Vietnam War, proponents argue, the resistance of soldiers, including the ultimate refusal to carry out combat missions in the field, didn't depend upon directives from union stewards or civilian "agitators." While perhaps not as consciously "political" as their wartime predecessors, today's young trooper seems even less willing to endure the arbitrariness of command authority.

In an essay on contemporary service life, Professor Ezra S. Krendel refers to recent Navy research that studied criteria for enlistment among 16 to 22 year olds. It found that "fate control," or dislike for authoritarian leadership, petty regulations, and the illicit use of power, was the main consideration in any enlistment decision. If this is so, then we've not heard the last word on military unions from those who are directly affected.

In These Times, September 28–October 4, 1977

Coalition Organizes Against Senate Bill

Designed to prohibit military unions, S-274 is so broad that it would prohibit almost any kind of support activity.

Seven national organizations engaged in protecting the legal and economic rights of American service members have formed a coalition to fight a bill (S-274) that they believe would abridge the Constitutional rights of both GIs and their civilian supporters.

The Washington office of the American Civil Liberties Union, the Center for National Security Studies, CCCO (Philadelphia), Citizen Soldier, *Enlisted Times* newspaper, the National Lawyers Guild, and the national president of the Association of Civilian (Guard) Technicians, have banded together in an effort to defeat the legislation in the House of Representatives.

Ostensibly designed "to prohibit the unionization of the armed forces," S-274 so broadly defines "labor organizations" that any group that assists individual soldiers with their grievances could be subjected to criminal prosecution. If S-274 becomes law, the coalition argues, such traditional GI organizing activities as discharge counseling, paralegal representation *vis a vis* administrative boards, not to mention the overt political associations formed by GIs and civilians during the Vietnam War, will become illegal. In addition, the mere advocacy of any collective action or self-organization for GIs would be outlawed.

Initial activities of the coalition include polling members of Congress as to their attitudes on this legislation. Few Representatives seem to have any understanding of the issues raised by the bill. Educational work will be combined with lobbying in the weeks ahead to identify potential allies.

In January the coalition plans a briefing for congressional staff members. Constitutional law experts and GI organizers will present arguments against the legislation. A campaign to mobilize the nation's law professors against S-274 is also being launched.

The coalition has established national offices at 600 Pennsylvania Avenue, SE, Washington, D.C. 20003.

In These Times, December 6–12, 1977

Unorganizing GIs

After months of vacillation and internal conflict, the national leadership of the American Federation of Government Employees, (AFGE), announced early in September that it was abandoning plans to organize members of the U.S. armed forces. Citing a four-to-one opposition vote by AFGE locals across the country, President Ken Blaylock declared that the union would not organize GIs now or "at any time in the foreseeable future." The decision represents a complete turnabout since the 1976 AFGE convention, when Blaylock fought for, and won, the constitutional authority to bring soldiers into the union. (See "A Union of Soldiers," *The Progressive*, March 1977.)

The union's talk of organizing soldiers had provoked intense opposition from both Pentagon and key Congressional committees. In the two months before the AFGE threw in the towel, both the Department of Defense and the Senate Armed Services Committee had mounted comprehensive legal attacks on any union activity by members of the armed forces.

On August 15, Defense Secretary Harold Brown announced regulations designed to limit severely, if not totally suppress, any organizing initiative by GIs or public employee unions acting on their behalf. The new regulations prohibit commanders from negotiation with any group representing soldiers and bar individual soldiers from conducting strikes, work stoppages, or other concerted activity that "obstructs or interferes with the performance of military assignments." Mere membership in a union is forbidden if the organization "presents a clear danger to discipline, loyalty or obedience to lawful orders."

Senator Strom Thurmond of South Carolina, leader of the anti-union forces in Congress, attacked Secretary Brown's regulations for not going far enough, and asked the Carter Administration to support his bill (S.274), which would make virtually all GI union activity illegal and impose criminal sanction for mere membership. Brown defended his preference for regulations over legislation by warning that the latter would be more vulnerable to "adverse court decisions" that could curb the military's ability to suppress union activity.

But, Thurmond's bill had fifty co-sponsors, and on September 16, S.274 was approved by the full Senate with only three dissenting votes. The bill now goes to the House where easy passage is predicted.

At stake in these efforts are fundamental questions concerning the constitutional rights of GIs to freedom of speech, association and privacy, as well as the rights of civilian society in its control of the military.

S.274 is designed not only to outlaw normal trade union activity in the armed forces, but also to strike a blow at any civilian group which might try to protect soldiers whose political or civil rights come under attack from the command. The bill does this by defining as a "labor organization" any group which has as among its objectives, "participation; in the process of resolving individual complaints or grievances in the chain of command." Thus, any civilian counselor who discussed a military-related grievance with an individual soldier could be prosecuted for committing a felony.

When AFGE president Blaylock was summoned before the Senate Armed Services Committee to defend his union's overtures to GIs, he promised the legislators that the AFGE would voluntarily surrender its representation of soldiers should a "national emergency" be declared. But a report accompanying S.274 advocated criminal sanctions and explicitly rejects the promises of labor leaders that they would withdraw in "time of war." As the report makes clear, S.274 is intended to give the military free rein, especially when the "necessity for emergency action" exists.

The bill would further isolate military society from such civilian institutions as labor unions by withdrawing the hard-won union recognition enjoyed by 60,000 civilian "technicians" of the National Guard.

The anti-union juggernaut in Congress has been assisted by the massive propaganda efforts of two organizations on the far Right—Americans Against Union Control of Government and Americans Against Big Labor. Using the direct-mail and polling techniques originally developed by the George Wallace campaign, these groups have flooded America's mailboxes with millions of "opinion surveys" warning against the "unchecked menace of union bosses," and soliciting responses to such loaded questions as, "Should soldiers disobey lawful orders from officers due to demands from union officials?" The "surveys" are accompanied by a strong pitch for funds to build a multi-million dollar anti-labor war chest. Any member of Congress who has felt the wrath of the "right-to-life" movement or the gun lobby is forewarned.

In February 1977, an Air Force study of enlisted and officer attitudes toward unionization was finally made public, following a freedom-of-information demand by *The Washington Post*. The study found that 36 percent of the enlisted airmen surveyed would join a union immediately, while another 32 percent were "undecided" about membership. Last spring, Citizen Soldier, a public interest organization working for GI rights, mailed a similar poll to 21,000 active-duty service branches. The results showed even stronger pro-union sentiment: 61 percent of the low-ranking soldiers and sailors favored immediate unionization, while middle-level and senior noncommissioned officers were only somewhat less pro union (41 percent: yes, 41 percent: undecided). Even among the lower echelons of the officer corps—lieutenants and captains—only half were flatly opposed to unionizing.

Citizen Soldier organizers conducted follow-up interviews with selected respondents, particularly the career NCOs, and found a striking degree of dissatisfaction and anger over conditions in the U.S. military. Erosion of pay and withdrawal of promised benefits were common complaints, but frustration with a "crisis of leadership" was also evident. The lower-ranking GIs tended to identify housing, assignment policies and problems with the military justice system as their biggest complaints.

Anti-union measures aimed at deepening the isolation of soldiers from the rights and values of civilian society will certainly not eliminate such grievances. Congress may be forgetting too soon one of the important lessons of the Vietnam War—that GI resistance can be a powerful force.

From *The Progressive*, vol. 41, no. 12, 1977.
Reprinted by permission of The Progressive, Inc.

A Victim of the Tests[1]

From the end of World War II until well into the 1960's, the U.S. Government detonated hundreds of nuclear devices at test sites in the western United States and the South Pacific. Tens of thousands of American servicemen were deployed at these tests, apparently in an attempt to "orient" them to nuclear warfare." Now, twenty years later, there is mounting evidence that GIs who were exposed to radiation at the tests are contracting leukemia and passing birth defects to their children at several times the normal rate.

One of the shocking cases to come to light in recent months is that of Sergeant Paul Cooper of Emmet, Idaho, who has been hospitalized since last September with incurable leukemia. Cooper participated in a nuclear test code-named "Operation Smokey" at Yucca Flats, Nevada, on August 31, 1957. He was in an advance party of 107 soldiers who were stationed only a mile-and-a-half from Ground Zero. Another 3,000 troops were deployed further back, at distance from two-and-a-half to eight miles.

Because Cooper is now too sick to be interviewed we talked with his wife Nancy, who gave the following account: Since the bomb to be detonated was about twice the strength of those dropped on Hiroshima and Nagasaki, it was placed atop a 750-foot steel tower in an apparent attempt to lessen the impact of the blast upon the immediate area. Like the other soldiers at the test site, Cooper wore no protective clothing—just his regular fatigue uniform and helmet. When the countdown began, the troops were told to lie on the open ground with their hands cupped over their eyes.

After the bomb was detonated, Cooper's unit was ordered to march toward Ground Zero. Nancy Cooper reported her husband's recollection of the steel tower. "It had melted into a twenty-foot-high red glowing blob." As the men marched forward, the heat became intense. Cooper said they stopped at a point where "it was like getting too close to a campfire with tight Levis on." He noticed that all the Atomic Energy Commission officials in the area were wearing elaborate protective clothing, hoods and gloves.

Before the explosion, AEC officials had briefed the troops, assuring

236

them that there was no danger and that they would be regularly monitored for any aftereffects. The promise of new uniforms after the test went unfulfilled. "I guess they didn't want to spend the thirty bucks that a new set of fatigues and boots cost back then," Cooper is quoted as saying.

Sergeant Cooper never heard from any Federal agency after the test, despite the fact that he served another seventeen years in the Army before he retired. Only after his claim to the Veterans Administration for disability payments for his leukemia condition attracted national publicity did the Army and nuclear safety personnel get in touch with him.

The Defense Department has joined with other Federal agencies to organize a crash study of the radioactive effects suffered by veterans of Operation Smokey. Of the 500 participants located at this writing, eight are known to have incurable leukemia—vastly higher than the normal rate. It is probable that more cases will be uncovered as more veterans are identified.

Today, Nancy Cooper waits at home with her three children. "I haven't seen Paul since September," she told us. "He was such a strong and determined man. He told his sister he didn't want us to see him as he is; he wants us to remember him as he was."

From *The Progressive*, vol. 42, no. 3, 1978.
Reprinted by permission of The Progressive, Inc.

Note

1. Citizen Soldier's campaigns on behalf of the Atomic Vets and the Agent Orange Vets were documented by Tod Ensign and myself in a series of articles that culminated in the publication of *G.I. Guinea Pigs*. By way of example, two of those articles are reprinted here.

Blowing the Whistle on Agent Orange

Maude de Victor works behind a cold, steel gray desk in the Benefits Section of the Veterans Administration regional office in Chicago. She is not your average paper shuffler. In recent months, Maude de Victor has joined the select ranks of whistle blowers—those heroic individuals who discover an outrage and, in defiance of bureaucracy or suppression, bring it to public notice.

The outrage Maude de Victor discovered was the shocking effect of dioxin poisoning of American veterans who came into contact with the herbicides that were used to defoliate more than five million acres of the Vietnamese countryside between 1962 and 1971. Her efforts have not only focused attention on the plight of these latest victims of the Vietnam War, but have also raised new warning against the domestic hazards posed by the herbicides.

Massive defoliation was a major tactic pursued by U.S. forces in Vietnam. It had two objectives—to deny guerrillas their jungle cover, and to destroy food crops so that the peasantry would be compelled to take refuge in controlled resettlement camps. The most widely used defoliant was Agent Orange, a mix of 2,4-D and 2,4,5-T, two herbicides used in the United States for many years to control crops and forest growth and to clear vegetation along roads and railroad tracks.

Dioxin—its full name is tetrachloro-dibenzoparadioxin, or TCDD—often appears as a by-product in the manufacture of trichlorophenol, from which 2,4,5-T is made. Dioxin is one of the most toxic contaminants known to humankind. Among the symptoms associated with exposure to the substance are a skin disorder called chloracne, liver abscesses, spontaneous miscarriages, numbing of limbs, reduced sex drive, personality changes and, defects among the children of those exposed. Dioxin poisoning is believed to have caused many birth defects in Vietnam in recent years, and a host of ailments among those who suffered exposure.

Maude de Victor, a thirty-eight-year-old black woman, had never heard of Agent Orange or dioxin when she took a random telephone call about a year ago from the wife of a Vietnam veteran named Charles Owens. Her husband, Mrs. Owens said, was dying of cancer, and he blamed it on "those chemicals from Vietnam." Four months later, Mrs. Owens called again to say that her husband had died—and that her claim for survivor's benefits had been refused by the VA.

That second call prompted Maude de Victor to try to find out about the chemicals which Charles Owens believed had caused his fatal illness. She called the office of the Air Force Surgeon General and spoke to Captain Alvin Young, who she points out, holds a Ph.D. degree in plant physiology. Young briefed her thoroughly on the U.S. military's defoliation program in Vietnam and on the symptoms believed to be associated with dioxin contamination.

Most of what we know about the toxic effects of dioxin on human beings has been learned from studying the victims of industrial accidents at plants producing trichlorophenol—especially the notorious accident in July 1976 at Seveso, Italy, where inhabitants were thoroughly doused with the poison. But there have been relatively few laboratory studies to determine the effects on animal systems of less concentrated exposure, and of dioxin's reported tendency to accumulate in the body's fatty tissue. One scientist who has conducted such experiments, Professor Val Woodward of the University of Minnesota, has asserted, "One thing is clear ... 2,4,5-T is a very effective teratogen [fetus-deforming agent]. It deforms mice in laboratory situations, and very clearly human beings who have been sprayed have a higher incidence of these deformities than people who were not sprayed."

Maude de Victor recalls that Captain Young described several major Vietnamese defoliation programs, such as Operation Ranch Hand, and that he said there was "no doubt" that anyone who participated in those operations would have been contaminated.

At this point, Maude de Victor was no longer merely following the bureaucratic routine of her job. She had a special reason for taking a special interest: In the 1950s, while serving with the Navy medical corps, she attended women with uterine cancer who were receiving experimental treatments with radium pellets. Twenty years later, she learned that she had breast cancer.

She underwent a mastectomy and has been given a clean bill of health, but she suspects that long-ago exposure to radiation may have induced her cancer.

At the VA, Maude de Victor receives an average of seventy telephone calls and personally interviews about fifteen veterans each day. After her talk with Captain Young, she began posing some questions to her clients: "You been in Vietnam? Got any kind of rash? Have any children with deformities?" Often they answered, "Yeah, how'd you know?"

With her supervisor's permission, she began logging these cases. In the first two months of 1978, she accumulated twenty-seven examples of this new disability. Her informal queries at the Veterans Hospital turned up about thirty more—all from the Chicago area. Suddenly, without explanation, her boss ordered her to stop logging potential dioxin poisoning cases; apparently, the higher levels of the VA were becoming concerned. Maude de Victor decided to tell what she had learned to a television news correspondent.

On March 23, WBBM, the CBS television affiliate in Chicago, aired an hour-long documentary featuring interviews with ailing veterans, research scientists, and the Air Force's Captain Young. Before the television cameras, he was less certain about the possible hazards of dioxin poisoning than he had been in conversation with de Victor. When asked about alleged dangers from 2,4,5-T, he said, "I don't think there is any supportive evidence."

Dow Chemical, a major herbicide manufacturer, released a statement after the broadcast denying any connection with alleged birth defects. Relying on a National Academy of Sciences study conducted in 1974, Dow asserted that "no conclusive evidence [exists] of association between exposure to herbicides and birth defects in South Vietnam." The statement made no mention of possible links between 2,4,5-T and ailments suffered by veterans, and Dow said it "fully supports further epidemiological studies of military personnel who have health problems associated with service in Vietnam." In previous statements, Dow had claimed the dioxin content in its herbicide was insignificant.

Scientists disagree about whether there are safe levels of dioxin exposure, and whether dioxins enter the human food chain and are stored in the body's fatty tissues. Using a solution far less toxic than that found in either Agent Orange or the 2,4,5-T herbicides used in the United States today, Dr. James Allen of the University of Wisconsin found that "low-level consumption even as low as five parts per trillion of dioxin in the diet was capable of causing an increased incidence of tumors in experimental animals."

Though Maude de Victor did not know it, American environmentalists have been fighting against the use of contaminated defoliants at home and abroad for years. While Vietnam was being defoliated, there was a sharp corresponding increase in the use of the same herbicides by state and local agencies. Since 1960, the U.S. Forest Service has made increasing use of defoliants containing 2,4,5-T in national parks and forests across the country.

For years this spraying program went unnoticed and unprotested, but in 1974 a group of citizens in northern Wisconsin banded together as the Chequamegon Concerned Citizens to fight the spraying of the two national forests near their homes. John Stauber, one of the group's founders, recalls, "We collected over two thousand signatures against the spraying in a short period. We really caught the Forest Service by surprise, they weren't used to dealing with opposition." Wisconsin's Attorney General entered the dispute and won a Federal court injunction against spraying on grounds where no proper environmental impact statements had been filed. In early 1977, the injunction was withdrawn after the state and the National Forest Service agreed on some ecological safeguards.

Around the country, groups have formed in a number of states to organize opposition to the continued use of herbicides. In February 1978, representatives from sixteen state groups met in Washington and formed the Citizens National Forest Coalition to coordinate and direct the fight against uncontrolled use of herbicides. Its goal was to win a national ban on all products containing 2,4,5-T and to seek an "ecologically sound and integrated forest management system."

One of the most active coalition members, the Citizens Against Toxic Spraying (CATS), has initiated a major court suit in Oregon which has stopped, for the time being, herbicidal spraying on Federal lands in that state.

Barry Commoner, the disgruntled environmental scientist, believes the burden of proof should rest with manufacturers of the herbicides—and with Government agencies that sanction use of the chemicals—to demonstrate beyond reasonable doubt that they are safe. He told WBBM, "It may well be found [that] soldiers who were exposed to dioxin in Vietnam accumulated [it] in their body fat with no symptoms ... except immediate skin symptoms. Let's say ten years later they become sick and lose weight. They would break down that fat, releasing dioxin into the body, and then symptoms would appear."

Commoner has proposed that when Vietnam veterans are interviewed for the 1980 Census, questions about possible dioxin exposure be included. "It is simply another cost of the war in Vietnam which we are going to have to pay, even this late," he says.

Michael Adams, a twenty-nine-year-old resident of Evanston, Illinois, is already paying the price. He served in Vietnam ten years ago as a combat engineer with the Twenty-fifth Division, and one of his duties was to clear forested area for base camps in the Central Highlands. Often his unit sprayed Agent Orange on the dense vegetation, using hand-pumps, and several times he watched as refitted C-123 aircraft sprayed defoliants on his unit's area of operation. Mike Adams believes he was exposed to the toxic herbicide during these operations.

Soon after he returned from Vietnam, large pimple-like sores began to form on his face. An Army medic told him they were "razor bumps" that could easily be removed, but the sores have persisted and are probably a form of chloracne, a common symptom of dioxin exposure. After his discharge in 1972, Adams began to experience numbness in his arms and shoulders. He had difficulty sleeping, and in the past two years he has lost more than sixty pounds. He also believes he has undergone a personality change: "Before I went to the 'Nam, I was an easy going, cheerful type; now, I often feel on edge and will blow up over just any little thing," he says.

Milton Ross, a twenty-nine-year-old computer programmer from Matteson, Illinois, who served two tours in Vietnam, is also paying the price. Not only does he suffer from some of the symptoms of dioxin poisoning, but his six-year-old son, Richard, conceived after Ross's return from overseas, was born with the last joints of his fingers and toes either deformed or missing. Ross and his first wife had a study made of their own genetic histories for possible explanations of their son's condition. The research uncovered no genetic disorders on either side.

Ross, who served with the Fifth Special Forces in the Central Highlands, told us, "Although I wasn't involved in the spraying operations, I was sprayed upon. The possibilities for exposure were unlimited. They sprayed a lot around the perimeter at Kon Tum, and often the wind would blow the clouds right over our camp." Ross has not been able to work since January, when he was hospitalized for a suspected heart condition, another possible consequence of dioxin exposure.

After he was interviewed on WBBM, Ross began hearing from other Chicago area veterans who also suspect they may be victims of Agent Orange. They are considering the formation of an organization that will battle the VA for disability benefits. Maude de Victor estimates that the Chicago VA has now received more than 500 calls, mostly from Illinois, from veterans reporting difficulties and requesting information and disability claim forms.

Both Milton Ross and Maude de Victor charge the VA is dragging its feet on these claims. "They've refused to examine these men; they haven't called them in," Ross complains. "I've gone over their heads to Washington and they tell me there'll be some results in a couple of months.

"The VA doesn't even have any rating criteria for chemical disabilities,"

Maude de Victor points out. "They're not doing anything on these cases because they don't have any standards for evaluation. Each case is either denied outright or 'diaried'—that is, placed in a computer where it's programmed to pop up every sixty days for re-review."

Meanwhile, de Victor is suffering the common fate of whistle blowers. She is excluded from staff meetings; "VA doesn't tell me anything anymore," she says.

From *The Progressive*, vol. 42, no. 6, 1978.
Reprinted by permission of The Progressive, Inc.

Excerpt from *G.I Guinea Pigs: How the Pentagon Exposed Our Troops to Dangers More Deadly Than War*

Introduction

In the last decade, the public's attitude about the development and use of science has undergone profound transformation. Gone are the days when a euphoric citizenry would sit transfixed before televised images of the astronauts taking mankind's first steps on the moon.

In the years before that dazzling event, each scientific discovery was acclaimed as a boost to national pride and potency—and, of course, private industry was quick to exploit each scientific "breakthrough" by marketing new products and services. Rare indeed was the scientist or public official who dared to raise questions about the environmental or social hazards presented by many of these scientific and commercial triumphs.

At first, only a handful of "health faddists" and "eco-freaks" bothered to learn about the havoc being wreaked upon the environment by many of these new products and technologies. When they warned that the earth's delicate eco-system was being irreversibly damaged by the uncontrolled use of pollutants, they were dismissed as "effete snobs" who wanted to turn back the clock by crippling economic growth.

The average American, weaned on the irresistible logic of economic growth, tended to regard ecological concerns as an exotic pastime, purchased only by those with the leisure and money to indulge such lofty ideals. The slow seepage of radioactive waste into a town's water supply was at first perceived as a threat by those who lived only miles away. The death of western poet Billie Shoecraft, after she was accidentally sprayed with a herbicide commonly used for forest and crop control, was regarded as an aberration unique to a particular community. Too many workers, particularly in the construction and energy industries, the environmentalists' protests seemed like callous invitations to join the ranks of the unemployed.

Rachel Carson's book, *Silent Spring* (1962) was the first exposé about the toxic effect of chemicals (DDT) to reach a mass audience. And as evidence of other environmental disasters accumulated throughout the Sixties, the number of concerned citizens grew proportionately. Ultimately came the dawning realization that each of us is being zapped by a growing barrage of gamma rays, microwaves, and X-rays, pesticides, preservatives, and ten thousand other chemicals. Even the basic staples of life are no longer safe— neither the air we breathe, the water we drink, nor the food we eat. Indeed the morning dew, age-old symbol of freshness and purity, is slowly turning to acid as a thousand pollutants infect the atmosphere. While the more industrialized societies are experiencing the effects of this massive poisoning first, eventually it will affect the entire human family.

Today, there is growing evidence that issues like radiation exposure and herbicide poisoning, to name just two apocalyptic vectors crisscrossing the nation, are beginning to get the hearing they deserve in that mythic realm of the pollsters, Middle America.

Opinion polls document the public's belief that the quality of life has badly deteriorated in recent years. The powerful myth that economic growth and scientific breakthroughs per se equals "progress" has begun to erode as an article of national faith, and coupled with this is a growing distrust of corporate and governmental decision making.

Of all the institutions, public or private, which have played a role in the development of science over the past forty years, none has been more active than the Pentagon. More than half of all scientific research in the United States today is financed wholly or in part by the Department of Defense, and the scope of funded research extends far beyond activities one would normally associate with the military mission. It is well known, for example, that many of the most significant scientific developments of the twentieth century—television, radar, microwave, satellite communication, penicillin, to name just a few—were results of military research.

In these pages, we will examine two products of Pentagon "research"— each claiming it's generation of guinea pigs. First, the program of atmospheric testing of nuclear devices (A- and H-bombs primarily) from 1945 to 1961; and second, the massive defoliation program in Indochina, during which five million acres were repeatedly doused from 1962 to 1971 with over twenty million gallons of highly toxic herbicides.

Before Vietnam deflated a robust tradition of Yankee patriotism, military service was an honorable calling. Young men routinely volunteered to fight to preserve our sacred way of life, no questions asked. Now it appears that a few questions might have been in order, given the generals' willingness to expose millions of GIs to highly dangerous substances and then justify such risk on the basis of "military necessity" and "national security."

The use of troops at the nuclear test blasts in Nevada provides a microcosm of this mentality. When the radiation-exposure standards imposed by the Atomic Energy Commission interfered with the commanders' desire for realistic nuclear battlefield training, they invoked these doctrines to justify taking control of safety standards. By arbitrarily raising the limits of allowable radiation, the Pentagon recklessly exposed the soldiers to even higher doses of radiation.

The toll for this lack of concern for the welfare of both GIs and civilians has only begun to be tallied in recent years. Today, countless World War II and Korean War vets may be suffering from disproportionately high rates of radiation induced cancers and leukemia. The hell-bent-for-leather, zap-the-Japs decision to drop the Big One in 1945 is finally bringing Hiroshima home to the American Heartland.

Unlike their counterparts from earlier wars, it has taken only a few years for the deteriorating bodies of Vietnam veterans to begin to tell the story of Vietnam in the only language that seems able to penetrate the consciousness of most Americans—the language of Death. Thousands of young vets who should be at the peak of physical health are instead coming apart at the seams. Some say there was just too much trauma to the collective psyche of all those zip-gun and deer-rifle warriors caught flatfooted in the Asian jungles, and proceeding on this assumption, the Veterans Administration has become the post-service quartermaster, equipped with its indispensable survival kit—Valium, Thorazine, and a host of other space-out medications, drugging veterans whose faraway eyes say they've never quite returned from Vietnam. But the undiagnosable traumas may not be entirely psychogenic in origin, the product of a million dreams which have mutated. A new culprit has been found, another piece of the puzzle, leading, as these things always do, back to the bigwigs who just couldn't say "No" to another war, no matter what the cost. This is the exposure of countless GIs to poisonous defoliant used in Vietnam.

In communicating their plight, the veteran/victims of radiation illness and herbicide poisoning whose stories are summarized herein will, we hope, win for themselves and others the consideration and relief they deserve. Although much of this book focuses necessarily on the military's abuse of science, the human dimension of the problem emerges in the experiences of America's warriors, who have been treated like so many no-deposit no-return soda bottles; once the contents are consumed, the empties are thrown on the junk heap. If they're lucky, they might get recycled.

The consequences of this massive negligence have been too long denied. Every dog soldier will have his day, and the day of the veteran-guinea pig is approaching. A critical mass of aggrieved victims of both nuclear testing and the defoliation program is rapidly being reached, and the inevitable explosion may have unforeseen results. In the short run, the victims must educate themselves, learn to articulate their experiences, and fight against the forces of anonymity, political impotence, and bureaucratic indifference. In the last analysis, their experience teaches another lesson more difficult to absorb perhaps than the lesson brought home by the abuse of their welfare. Once a nation's military command throws its own soldiers into the path of its weapons of destruction, has it not already forfeited the support of its own people as well as its capacity for defense?

Michael Uhl, Tod Ensign, New York City, 1979

Chapter 7—The Ranch Hands: "Only We Can Prevent Forests..."

It was a suffocatingly hot July day in 1962 when 900 soldiers from the Fourth Infantry Division became the first troops to conduct nuclear maneuvers at the Nevada test site since the Plumb Bob series with its ill-fated "Smoky" shot in 1957. As it turned out, they were also among the last GIs to participate in an atmospheric bomb test. Joining them on the sunbaked desert that day were two high-ranking members of the Kennedy administration—Attorney General Robert Kennedy and General Maxwell Taylor, special military advisor to the president.

These men had taken time from their busy schedules to witness the testing of the new "Davy Crockett" atomic mortar shell. While the Kennedy administration was eager to show the nuclear flag in response to Soviet A-test initiatives, it's likely that the attention of the two men may have strayed to a real life battlefield, 10,000 miles away—Vietnam.

At the time, Kennedy and Taylor were serving as co-chairmen of the Special Group Counter-Insurgency, an ultra-secret planning group created by President Kennedy to organize America's effort to fight revolutionary guerrilla movements in Vietnam and other parts of the world. As two architects of the grand American scheme to intervene in Vietnam squinted into the bright Nevada sun, the first sorties by air-force defoliation planes made lazy arcs over Vietnam's canals and roadways.

John Kennedy had won the presidency by a narrow margin, and he attributed his success in part to his campaign pledge to restore America's military supremacy over the Soviet Union. During the campaign, he had charged that the Eisenhower–Nixon administration had allowed U.S. military strength to erode. In his three years as president, Kennedy substantially boosted military spending in all sectors, including a tripling of spending on the development of weapons for chemical and biological warfare.

It had become an article of faith since World War II that the immense technological capacity and inventiveness of American industry allowed American policy makers to shape, and often control, events in even the remotest corners of the globe. In his inaugural address, John Kennedy asserted not only the ability but the *right* of America to do so. "Let every nation know ... that we shall pay any price, bear any burden, meet any hardship, support any friend, oppose any foe to assure the survival and the success of liberty. This much we pledge—and more."

Over the next fifteen years, this presumptuous arrogance would bring death and destruction to Indochina. Only after a savage bloodletting, in which millions perished and much of Indochina was blasted to smithereens, would it be seriously challenged.

Defoliating agents had been developed originally for use in the South Pacific against the Japanese. These defoliants were to destroy vegetation in order to deny concealment to the enemy and to open up "fields of fire" around defensive positions and along transport routes. They also were to destroy food crops which might be of use to an enemy. But their military debut was delayed when atomic bombs brought World War II to a rapid conclusion.

After the war, army chemists continued to refine the technology by testing over 12,000 different compounds for their defoliating properties. (It wasn't publicized at the time, but Britain enjoys the distinction of being the first country to employ defoliants as a military weapon, using them in its campaign to suppress the communist insurgency in Malaya in the early 1950s.)

It must be stressed that when they decided to utilize chemical warfare in Vietnam, the Kennedys were only expanding upon an American tradition begun at Hiroshima and Nagasaki. After all, once you've poisoned whole cities and sown the heavens with deadly plutonium and other radioactive toxins, who's going to worry about the long-term effects of a few "weed killers"? The relentless development of nuclear weapons contributed to an attitude of moral agnosticism among most, but by no means all, American scientists. Given this moral climate, an entire subcontinent cold be turned into a virtual laboratory for testing terrifying new weapons with scarcely a whimper of protest.

In October 1961, Kennedy's most trusted military adviser, General Maxwell Taylor, returned from an inspection tour of Vietnam with a deeply pessimistic report. The regime of Premier Ngo Dinh Diem was in serious danger from a determined insurgency led by the National Liberation Front. Anxious not to lose an ally to communism, Kennedy resolved to tilt the scales in favor of the Diem government.

Historian Arthur Schlesinger, a Kennedy intimate, reports in *A Thousand Days* that Kennedy made a priority of developing a counter-insurgency program for the U.S. military. He ordered Special Warfare Centers to be established at Fort Bragg (for Green Berets) and at U.S. bases in Panama, Okinawa, Vietnam and West Germany. Among the new programs he personally approved was Operation Hades, code name for a program under which a squadron of cargo planes would defoliate guerrilla-controlled area of Vietnam from the air. According to the military, Operation Hades would "clear jungle growth and reduce the hazards of ambush by Viet Cong forces ... destruction of food [would be] undertaken only in remote and thinly populated areas under Viet Cong control and where significant denial of food supplies can be effected...."

The defoliation scheme had been developed by the Pentagon's Advanced Research Projects Agency (ARPA). In May 1961, teams of scientists from Fort Detrick's plant-science labs were sent to Vietnam as part of Project Agile to conduct field experiments on the susceptibility of Vietnam's flora to various types of defoliants such as 2,4,5-T and 2,4-D. Experts from the Department of Agriculture and the U.S. Forest Service, as well as the air force's armament labs at Eglin Air Force Base, were also called in to lend expert advice. Evidently the project's name, Operation Hades, was too strong even for hardened military stomach, for it was soon changed to Operation Ranch Hand. The satanic theme survived, however, at least on the shoulder patches worn by some Ranch Hands depicting a smiling devil with a pitchfork.

The Pentagon Papers tell us that Kennedy agreed to a substantial increase in U.S. commitment in Vietnam without having pinned Premier Diem down to a unified strategy for fighting the rebels. "By early 1962, however, there was apparent consensus ... that the Strategic Hamlet program represented the unifying concept." By mid–1963, Premier Diem claimed the seven million Vietnamese (nearly half the population) now lived in 7000 such hamlets.

At the time the spray program began, two-thirds of South Vietnam's land surface was covered with forest, much of it extremely dense triple-canopied jungle, This dense foliage afforded the anti-government guerrillas excellent cover and relatively safe bases from which to operate. Furthermore, nearly four-fifths of Vietnam's population (the "hearts and minds" the U.S. so piously urged the Saigon government to win) lived in these rural areas. Over the next nine years, more than a third of this forestland would be sprayed at least once, while at least 15 percent of the croplands also was doused.

Once it was decided to organize a defoliation program, the air force naturally turned to its Special Aerial Flight, a unit that had been flying insect-spray missions since the Korean War, using C-47 cargo planes. They flew missions throughout the United States and the Caribbean whenever aerial spray was needed on an emergency basis. When the air force adopted the two-engine C-123 "Provider" as its basic cargo and troop-transport plane in 1960, the "spray birds," as they were called, switched over to this plane also.

We met some of the original pilots at the twelfth annual reunion of the Vietnam Ranch Hand Association in Fort Walton Beach, Florida, on an October weekend in 1978. The Ranch Hand Association is sort of an alumni club for the men who flew missions with Operation Ranch Hand from 1962 to 1971. Unlike veterans of earlier wars, there've been few reports of Vietnam vets getting together to reminisce about the "good old days"; many of them threw away their uniforms and medals when they came home and tried to forget the whole thing. The men who flew the defoliation missions, however, are apparently an exception. Of the 1200-odd pilots and flight engineers eligible for membership in the Ranch Hand Association, nearly a quarter are on its active mailing list. Every fall, a number of these men travel hundreds, sometimes thousands, of miles to spend a weekend eating, drinking and swapping stories about their exploits on what they affectionately call "the Ranch." At various times during the weekend, we noticed that nearly all of the thirty-odd men attending wore special shirts, scarves and flight suits emblazoned with the Ranch Hand crest—a bright green patch bisected by a defoliated stripe of brown.

One of the pilots we met at the 1978 reunion was William "Robby" Robinson. Robby today is a desk-bound warrior in the battle for insurance sales near Houston, Texas, but for twenty-one years he flew air-force planes, several of those years as a spray pilot. Despite his office pallor, he still retains the rugged bearing of an air-force career officer. Another pilot we met was Jack Spey, the association's president and its principal spark plug. Spey best fits the popular stereotype of the aviator hero—a reincarnation of Terry and the Pirates. Blond, tanned, and trim with boyish good looks just starting to harden around the edges, he talked with enthusiasm about his record eleven years with the defoliation program, Robby and Jack are the two most senior Ranch Hands, still alive and kicking. Together, they flew two of the original six C-123s on their maiden voyage to Vietnam near the end of 1961. Over nonstop screwdrivers, they sat down and reminisced about the birthing of Operation Ranch Hand.

In 1961, Robby told us, one of the men in his spray unit, Captain Mario Cadori, was sent to Vietnam to train the Vietnamese in the techniques of defoliation. According to Robby, Cadori decided, after taking the Vietnamese pilots up on a few test runs, that American pilots would be needed. "He told us that the Vietnamese would fly their planes at the proper altitude, just above the treetops, for a while, then they would start to inch higher, losing the effective spray application." Whether or not the decision to use American spray pilots was based on the alleged cowardice or simple ineptitude of the Vietnamese, the air force actively began to recruit American crew members for Vietnam in the fall of 1961.

Apparently the obsession with "national security" that pervaded the atomic test program carried over to the defoliation project as well. Jack Spey remembers that when the air-force recruiters came to Pope Air Base looking for prospective crew members, they made the applicants sign statements that they wouldn't divulge anything that was said during the interview.

"After all that," Jack said, "they told us precious little about the mission. We didn't even know where we'd be sent if we were picked. Just a few days after we were chosen, we were told to be ready to ship out immediately."

The day after Thanksgiving, 1961, the six C-123s which had been specially refitted for defoliation missions, took off for Vietnam. Designed for troop hauling and cargo, the planes were stripped of all extraneous equipment, and a cylindrical 1000-gallon tank adapted from the B-50 was added. Spray booms with sixteen nozzles each were mounted under each wing and a small gasoline engine was installed to pump the defoliant through pressurized hoses from the tank to the wing racks. (Later, after field testing in Vietnam, a third spray rack was added across the rear, beneath the cargo door.) Each plane's crew consisted of a pilot, copilot and a flight engineer. The engineer rode in the cargo hold and operated the spray machinery. A fourth crew member, a navigator, was added to the lead plane on each mission, to direct the planes to the target.

To accomplish the long trek across the Pacific, extra gas was stored in the defoliant tank. The planes island-hopped, first to Hawaii, then Johnson, Wake and Guam before finally landing at Clark Field in the Philippines. According to Robby, only two planes went on to Vietnam, and the rest remained at Clark because the defoliation program still was a "touchy" situation in diplomatic circles. James Camden of Greenville, South Carolina, was a flight engineer with the original party. He recalls that the Vietnamese would only allow three planes and their crews to be in Vietnam at any one time. This meant that crews had to shuttle back and forth to the Philippines when one group was to relieve another. The spray crews were listed as members of the U.S. Embassy in Saigon.

Just weeks before Robby Robinson and Carl Marshall landed the first C-123s at Tan Son Nhut Airbase, a unit of thirty-three American helicopters and 500 crew members had arrived. This unit represented the first U.S. personnel sent to Vietnam for purposes other than training or technical assistance. When Robinson and Marshall arrived, they were assigned to a hut on the sprawling base. Before long, someone had nailed a plaque over its door with the motto of the Twelfth Air Commando Squadron: It pictured Smoky the Bear with the legend "Only We Can Prevent Forests."

From the beginning, the spray missions operated subject to a complicated set of instructions and procedures, called rules of engagement. Robby remembers that every mission had to be cleared through various levels in the Vietnamese and American command structure, up to, and including, the White House. "After all that," he lamented, "the enemy knew exactly what we were planning and was usually waiting for us when we got there." The complicated rules, called Project Farmgate, created problems. For example, since it was impossible to tell which crops were, in fact, intended for enemy soldiers, crop destruction was disguised as a South Vietnamese activity, and the planes were flown with South Vietnamese markings and with a Vietnamese observer aboard.

The Ranch Hands were presented with an unusual mission in that no country had ever conducted massive defoliation as an instrument of war. "It was all new," Jack Spey remembers. "That's what helped develop our unit's camaraderie and esprit de corps; there weren't any manuals, we had to figure it out for ourselves." So, with good ol' Yankee ingenuity, the small band of pioneering aviators set out to accomplish what no one had ever done before: systematically destroy millions of acres of foliage from the air under combat conditions.

John Lemanski showed up at the reunion wearing a bright purple jumpsuit that would have won the prize for most unusual uniform had one been offered. Large Chinese characters which translated as "purple" (referring to the defoliant called "Agent Purple") were stitched on the back in white thread. Over his heart, John wore the Ranch Hand emblem. John and several buddies had designed the uniform themselves and then sent the patterns to a custom tailor in Hong Kong. John described to us the standard operating procedures for defoliation missions.

Excerpt from G.I. Guinea Pigs

"We'd take off while it was still dark. Arriving near the drop area, we'd circle at a relatively high altitude until the sun came up. Just at daybreak, we'd swoop down over the target. We did this for two reasons: one, to try and keep the enemy gunners off-balance; two, you had to dump early in the day—later on, the intense ground heat would keep the spray from settling properly. We'd return to base, reload, and often make another run before it got too hot.

"The spray operator was a recycled flight mechanic," John continued. "He'd start the twenty-horsepower motor once we were aloft; after checking the valve and hose pressure, he'd radio the pilot that everything was ready. The pilot would activate the spray mechanism once we'd arrive over the target."

Like the other pilots at the reunion, John talked in a casual, offhand way about what must have been some rather hairy flying experiences.

"We'd fly with both cockpit windows and the rear cargo door open. We left the cabin windows open so that a stray round wouldn't shatter the Plexiglas in our faces. Also, the air conditioning didn't work well at low altitudes and it was hot as hell in there. The cargo door was left open so the flight mechanic could visually check the spray pattern. Also, he could throw out smoke grenades to mark 'hot' areas which were giving us fire."

Lemanski emphasized that the spray missions required some very demanding precision flying. "We'd come in over the target in tight formation, sometimes with as many as eight or ten planes flying just above stall speed." Another flyer estimated that the planes were often no more that fifteen or twenty feet apart during spraying.

As the C-123 was intended for cargo hauling, not combat, it carried no armament and had armored plating only in the pilot's cabin. Flying at about half its normal cruising speed—"low and slow" as the Ranch Hands called it—the craft was vulnerable to small-arms fire from the ground. John summed it up: "If the enemy had ever learned to wait and 'lead' the airplane before firing, we'd have been in big trouble."

Robby Robinson remembers flying the very first defoliation mission just days after arriving, as old Vietnam hands use to say, "in-country." They sprayed along both sides of Highway 15, which runs south forty miles from Saigon to Vung Tau on the sea. This route was chosen because it offered several different types of foliage as test targets, and also because the area had recently been infiltrated by National Liberation Front guerrillas. A few days later, scientists from the Army Chemical Corps visited the spray sites, taking samples and photographing the effects of the sprays.

A month or so later, the unit flew another series of test missions, this time spraying mangrove forests and nipa palm in the Ca Mau peninsula in the Delta. Just after the other four planes arrived in Vietnam, the squadron suffered its first loss when a plane went down in the Delta with all hands lost.

"They thought it was mechanical failure, but they never found out; given the terrain and possibility of 'unfriendlies,' you couldn't do the type of accident investigation you would in the States," Jack Spey observed without emotion. "In the early days," he added, "the program wasn't much. Both the ARVN [South Vietnamese] and the Americans had to learn that it existed and what it could do. You start slow, just like any new program that has merit."

Listening to Jack, one gets the uneasy feeling that he could be describing a sales campaign for a new type of aluminum siding, instead of a vast program for devastating the foliage of half an entire country. In any case, the official figures confirm Jack's recollection. During 1962, only 4940 acres were sprayed, mostly in the Delta region in the south. The following year, this increased to a total of 24,700. The air force estimated acreage sprayed by calculating the amount of ground area each sortie could be expected to cover if everything went according to plan.

From August 1965 onward, the air force maintained a computerized history called the HERBS file which logged missions of both spray planes and helicopters in considerable detail. Each entry lists the date, type and quantity of herbicide used and it classifies each mission as to type—for example: crop, supply route, military installation and the like. The exact geographical location, called a Universal Transverse Mercator Grid Coordinate, for each mission is also listed. The HERBS file, which runs to 315 computer pages in length, could be a valuable document in tracing personnel exposures. At first, the spray mechanism was set to disperse at one gallon per acre, but Jack recalls that this had been increased to three gallons per acre by the end of 1963. Flying under ideal conditions, each plane cold lay down a 250-foot swath over an eight and a half mile stretch in three and a half to four minutes. A special valve allowed the pilot to dump the entire load of herbicide in just thirty seconds. This was activated whenever a plane developed serious mechanical trouble or was badly hit by ground fire.

The Pentagon continues to minimize the frequency of such emergency dumping. Spokesperson Tom Dashiell stated in a September 1979 interview that, according to military records, only thirteen such dumpings occurred during the entire war. Based on the accounts of the small number of pilots we interviewed, his figure seems a gross underestimate.

The navigator was essential to the success of defoliation missions. It was his job to receive target orders from command, plan the mission, direct the planes to the target, and oversee the actual spraying. As already mentioned, he rode in the lead aircraft, with a backup navigator usually along in another plane in case the first one went down or had to turn back. We talked to one former navigator, Aaron Valenzuela.

Aaron is a Chicano who now practices law in San Antonio, Texas. Since returning from Vietnam, Aaron's had no contact with other Ranch Hands, although he was interested when we told him about the Ranch Hand reunions. Aaron flew as a navigator on the "spray birds" during the last half of 1969 and early 1970. He described his job: "It was a tough mission, all map reading at low levels; this was unusual work for an air-force navigator. I would ride astride the radio on top of an armor-plated box between the two pilots."

Asked about the process of preparing missions, he told us: "We would get target requests in from MACV [Military Assistance Command—Vietnam]. They would tell us what herbicides they wanted used and give us a target number. By the time I got over there, practically the whole country had been targeted. So you'd go into the safe and pull out the folder for that particular target. There were a few new targets, and on these we'd have to fly out and rec it ourselves.

"After planning the mission, I'd conduct the briefing for the flight crews, giving them the flight time, geographical coordinated, airspeed and details about the spraying itself. After the first drop, sometimes we'd put in at a satellite base where we'd pick up more herbicides and go out to hit another target."

Aaron remembers targeting spray missions around "friendly" base camps on many occasions. "We flew around their perimeters to destroy foliage—this would prevent guys from sneaking in. We'd also spray along likely avenues of approach to the camps."

The soft-spoken lawyer recalls having some second thoughts about the safety of the chemicals while in Vietnam. "It was strange seeing loaders wearing protective clothing at one refueling base at Ben Hoa," he recalled, "the Vietnamese loaders usually wore only shorts. We normally flew with the plane windows open, so we'd often get hit with spray from the planes in our formation."

Charley Hubbs, who piloted spray planes for two years, put it more graphically: "You could always tell a Ranch Hand—by the way he smelled. You'd get hit [through the windows] with four minutes of whatever you were putting out." According to Charley, the crew also could get doused if their plane's spray system got hit by ground fire. "If you open the rear window of a station wagon when the front windows are already open, where's the air going to go? It's the same in a plane, the spray in the cargo hold would get sucked up into the cabin. It was very common to get fogged out this way." Charley served as deputy commander of the Ranch Hands during

1966 and 1967. Now retired from the air force, he works as an air crash investigator with the National Transportation Safety Board.

Navigator Valenzuela remembers one time he was acutely exposed to the chemicals. "They didn't get the top back on the tank and it came off just as were taxiing for takeoff. The flight engineer and I got soaked before we could get it back on." Three years ago, Aaron was forced to retire from the Air Guard reserve when doctors found he had Cryptococcus—a fungus like condition in his lungs. He wonders if this condition wasn't somehow brought on by his service with the spray birds.

Flight-crew members, other than navigators, apparently knew practically nothing about the chemicals they were dumping all over Vietnam every day. "Any evaluation of effectiveness was done by the army's Chemical Corps; we didn't get into evaluation—our job was to put the chemicals where they wanted it," Jack Spey summarized.

Lieutenant Colonel Dick Peshkin from Great Neck, New York, served as Ranch Hand operations officer during 1965 and 1966. He confirmed their ignorance about the chemicals: "I never saw any technical data on 2,4,5-T [a compound that is a major ingredient of Agent Orange] or the other herbicides. It was strictly a 'You call, we haul' type of situation."

Hal Underwood, another Ranch Hand pilot, who flew his own small plane all the way from his Montana home to the reunion, agreed with Peshkin. "Before each mission we were briefed only on the geographical characteristics and coordinates of the target area. We were never told what was beneath the foliage, nor were we ever told what type of defoliant we'd be using on a particular day. You couldn't mistake rice crops, however. They were a bright green—almost chartreuse."

At the same time that Agent Orange was being routinely sprayed along Vietnam's canals and waterways, Dow Chemical, a principal manufacturer of 2,4,5-T, was affixing the following warning to each can produced for domestic use: "Do not contaminate irrigation ditches or water used for domestic purposes. Caution. May cause skin irritation. Avoid contact with eyes, skin and clothing. Keep out of reach of children." No one we've interviewed, however, has ever mentioned seeing any sort of warning on any herbicide used in Vietnam. It's apparent that no effort was made to educate any of the flight crews as to the toxic properties of any of the defoliants. Instead, it appears that the command constantly repeated the theme that they were harmless to animal life. To this day, many of the Ranch Hands seem to cling to this dubious assertion.

The defoliants were relatively slow to take effect. It took a least a week for highly susceptible mangrove trees to die, while it took nipa palm trees up to five weeks to lose all their leaves. Jack Spey remembers that, depending on the time of year and weather, you might begin to see a slight discoloration of the leaves of hardwood trees a day or two after spraying. If the trees were exposed during growing season, the defoliant's effects would register more rapidly than they would otherwise; but it took anywhere from one to three months for the full impact to take effect.

This meant that the spray program had no immediate tactical value to the military strategists: one couldn't spray a forest area in the middle of a battle hoping to unmask a concealed enemy. Its only value was as part of an overall plan for denuding areas over a long period. Of course, crops could be spoiled immediately by contact with the sprays.

Some of the Ranch Hand pilots expressed serious doubts about the value of the whole program. Hal Underwood, who flew in both World War II and Korea before Vietnam, told us that he noticed that "we were flagged [ordered] to return to the same area over and over." This caused him and others to doubt the effectiveness of the defoliating sprays, on both a short-term and long-term basis.

The history of the defoliation program can be divided into two distinct periods. The first phase from 1962 to early 1965, consisted of relatively limited spraying of selected targets, mostly in the Delta region, by a squadron of about eight planes. The second phase, which coincided with the rapid buildup of U.S. combat forces in Vietnam, dwarfed the first period in both the size and scope of the spraying. Eventually the squadron grew to thirty planes which flew missions in all four military corps areas of South Vietnam, from Bien Hua, Phu Cat and Da Nang, which the men called the "Mountain Range."

Jack Spey spoke nostalgically about the Vietnam he remembers from the early days. "Saigon had a very sleepy atmosphere; it was very much a Vietnamese city, not yet Americanized as it later became. I remember its tremendous restaurants and the French-colonial atmosphere of many of the buildings. Prices were very, very low by comparison with later years. We were urged to wear civilian clothing downtown to maintain a low-keyed presence. We didn't want to look like an occupying army.

"At the time, most of the Americans were army; we had only a few air-force elements there, helping out in the air tower and doing training.... There was no security problem in any of the large cities or in most of the provincial towns. You could safely drive to Vung Tau, and the train was still running north along the coast. You could still go hunting around Ban Me Thout for lion, tiger or peacock. The insurgency was at a very, very low level by 1965 or 1966 standards.

"Most of the officer corps was billeted downtown, while the enlisted men were quartered in a tent city out at Tan Son Nhut Airbase. Three or four of us officers would find a building down-town and rent it from a local owner, just like you would in any city in the world. A lot of the houses were passed down through the same unit; when a guy would leave, his replacement would just move right into his bed."

Jack's recollection of a peaceful and "secure" South Vietnam would have surprised General Taylor, whose pessimistic situation report to President Kennedy triggered the U.S. buildup in late 1961.

Being a mountainous country in a tropical zone, Vietnam presented the pilots with many diverse flying situations for which the Ranch Hands had to develop or adapt techniques. Jack recalls: "When we first started to spray in mountainous terrain, I can remember going down a hill spraying a power line near Dalat. We tried to hold it to the proper airspeed, but were doing a hundred and seventy knots by the time we got to the bottom. The second time down, we were able to hold it to a hundred and fifty; then we got smart and the third time kept it to a hundred and thirty. We were feeling our way along, devising various techniques on the spot."

One experiment that didn't work out was an attempt to fly defoliation missions at night. It was hoped that this would increase the element of surprise and make it more difficult for enemy gunners. Jack flew on one of the test missions and says, "It was very scary because you could see the muzzle blasts from gunners on the ground; during the day you didn't hear or see anything until the slugs hit the plane. The experiment was ended because it became very evident that a successful rescue would be almost impossible if a plane did go down. Also, navigation was a problem, because at such low altitudes you're doing it all visually ... once you got into a target area at night, you could get so lost you'd have chemicals where you didn't want them—it would be a real bucket of worms."

As the rate of missions increased so did the intensity of small-arms fire from the ground. The crews soon learned under what conditions they could expect hostile fire. "It depended on the area you were flying in," Jack noted. "If it's real dense jungle, you can't see them and they can't see you, and you don't get shot. If an area's unpopulated, like mangrove swamps, there's no problem unless you run across a military unit that's in transit. If you're working in or around populated areas, the probability of receiving opposition increases. Opposition also increased as you got into crop destruction; if you got crops, you got people who plan to harvest them."

Jack and the other Ranch Hands seemed strangely oblivious to the consequences of their actions. Like many who've spent years in government service, they tend to lapse into a jargon that is utterly devoid of any real feeling. "Unfriendlies," "suppressing fire," "hostile-incoming," and "crop denial" are some examples of terms commonly used by Ranch Hands. They would talk about encountering "opposition" while they were destroying six months of a farmer's labor as if the problem were simply a banal fact of life, like rush-hour traffic on the Long Island Expressway. Perhaps in this way they insulated themselves from the human consequences of their actions, thus avoiding what might be a very painful accounting.

They quickly learned to expect ground fire if they were operating in an inhabited area, but apparently that never caused them to question their assumption that America's military effort had but one objective: to protect the Vietnamese from a ruthless invader.

According to Jack Spey, the Ranch Hand pilots developed tactics for evading ground fire as they went along. "We tried everything we could think of to get through the 'small-arms envelope' that can eat you alive. Above twenty-five hundred feet, you're relatively safe as far as small-arms fire; below that, you're vulnerable. Assuming we expected opposition on a run, we'd fly out there above that altitude and then, when we had the target in sight, we'd make a very rapid descent to spray altitude and start spraying. As soon as we were finished we'd make a rapid climb back above the twenty-five hundred threshold.

"Another technique we used was much more difficult from a navigational standpoint. This was the 'pop-up' technique, where you'd make a rapid descent right onto the deck about five or six miles out from the target. You'd scoot across the ground just as low as you could go without knocking things down, at as fast a speed as you could manage. Then, at the pop-up point, which hopefully was easy to identify, you'd pop up to a hundred and fifty feet and flip on the spray switch. The problem was that if the terrain didn't have features that stood out, you were going to pop up and be way out in left field, with no choice but to abort it. Sometimes you could look at a map or aerial photograph and pick out approach aids, but a lot of targets weren't suited for it and it was easy to get lost and botch the deal."

Since the Americans enjoyed virtually total control of the air, the powerful jet fighters that accompanied the spray birds on many of their missions had a relatively easy time of it. Jack said that "if we expected any opposition, we'd normally request dust-off [rescue] helicopters to stand by in the area. Sometimes we'd also request and FAC [forward air controller] to come along and, if the navigation was difficult, to mark the start of the target.

"Our flight commander would decide if fighter support was needed, and, if so, how it was to be deployed. We'd always get fire in the Delta, because that's where the people and crops were. Sometimes the fighters would sit high and dry and would respond only if we threw out smoke grenades. Also, the FAC [forward air controller in a small plane] would try to pick out where hostile fire was coming from and he might employ fighters.

"Sometimes we'd even request that the fighters hit an area before we sprayed; this negated the element of surprise, but there were a few places where it was worth it. Sometimes, the fighters would strafe alongside us as we sprayed; they'd sit there and sparkle right in front of us. We'd have empty twenty-millimeter cartridges fall right through the holes of our fuselage as the A-1 fighter opened up above us."

When the massive buildup of U.S. forces began in March 1965, defoliation operations increased accordingly. Total acreage sprayed that year was more than double the figure for 1964. For the first time, significant stretches of croplands were destroyed—nearly 66,000 acres in 1965 alone. In 1966, the program again expanded, with the total acreage sprayed quadrupling. The 1967 program was the largest ever, with 1.5 million acres of foliage and 221,000 acres of croplands hit. The heavy spray continued during the next two years at only slightly lower levels. That 19,000 sorties (one flight by one plane) had been flown by the end of 1968 gives some idea of the intense activity. By the time the spray program finally ground to a halt in 1971, an estimated 6 million acres, of which 10 to 15 percent was cropland, had been doused by a total of 107 million pounds of herbicide.

Herbicide manufacture became one of the "growth" industries spawned by the Vietnam War. Annual sales increased from $12.5 million in fiscal 1966 to $79.8 million in fiscal 1969. Eleven chemical companies shared the booming business: Dow, Hercules, Northwest Industries, Diamond Shamrock, Private Brands, Thompson Chemical, Monsanto, Ansul, Trans-Vall, Hooker and Velsicol. Evidently Hercules, a huge multinational conglomerate, had good sources within the Pentagon, for it had the foresight to purchase a herbicide-manufacturing operation, Reasor-Hill, Inc., in December 1961, as the first C-123s were winding their way across the South Pacific. So great did the war-demand become, according to journalist Thomas Whiteside, who wrote the first articles questioning the safety of Agent Orange, that 2,4,5-T and 2,4D (the principal ingredients of Agent Orange) became extremely scarce on the U.S. domestic market after 1968.

Two air force buddies who flew during those years of heavy spraying were reunited at Fort Walton Beach. At first glance, Jim Pochurek and Ralph Dresser couldn't be less alike. Jim is a mild-mannered forty-five-year-old who, in his polyester leisure suit, could easily pass for a real-estate salesman—which, in fact, he is. Ralph, by contrast, has "soldier" written all over him. Decked out in his black Ranch Hand jumpsuit, with the unit's purple scarf knotted around his neck and a thick stogie clenched between his teeth, Ralph still stands tall. A full bird colonel, Ralph was the only reunion guest who still takes jets up every day. But for two years, from 1965 to 1967, Jim and Ralph flew spray missions together.

Ralph and Jim fell to reminiscing about their years on the Ranch, and Jim couldn't conceal his delight when he told us about the day he took Dan Rather of CBS News along for a ride. It seems that journalists were forever visiting the Ranch Hands in search of a different angle for a story. As Jim tells it, Rather's first trip up was very quiet, but when they went out on a second run, all hell broke loose, with ground fire coming in from all direction. "You should have seen Rather's face," Jim recalls with a wicked grin. "He didn't make a peep until we finally set the gooney bird back on the ground."

Once safely back on the tarmac at Tan Son Nhut, Rather questioned them about National Liberation Front allegations that the defoliants were a hazard to health. Ralph took a sip of the herbicide to show Rather what he thought of such "commie propaganda."

The reunion we attended took place just two days after the House Veterans Affairs Committee had conducted the first congressional hearings on the growing controversy over whether defoliants may have impaired the health not only of the Vietnamese but also of many of the 2.8 million Americans who served there. We asked Ralph what he thought of this controversy. He recalled that on at least two occasions in Vietnam he was confronted by other American commanders who complained that his spray planes had made their troops sick. "I told them, Bullshit," he growled. "I'd grant that the stuff tastes bad, but I'd dip my hand in and drink it for chrissakes, to show them it was harmless."

Like the Apostle Thomas the Doubter, Ralph Dresser is a man of the senses, and for him, personal experience is the final arbiter in the controversy over Agent Orange. Looking at Dresser, it's conceivable that he could drink poison, the way some people eat glass or chew nails. In his opinion, guys who now complain of health problems have been "psyched out" by communist propaganda.

"The Viet Cong charged that we were waging chemical warfare so they could turn international opinion against us. They told the Vietnamese that they could prevent maladies by putting plastic bags on their bodies when the planes came over," Dresser chortled. "They even had some crazy antidotes. They told people to rub onion and garlic mixed with urine on the exposed parts. They thought this would bring the toxic chemicals to the surface!"

In the early days of the defoliation program, the Viet Cong weren't the only ones concerned about the possible health effects of these toxic chemicals. According to Dresser, the South Vietnamese also insisted that their workers wear protective gear whenever they worked around the herbicides. Eventually, the Americans' repeated assurances that the defoliants were harmless won the Saigon government over and safety precautions became very lax.

Asked if he believed that any of the Ranch Hands had been harmed by exposure, Ralph gestured toward his fellow cowboys: "Look at these guys. They lived and worked with the stuff every day; there's nothing wrong with them," he laughed.

As we talked further with Ralph, he grew more serious. Judging from the obvious respect the others accorded him, he must have been a good commander, a man others would trust with their lives. These reunions, he felt, took place only because of the uniquely high morale among the Ranch Hands in Vietnam. This, in turn, stemmed from the shared dangers and unprecedented nature of their mission. He acknowledged that since the opposition didn't have antiaircraft defenses in southern Vietnam, the odds of survival for his flight crews were much greater than they would have been, say, during World War II.

When he took command of the Ranch in 1965, Ralph recognized that the anomalies of the mission required a flexible command structure. He allowed responsibility to shift from person to person, depending on the needs of the moment. From Thailand he brought a carved wooden statue of a man with his head up his ass. This became the Master Magnet Ass Award, which was given to the pilot whose plane had taken the heaviest beating from ground fire the previous week. This crude barracks humor had a point: Rather than chew out the offending pilot, Dresser figured that the prizewinner would analyze his mistakes and take corrective action. "It made something positive out of something negative," Dresser explained.

One plane earned the name "Patches" because she'd taken so many hits. At the reunion we saw a home movie that recorded the homecoming of "Patches" at the previous reunion. It was strangely moving to watch as the Ranch Hands walked up and down the plane, fondly stroking her much-battered fuselage.

The elements of nature seem mixed in Colonel Ralph Dresser: part Dr. Strangelove stereotype of the macho invincible career soldier; part man of human responses, warm and congenial to his friends, competent and effective within the limits of his mission. Ralph doesn't seem to have the Big Picture, however, and his scoffing at the thousands of sick vets who got caught in the prop wash of the cowboys' jungle hose-down seems self-serving and protective of his super pilot image.

The fact is, once the fateful decision was made to have Americans take over most of the war effort, troops, equipment and armaments poured into Vietnam on a truly massive scale, and new means for conducting defoliation—principally helicopter, but also spray trucks, riverboats and even backpacks—

were rapidly introduced wherever U.S. troops were deployed. UH-1 "Huey" helicopters were converted for spraying by attaching 200-gallon fuel tanks and gravity-feed sprayers. Flying at fifty-five knots, they could lay down one and a half gallons per acre from an altitude of 100 feet.

Ed Kernea, who now lives near Rickman, Tennessee, served as an army chemical officer in the First Air Cavalry during the period 1969-70. Ed's not a member of the Ranch Hands Association and his views differ markedly from those of some of its members. When asked about the government's claim that the spraying was always done in remote areas where U.S. troops were unlikely to be exposed, he responded: "Completely false; we sprayed around the perimeters of our base camps on many occasions. I often did the spraying myself, using a backpack. We'd spray in real close to the bunkers; anyone in the camp could have been exposed."

Ed also went out on many missions where helicopters were used to spray crops suspected of belonging to the enemy. "Often we'd get splashed when we loaded the chopper's tank from the fifty-five gallon drums. We never wore any protective gear or gloves. We'd often go back and hit the same areas again, especially where rice was growing."

Ed's job was not unique: "There were at least four or five other chemical officers in the division, each doing exactly the same thing I was, only in other areas." He remembers being told that the air cavalry also used tanker trucks for spraying, although he never actually saw them in operation.

Ed is one of the few handlers we encountered who seems to have allowed himself second thoughts about his actions in Vietnam.

"I think about the program now and wonder how the hell I ever did it. To see the whole countryside just dead from that stuff, it was very sad. I never wanted to do crops, but I had to do it—following the old orders, ya know."

Since returning from Vietnam, Ed has suffered from a chronic skin condition. He's furious that the VA director in Nashville responded to a White House query about his case by denying that Ed had ever worked with defoliants in Vietnam.

Gerry Cece and another enlisted man who attended the reunion privately confided to us that they had a series of personal health problems which could, conceivably, be related to acute exposure to herbicides. As flight mechanics, or loaders, they routinely rode in the cargo hold, where they were often doused with the chemicals in the course of performing their duties.

Jan Soroka of Dallas, Texas, had the same job in Vietnam as Ed Kernea, although he served with the army's Ninth and Twenty-fifth Infantry Divisions. He confirms Ed's account of using army trucks to spray around "friendly" base camps. "We'd take barrels of the defoliants out on trucks and use a gas-driven pump to spray everything around a base camp. No one wore any protective gear—there wasn't any."

Soroka went along on many helicopter flights in which defoliants were sprayed along river banks. Since the helicopters had no doors, spray drifting back into the cabin was a constant irritant. He also remembered an incident which demonstrated the danger from spray drifting to the ground. "This pilot refused to fly low and he released the spray from about 500 feet; this killed everything for a mile back from the river.

Jan, who works as an industrial chemist today, has experienced some health problems since Vietnam. "I keep feeling congestion at the top of my lungs; I'm always trying to clear my throat." After an examination at his local VA hospital, he was told they could find nothing wrong.

Lee Jurney commanded a helicopter unit attached to the 199th Light Brigade, (nicknamed the "Red-Catchers"), in Vietnam during 1968 and 1969. His unit's area of operations was a twenty-five mile arc around Saigon. For six months, Lee flew spray missions for the brigade's chemical unit. "At the end of six to eight hours of flying, we'd have the stuff stuck all over us. It was a white creamy fluid and smelled like a horse lathered down real bad. Your eyelids, the fingers of your gloves, stuck together like glue. We inhaled it, yet we weren't provided with any type of mask; it was a real bummer. All eight pilots in my unit rotated on these spray missions, but I flew a lot of them because I was an experienced low-level pilot. I probably got in over a hundred hours with defoliants. A month or two after I started these missions, our choppers were refitted with 200-gallon tanks, with very long booms protruding out each side. Before that, we had dumped the defoliant directly from the 55-gallon drums.

"We conducted lawn-mower style spraying. When I returned to Vietnam for another tour three years later, I could still tell easily where we'd sprayed."

Lee remembers the names of two U.S. firebases, (Stephanie and Pineapple), around which he sprayed within a hundred yards of the emplacements, but he says that there were several others that got the same treatment.

Lee Jurney is a bitter man today. He's convinced that a tumor, which doctors discovered in his pituitary gland, was caused by his massive exposure to the defoliant. His experience with herbicides has "raised his consciousness" about other environmental concerns, Asked where he works now, Lee says, "Babcock and Wilcox. But," he hastens to add, "not in their nuclear reactor division."

Paul Steinke lives in San Diego today, where he attends law school. His wife has suffered four consecutive miscarriages which her doctors cannot explain. Paul feels that he underwent what he calls a "personality change" after he came home from Vietnam. He'd flown a helicopter there in support of the 101st Airborne Division in the northern part of South Vietnam. On several occasions he flew defoliation missions during which "we sprayed around friendly hamlets and firebases." Steinke remembers that the rotary blades of his helicopter would sometimes suck the spray right into the doorless cockpit.

So, with each pilot we interviewed, the evidence accumulated that the possibilities for exposure for U.S. service members was much greater than the U.S. government has yet been willing to admit. In keeping with the contention that only a small group, (the spray pilots), risked any substantial exposure to herbicides in Vietnam, President Carter announced on Memorial Day, 1979, that the Air Force would launch a study of the 1200 Ranch Hands. Jack Spey pledged the Ranch Hand Association's full cooperation in conducting the study. Within a month, nearly half of the spray unit veterans had been located, and the search continues.

In a sense, the issue has come full circle. The men who followed orders and dumped the chemicals, now find themselves the subject of the *only* epidemiological study of GIs which the government has been willing to undertake so far. Even by the end of their reunion in October 1978, there were signs that many of the Ranch Hands were feeling more sensitive to the health allegations, despite their posture of indifference. As the long weekend of boozing and eating drew to a close, we went out to a farewell dinner of enchiladas and tostadas with Jack Spey, Robby Robinson and Hal Underwood. Several stacks of tortillas and rounds of Dos Equis beer later, we said good-bye to our hosts. Still uncomfortable with us and our opinions, Hal Underwood called us aside in the restaurant parking lot. There was just a trace of a plea in his voice as he shook our hands once more: "Don't forget, be good to us, won't you fellas?"

Chapter 10—The VA Fiddles While Agent Orange Burns Vets

Maude DeVictor works behind a cold, steel gray desk in the Benefits Section of the Veterans Administration regional office in Chicago. Maude, a thirty-eight-year-old black woman, had never heard of Agent Orange or dioxin when she took a random telephone call about a year ago in the summer of 1977. Mrs. Charles Owen was on the line. Her husband, she told Maude, was dying of cancer, and he blamed it on "those chemicals from Vietnam." Charley Owen, a black man from Chicago's South Side had made a career of the Air Force, spending twenty-seven years on active duty, including a tour in Vietnam. He had retired and returned to college when his doctor gave him the bad news—terminal lung cancer. Maude gave Mrs. Owen what information she could, although she knew the VA had no disability rating for exposure to military herbicides.

In October, Ethel Owens called again, in tears. Charlie had died, and the VA had denied her claim that his death was service connected. Maude was confused and angry. Could it be that some weapon used in Vietnam *could* cause cancer, she asked herself? She decided to do a little investigating on her own.

When Maude called the office of the Air Force Surgeon General, she was told that they didn't know what she was talking about. The next morning she was called by Captain Alvin Young, an Air Force plant physiologist. Young gave her a full run down on the defoliation program, including descriptions of the health symptoms that scientists have attributed to dioxin exposure. Maude didn't know it at the time, but she was being briefed by one of the Air Force's resident experts on herbicides and their long-term effects. A claims worker in an obscure government niche, she must have felt a little awed by the attention which her innocent inquiry had generated.

She began to prepare memos for her supervisors, sharing her newly acquired information about this mysterious issue. At this point, it should be noted, Maude was no longer following the bureaucratic routine of her job; her unusual curiosity had a personal basis. While serving in the Navy's medical corps in the 1950's she had attended women with uterine cancer who were receiving experimental treatments with radium pellets. Some years later, she herself had developed breast cancer and had undergone a mastectomy. Since then, she'd lived in the shadow of a cancer she suspected was induced when the Navy exposed her to dangerous levels of radiation.

Armed with some basic information about herbicides and their potential for long-term health effects, Maude went to her supervisors and obtained their permission to conduct an informal investigation within her VA facility. Working in the intake office, she talked with sixty or so veterans over the phone on an average day. She also conducted personal interviews with an additional ten to fifteen claimants. Whenever she encountered a vet who's served in Vietnam, she began asking questions, "Ever had a persistent skin rash?" "Have any kids born with deformities?" "Do your arms and/or legs tingle and go to sleep?" Often the vet would answer, "Yeah! How'd you know?"

During Christmas, Maude was temporarily assigned to the VA's West

Side hospital for a few days. Just checking records informally, she identified eight patients whose symptoms indicated they could be suffering from dioxin poisoning. In the first two months of 1978, she identified twenty-seven other Vietnam veterans through her own sleuthing at the benefits office. Then, suddenly, without explanation, her boss told her to stop logging cases. Apparently, the VA higher-ups were becoming concerned about her findings.

Angry at what she calls "bureaucratic ass-covering," Maude decided to tell what she knew to Bill Kurtis, a respected anchorman with WBBM-TV News in Chicago. Kurtis, at first, wasn't too impressed. "Frankly, I had filed away the herbicide problem as no story," he remembers. But when he saw Maude DeVictor's research, "it just hit me between the eyes like no other story."

On March 23, 1978, WBBM telecast a one-hour documentary which focused on the allegations of several Chicago-area veterans that they or their children were suffering from dioxin's long-term effects. Kurtis interviewed scientists who had demonstrated dioxin's toxic effects on lab animals, and also spoke with government representatives and with scientists employed by the herbicide manufacturers. On camera, the Air Force's Dr. Young was less forthcoming then he had been earlier with Maude DeVictor. Asked about alleged dangers from 2,4,5-T, he stated. "I don't think there's any supportive evidence."

Response to the broadcast was immediate. Several hundred Vietnam veterans called or visited the VA's Chicago's facilities, complaining of ailments like those discussed on the program and seeking information and examinations. Predictably, Dow Chemical issued a statement denying any connection between their herbicides and the veterans' health problems. And on the day of the broadcast, the VA issued a press release which emphasized that out of a total of 2.5 million claims decided annually by its fifty-eight regional offices, only twenty-seven were based on herbicide poisoning, and these all had been filed in one office—Chicago. The VA's logic was clear. No health problems existed since only a handful of people had complained and these probably were stimulated by an individual or group in just one city.

Two veterans located by Maude were featured on the show. Their Vietnam experiences were typical of the experiences of many of the vets who later came forth in response to publicity. One was Michael Adams, twenty-eight, of Evanston, Illinois, who served in Vietnam as a combat engineer with the Twenty-fifth Division in 1968. He also remembers watching as C-123 aircraft sprayed defoliants near his unit on several occasions. After he returned to the States, large pimple-like sores began to appear on Mike's face. An Army medic told him they were "razor bumps" that would go away. But the sores have persisted and are probably chloracne, one of the most common symptoms of dioxin exposure. Chloracne is similar to the acne which plagues many teenagers. It appears on the face, neck, shoulders, and upper part of arms as festering pimples and blackheads that periodically erupt. All scientific authorities agree that exposure to dioxin can produce a chloracne condition in those exposed.

After he was discharged in 1972, Mike's shoulder and arms began to go numb for periods of time. He had difficulty sleeping and in the past two years he's lost more than sixty pounds. He believes he's undergone a personality change as well. "Before I went to Nam, I was an easy, cheerful guy; now I often feel wound up real tight, and I'll blow up over just any little thing."

Agent Orange may have affected not only Milton Ross, thirty-four of Matteson, Illinois, but his son Richard, as well. Milt served with the Fifth Special Forces in Vietnam's Central Highland, and he told us, "Although I wasn't involved in spray operations, I was sprayed upon. They sprayed a lot around our defense perimeter at Kon Tum to keep a clear 'field of fire' open. Often the wind would blow the spray right over our camp."

Milt's son Richard, who was conceived after Mike returned from Vietnam, was born with the last joints of his fingers and toes either malformed or missing. Milt and his wife consulted a genetic counselor who took a detailed genealogical history from both parents. Her study uncovered no genetic disorders in the family history which might explain Richard's condition.

Despite the hundreds of new claims, the VA hadn't formulated any criteria for rating disabilities possibly brought on by the herbicides. According to Maude DeVictor, "Nothing was done with these new cases, since they didn't have any standards for evaluating them. Some were denied outright, but most were "diaried"—that is, placed in a computer which was programmed to print them out every sixty days for review.

A few weeks after the show, Maude got her "thanks" from a grateful employer; she was transferred to a back office and given a job of answering telephone inquiries about missing disability checks. Such is the fate of government "whistle blowers."

Ralph Metcalfe, a black congressman from Chicago's South Side, became interested in the controversy and asked the General Accounting Office (GAO), Congress's investigative arm, to probe both the Pentagon's use of herbicides during the Vietnam War and the VA's handling of disability claims based on Agent Orange exposure. The GAO published the first half of its report three months later, just prior to Metcalfe's untimely death. It basically just repeated what the Pentagon had said, that no scientific testing of the chemical was done prior to use, since the herbicides already were widely used in the U.S. It passed along, without comment, the Pentagon's conclusion that, despite several studies done after 1967, "no firm link has been made between long-term adverse health effects and exposure ... in Vietnam." The report ended by noting that the Defense Department has no plans to conduct epidemiological studies on military personnel who may have been exposed. This would remain the Pentagon's position until 1979, when President Carter directed the Air Force to conduct a study of the 1,200 men who served with Ranch Hands in Vietnam.

As staff members of Citizen Soldier, a GI and veterans' rights organization based in New York City, the authors were contacted by friends in Chicago who knew we'd be interested in this emerging controversy. Based on a decade's organizing among GIs and veterans, we suspected that the problems being reported in Chicago were not unique to that city but probably we're shared by veterans across the country. On May 5, 1978, Citizen Soldier held a press conference in New York to announce its "Search and Save" campaign (to be contrasted with "search and destroy"), which would identify and alert ailing Vietnam vets, by offering a toll free "800" phone service. The distinguished environmental scientist, Dr. Barry Commoner, who directs the Center for Biology of National Systems at Washington University in St. Louis, joined several Vietnam veterans who were suffering from ailments associated with dioxin poisoning. Dr. Commoner drew the broad implications of the fight for Agent Orange victims. "My knowledge of the industrial accident in Italy two years ago, when a cloud of dioxin vented from a factory and settled over Seveso, convinces me more than ever that all dioxin-related pesticides and chemicals should be immediately banned from further use."

As wire-service stories and broadcast media spread the word about the toll-free "hot line," the calls began to pour in from across the country. An article in the *National Star*, a tabloid weekly with over two million readers, stimulated many calls. Soon the phone lines were jammed beyond capacity. In just five weeks, 2000 calls were taken from worried veterans and their families. Unfortunately, the huge phone bills and the crushing burden for a small staff of handing so many calls, caused the service to be terminated, but not before an important point had been made: There apparently were tens of thousands of Vietnam veterans who were suffering in silence from a common set of symptoms.

Although Agent Orange was rapidly evolving from a local to a national issue, the VA's policy makers continued to act as if they thought the issue would go away if they minimized its significance. On May 18, a policy memo by Dr. Garrit Schepers, deputy chief of Health and Medical Services, was circulated to all one hundred seventy-two VA hospitals and fifty-eight regional offices. After providing a brief history of the defoliation program in Vietnam, Dr. Schepers drew the following scientific conclusions: "The herbicides have a low level of toxicity ... they appear to be rapidly absorbed and completely excreted in both humans and animals." (He also states as fact that dioxin is eliminated from the body "fairly rapidly" and that "all available data" suggest that it's not retained in the body tissue after contact). "Humans exposed repeatedly may experience temporary and fully reversible neurological symptoms, however the only chronic condition definitely associated with exposure ... is chloracne." (A few weeks earlier, the VA had issued a new rating memo stating that only chloracne was to be recognized as a basis for a granting of disability.)

Dr. Schepers' memo dismisses fifteen years of research by Dr. Ton That Tung, a Vietnamese scientist who has received numerous international awards for his work on dioxin, by stating that comprehensive animal studies "failed to confirm the [Vietnamese] suggestion" that liver cancer, miscarriages, and birth defects can be caused by exposure to dioxin.

In cases where a veteran manifests health symptoms that cannot be explained by reference to defined disease, Schepers instructs the staff to take a detailed medical history, including any exposure to herbicides. "If [he] has no objective symptom or sign, simple reassurance should be offered. The veteran should be told that a record will be kept ... but if [he] doesn't have symptoms and didn't previously experience any, the likelihood of herbicide poisoning is virtually zero."

The medical staff, however, is cautioned not to make any entry in a patient's file which suggests "a relationship between a veteran's illness and defoliant exposure, unless unequivocal confirmation ... has been established." If such a case is found, it is to be reported immediately to VA headquarters. On the subject of conducting outreach for ailing veterans, Schepers is adamant; under no circumstances is a VA facility to initiate examination of any veteran for dioxin poisoning. Field staff is also warned not to make any public statements about Agent Orange unless they're first "reviewed" by headquarters.

The good doctor then waxes philosophical about this whole problem, lamenting that "a great deal of concern has been engendered among veterans and their families ... by media presentations." His implication seems to be that this issue has been created by a sensationalist press which has been bombarded the public with "scare" stories.

The underlying message which permeates Schepers' memo must have been clear to all but the densest bureaucrat: This whole controversy is prob-

Excerpt from G.I. Guinea Pigs 271

ably a hoax, but we're getting some heat, so we've got to appear to be doing something. If you can find *any* other explanation for a veteran's health problems, use it. If you can't, send the case to Washington immediately!

As the Schepers memo was being distributed internally, the VA continued to issue statements to the press which minimized the problem. A United Press International dispatch quoted an unidentified Veterans Administration spokesman as claiming that there was no proof of any long-term effects from herbicide exposure. He added that the toxicity of Agent Orange was "no higher than that of aspirin." This phantom spokesman pointedly observed that the "primary source" for reports of herbicides causing birth defects was "North Vietnamese propaganda." Some of the armchair warriors at VA headquarters were still using the old Johnson/Nixon formula that any criticism of America's involvement in Vietnam must originate in Hanoi. Like the Japanese soldiers who occasionally turn up on isolated Pacific islands, maybe they haven't yet heard that the war is over.

A few weeks later, the administrator of the VA, Max Cleland, attended a Fourth of July celebration in Indianapolis. Cleland has made much of the fact that, since he's a paraplegic due to Vietnam War wounds, he wants the truth and nothing but about Agent Orange. According to a VA worker who was present at the patriotic wiener roast, Cleland immediately bristled when someone asked him if he thought the agency was doing enough for the vets who may have been exposed. He intoned the litany about how no scientific studies have established any long-term health effects, and he added his opinion that the issue was largely the creation of irresponsible environmentalists.

As the phone calls and letters poured in at Citizen Soldier, the media continued to follow the story, often conducting in depth interviews with hometown veterans who'd called in response to previous stories about the "hot line." It is probably part of the legacy of Watergate that daily newspapers in cities large and small have reporters who are eager to write articles about an important issue of public policy. From the Lawrence, Massachusetts, *Eagle-Tribune* to the Albuquerque *Journal* to the *Seattle Times*, the story of Agent Orange was told.

By the end of summer in 1978, Citizen Soldier had logged over 3000 calls and letters from veterans. Working with the help of environmental scientists like Dr. Susan Daum of Mount Sinai's Environmental Science Labs and Drs. Jeanne and Steve Stellman of the American Health Foundation, Citizen Soldier designed a six-page self-administered medial questionnaire. The survey form asked veterans detailed questions in five areas: military service history, herbicide exposure, personal health history, past medical history, and family history, with emphasis on stillbirths, miscarriages, and congenital birth defects. A questionnaire was sent to every veteran who called in or wrote, and copies were distributed in bulk to hundreds of veterans groups, trade unions, and counseling centers across the country.

About the time, Paul Reutershan, 28, of Lake Mohegan, New York, read the allegations about Agent Orange in his local newspaper. Paul had flown a helicopter in Vietnam, and his chopper had passed through defoliant mists being laid down by C-123s. Back home, Paul found a job as a conductor on ConRail commuter trains and was planning to be married when doctors gave him terrible news: he had less than two years to live. When Paul first learned that his abdominal cancer was terminal, he was incredulous. He'd always been a bit of a "health nut," and he neither drank nor smoked. So, when he read over the symptoms some doctors associate with dioxin exposure, it hit him with enormous force. Thinking back to Vietnam, Paul remembered that he'd developed chloracne on his back just before coming home.

Bitter at the fading of the light, Paul threw himself into a frenzy of activity, speaking about Agent Orange wherever and whenever someone would listen. Starting off with late night cable TV in New York, before long Paul was being interviewed on the "Today Show" and other national programs. It was painful to listen as Paul exposed his deepest feelings about being used callously by the U.S. military. In his rage at the cruelty of his fate, Paul was disturbingly eloquent: "I got killed in Vietnam; I just didn't know it at the time."

With the help of his sister, Joan Dziedzic and other Vietnam veterans, Paul formed an organization for those most affected by defoliants, calling it Agent Orange Victims International. It was his dream that this group would unite victims of U.S. spraying in Vietnam with civilians who had been harmed by the domestic use (for crop and brush control) of the same herbicides.

On Capitol Hill, as constituent mail from "back home" increased, Congress slowly stirred. Since the veterans' affairs committees in both the House and Senate tend to be dominated by conservative partisans of the military, there was not much enthusiasm for prying open what might prove to be another can of military worms. However, when the traditional veterans' groups such as the Veterans of Foreign Wars and the Disabled American Veterans began to make inquiries about Agent Orange, even the most reactionary lawmakers had to pay some attention. Some of the more liberal members of the House committee circulated a joint letter to their chairman, asking that the Veterans Administration furnish the panel with a detailed report on its handling of the Agent Orange claimants, as well as a summary of the scientific research being performed on the issue within the federal sector for the VA.

Nothing more was heard publicly in Washington until early October 1978, when the leadership of the House Veterans Affairs Committee announced that it would hold a one-day hearing on Agent Orange the following day. The witness list was no surprise, however; spokesmen for the Veterans Administration, the Air Force, and the National Cancer Institute dominated the proceedings.

Major General Garth Dettinger, the deputy surgeon general of the Air Force, set the tone for the day's proceedings; he offered the reassuring news that four times as much dioxin was dumped on rangelands and forests in the U.S. as was used in Vietnam from 1962 to 1971. Taking the hard line, he flatly asserted that the use of herbicides in Vietnam or the U.S. "has not resulted in a documented increase in illness among users or the general population."

The general then turned to the risk faced by GIs during the Vietnam defoliation program: "The potential for exposure of U.S. military personnel is *highly* [his emphasis] unlikely." This, he explained, is because Vietnam's dense canopied cover would have prevented all but 6 percent of the total herbicide applied from actually filtering through to the forest floor. This level of exposure would be the same, he reassured us all, as that routinely encountered by persons entering sprayed rangelands in the U.S. Besides, Dettinger explained, ground combat troops would be unlikely to enter a sprayed area for several weeks after treatment, because "defoliation didn't occur until three or four weeks after treatment." The general apparently thought that because defoliation was not used as a *tactical* weapon, as artillery or an air strike would precede a ground assault in a target area, soldiers would not enter a recently sprayed area. But since Vietnam was primarily a guerrilla war, characterized by hit-and-run assaults and constantly shifting battle lines, GIs were required to pursue the enemy anytime and anywhere.

Regarding what portion of the 2.8 million troops might actually have been exposed, Dettinger demonstrated even greater rigidity, and even less knowledge. According to him, only insecticides and smoke screens were aerially applied in areas where U.S. ground troops operated. "I want to stress," he declared, "that herbicides were *not* [his emphasis] used in this fashion."

As was shown in chapter 7 about the Ranch Hands, there are many eyewitness accounts of routine spraying of defoliants around "friendly" base camps and firebases. Perhaps it is the spirit of inter-service rivalry which prevents the good general from taking any notice of what the army and marine helicopter and spray trucks may have been doing with their supplies of herbicides, but at least one account claims that the Air Force C-123s themselves gave large numbers of U.S. troops an unwanted bath of Agent Orange. John East, of Santa Rosa, Californian, never will forget a morning in the fall of 1967 when he was standing with five hundred other marines on a hillside firebase in the northern I Corps sector. "Three planes were flying abreast as they came right over us. They were flying into the winds and as they released the spray it blew back over our base. I felt it dampen my shirt and I was quite upset that it blew onto me. Everyone on the hill got a shot of it. None of the officers said anything about it; it was just shrugged off." Further refutation of Dettinger is found in a GAO report, which we summarize below.

Dettinger offered one further argument whey the spray poses little danger. "Photodegeneration has been shown to destroy dioxin within a [few] hours." Photodegeneration is defined as "chemical degradation in the presence of light." In other words, Dettinger was saying that a few hours of sunlight rendered dioxin harmless.

This argument seems dubious in light of a number of studies which found that dioxin resists decomposition and is soluble in human body fat. One study found that, after one year, approximately 59 percent of the dioxin was still present in two moist soil samples, regardless of the amount applied or the type of soil.

The deputy surgeon general did acknowledge that a relatively small group, the spray handlers, could have encountered significant exposure, but he argued that "closed transfer systems" [for defoliant loading] and the use of *protective equipment* [his emphasis] employed during ground loading" would have kept such risk to a minimum. To buttress Dettinger's testimony, the Air Force released an extensive 247-page report which had been written for the surgeon general by Captain Alvin Young (the plant scientist Maude DeVictor talked to) and three other Air Force scientists. It echoed Dettinger's claims: "[Handlers] were indoctrinated in appropriate safety precautions, including gloves and face shields.... [They] were encouraged to take normal safety precautions ... and to avoid skin and eye contact with the material. Contaminated clothing was to be washed before re-use. Spillage on skin was to be rinsed copiously...."

While the Veterans Administration and Congress continue to regard this report as authoritative, the surgeon general's office seems to have backed away from some of its assertions. In an interview with the authors in August 1979, Major Phil Brown, an official spokesman, stated, "I'm not aware of any directions to the men [in Vietnam]: 'Thou shalt wear protective gear.'" Brown also injected a note of skepticism about Dettinger's claim that a

Excerpt from G.I. Guinea Pigs

"closed transfer system" for loading would have kept risk of exposure low. "There's a fairly long period of time when they did hand pump from fifty-five gallon drums into the fuel trucks," he stated.

Ranch Hand, Charley Hubbs, quoted previously in chapter 7, served in Vietnam until the end of 1967. He sat in on our interview with the surgeon general's staff. When we asked him if the men actually hand pumped each plane's 1000-gallon tank, he nodded and laughed, stating that "we had some pretty tired folks." Charley feels that the Ranch Hands were poorly equipped. "You could sum up what they did for us over there in a word—nothing! Other squadrons had all kinds of planes and support units; we just had to live hand to mouth."

The Air Force's recitation of precise regulations mandating the use of protective gear and safety procedures reminds one of the policy statements the Pentagon issued whenever evidence surfaced of war crimes, like My Lai. A whole list of instructions that each GI was given regarding the Geneva Convention and Rules of Land Warfare would be rattled off, as though such training shifted all responsibility for what might happen on the battlefield from the commanders to the individual soldiers. It's easy to imagine that in the early days of the spray program someone in the Air Force legal office foresaw the need for some "boilerplate"—as it is called in the legal trade—whose sweeping language could be used to cover up any future situation in which a claim for damage might arise.

Charley Hubbs was very candid about the total disregard for safety measures in Vietnam. "They may have said, 'do these things,' but I guarantee you that over there no one used any such gear. Loading, flying, getting shot at, spraying, we all wore the same thing, a T-shirt."

One fuel supervisor who worked at Phu Cat in 1970, Donald Martin of Tampa, Florida, told us that the American GIs who loaded the planes got "drowned" a number of times while transferring herbicides from storage barrels to loading tanks. "No one wore gloves or protective gear, just combat fatigues; most guys didn't even wear shirts 'cause it was so hot. When a guy got splashed, he just kept on goin'." Don Martin doesn't remember any training in the proper handing or use of herbicides. Although he served in Vietnam after the Pentagon publicly had announced spray restrictions due to disquiet about the use of herbicides, this doesn't seem to have resulted in any increased concern for the handlers' safety. Don today suffers from a severe arthritic condition which has rendered him unable to work. Several doctors have given him statements that his disability may have been brought on by his daily contact with the chemicals.

Dr. Paul Haber, the Veterans Administration's chief medical officer for professional services, also testified at the House hearings in October. His testimony basically echoed that of the Air Force. He stated that "the only human disorder linked to herbicide is chloracne." Temporary symptoms such as nausea, diarrhea, headaches, and the like, "disappear after a short period of time." But apparently the VA brass had had some second thoughts about the accuracy of some of Dr. Scheper's scientific opinions, because Haber now acknowledged in his statement "a main scientific concern is whether ... dioxin may persist in body tissue for protracted periods." To seek answers, he announced that the VA would conduct a study to compare fat tissue taken from a small number of Vietnam veterans with vets who hadn't served in Vietnam.

Preliminary results from this study released at a VA scientific meeting in December 1979 confirmed that measurable levels of dioxin were present in some of the exposed veterans. Fat tissue was taken from thirty-three veterans, including a group of ten who hadn't served in Vietnam. Among twenty-two samples analyzed, dioxin has been found in ten cases.

Haber then presented a newly revised medical circular that was being sent to all VA facilities. He explained that its purpose was to "insure that each veteran who alleges exposure will immediately receive proper administrative and health care management." Obviously, something had happened between April and September which accounted for the changed attitude at the Veterans Administration. That "something" was likely the fact that thousands of veterans had come forward to complain of health problems. They were proving impossible to sweep under the bureaucratic rug.

The September 13 circular ordered all VA facilities to submit quarterly reports to headquarters detailing all Agent Orange claims filed, along with copies of medical files in any case where disability for herbicide exposure was granted. This reporting was a dual-edged sword, however. While it could help the VA headquarters stay abreast of national developments, it also made any disability grant subject to the immediate review of headquarters brass. This would likely have a chilling effect on even the most dedicated VA worker. To no one's surprise, the VA announced later in the year that not one single claim for herbicide-related disability had been granted in the entire country. While the VA had altered its policy to create the appearance of greater sensitively to the issue, the net effect of its *de facto* policy of discouraging all such claims continued unchanged.

Dr. Haber also told the committee that the Armed Forces Institute of Pathology had begun to receive and store body tissues that were taken from Vietnam veterans who underwent operations at VA medical centers. He also described a review of in-house data on cancers, skin problems, and other medical categories which the VA staff was conducting.

Dr. Haber's statement also contained a reference to a request that the

VA had made of the Pentagon "to furnish us with complete maps of each herbicide mission, the dates they were carried out, units performing the spray missions, the unit present in the area at the time of the mission or those units entering the area after they were sprayed.

In his testimony, Dr. Haber referred to an "informal group" that had been meeting to collect scientific data on herbicides and formulate health care policy. It included representatives from every federal agency with regulatory responsibilities concerning toxic chemicals, as well as "consultants" from Dow Chemical Corporation and various universities. He neglected to mention that the VA had been threatened with a lawsuit, since Haber's informal panel violated the Federal Advisory Committee Act. Enacted a few years ago, this legislation is an attempt to deal with the problem of "stacked" committees which produce predetermined conclusions and recommendations. The National Veterans Law Center in Washington, D.C., demanded that the Veterans Administration comply with the act, which specifies procedures for the organization and composition of such bodies with an eye toward encouraging reasonable diversity. Apparently Haber's lawyers advised him to scrap his informal panel and start over, which is exactly what he did.

No independent scientist—much less a potential victim—was invited to testify before the committee. The one veteran who represented Veterans of Foreign Wars, issued a cautious statement politely asking for more outreach and treatment. The one-day hearing was over.

By November, over a thousand Citizen Soldier questionnaires had been completed and returned. The American Health Foundation coded the responses to the first 536 and then analyzed them by computer. Volunteers at Citizen Soldier then spent many hours checking each reported case of cancer or birth defect with local physicians or medical records. In an open letter to the veterans, Drs. Jeanne and Steven Stellman of the American Health Foundation summarized their findings.

There were 35 cases of cancer reported, which included three cases of kidney cancer, a very rare disease for this age group; three testicular cancers, and a number of cancers of the lymphatic system. There were 77 children reported born with defects, ranging from missing or deformed fingers to heart defects to unusual skin and hearing disorders. One of the most unexpected findings was the large number of veterans who complained of changes of skin color and sensitivity to light, as well as nervous system difficulties."

A week before Christmas, Paul Reutershan succumbed to his abdominal cancer. Just before his death he was granted a service-connected disability for his condition, but dioxin exposure was never mentioned. That day after he was buried, his sister received a phone call from a VA official. He warned her not to cash the disability check they'd sent Paul, since his claim against the government expired when he did. Bureaucratic duty performed, he hung up.

In early 1979, two network shows, ABC-TV's "20-20" and Public Broadcasting's "For Your Information," both aired programs featuring the Agent Orange controversy. When Geraldo Rivera described Citizen Soldier's questionnaire and read its address on "20-20" he stimulated another 1,500 calls and letters from veterans.

The avalanche had started.

Appendix: Author's Testimony Before the House Committee of Government Operations Hearings on the Phoenix Program

HEARINGS BEFORE A
SUBCOMMITTEE OF THE COMMITTEE ON GOVERNMENT OPERATIONS
HOUSE OF REPRESENTATIVES
NINETY-SECOND CONGRESS
FIRST SESSION

July 15 {a.m., p.m.}, 16, 19, 21; and August 2, 1971

Printed for the use of the Committee on Government Operations

U.S. GOVERNMENT PRINTING OFFICE

68-870 WASHINGTON: 1971

COMMITTEE ON GOVERNMENT OPERATIONS

Chet Holifield, California, *Chairman*
Jack Brooks, Texas
L. H. Fountain, North Carolina
Robert E. Jones, Alabama
Edward A. Garmatz, Maryland
John E. Moss, California
Dante B. Fascell, Florida
Henry S. Reuss, Wisconsin
John S. Monagan, Connecticut
Torbert H. Macdonald, Massachusetts
William S. Moorhead, Pennsylvania
Cornelius E. Gallagher, New Jersey
Wm. J. Randall, Missouri

Benjamin S. Rosenthal, New York
Jim Wright, Texas
Fernand J. St Germain, Rhode Island
John C. Culver, Iowa
Floyd V. Hicks, Washington
George W. Collins, Illinois
Don Fuqua, Florida
John Conyers, Jr., Michigan
Bill Alexander, Arkansas
Bella S. Abzug, New York
Florence P. Dwyer, New Jersey
Ogden R. Reid. New York
Frank Horton, New York
John N. Erlenborn, Illinois
John W. Wydler, New York
Clarence J. Brown, Ohio
Guy Vander Jagt, Michigan
Gilbert Gude, Maryland
Paul N. McCloskey, Jr., California
John H. Buchanan, Jr., Alabama
Sam Steiger, Arizona
Garry Brown, Michigan
Barry M. Goldwater, Jr., California
J. Kenneth Robinson, Virginia
Walter E. Powell, Ohio
Charles Thone, Nebraska
Herbert Roback, *Staff Director*
Christine Ray Davis, *Staff Administrator*
James A. Lanigan, *General Counsel*
Miles Q. Romney, *Associate General Counsel*
J. P. Carlson, *Minority Counsel*
William H. Copenhaver, *Minority Professional Staff*

FOREIGN OPERATIONS AND GOVERNMENT
INFORMATION SUBCOMMITTEE

William S. Moorhead, Pennsylvania, *Chairman*
John E. Moss, California
Torbert H. MacDonald, Massachusetts
Jim Wright, Texas
John Conyers, Jr., Michigan
Bill Alexander, Arkansas

Ogden R. Reid, New York
Frank Horton, New York
John N. Erlenborn, Illinois
Paul N. McCloskey, Jr., California

Ex Officio
Chet Holifield, California
Florence P. Dwyer, New Jersey
William G. Phillips, *Staff Director*
Norman G. Cornish, *Deputy Staff Director*
Harold F. Whittington, *Staff Consultant*
Dale E. Moser, *Supervisory Auditor, GAO*
Martha M. Dott, *Clerk*
Mary E. Milek, *Secretary*

(II)

August 2 1971 hearing, pages 287-362

Witnesses:

Michael J. Uhl
K. Barton Osborn
Jerome R. Waldie {p.287}

U.S. Assistance Programs in Vietnam

Monday, August 2, 1971
House of Representatives,
Foreign Operations and
Government Information Subcommittee
of the Committee of Government Operations,
Washington, D.C.

The subcommittee met, pursuant to recess, at 10 a.m., in room 2203, Rayburn House Office Building, Hon. William S. Moorhead (chairman) of the subcommittee presiding.
Present: Representatives William S. Moorhead, Ogden R. Reid, and Paul N. McCloskey, Jr.
Staff members present: William G. Phillips, staff director; Norman G. Cornish, deputy staff director; Harold F. Whittington, staff consultant; Dale E. Moser, supervisory auditor, GAO; and William H. Copenhaver, minority professional staff, Committee on Government Operations.

Mr. Moorhead. The Subcommittee on Foreign Operations and Government Information will please come to order.

While waiting for other members to arrive, I will make an opening statement.

During the past several weeks, we have been looking into the economy and efficiency of the operations of the U.S. assistance programs in Vietnam, Cambodia, and Laos. We have reviewed the degree of inequity in the exchange rates in the currency of these countries with the U.S. dollar. We have begun our inquiries into the long-range implications of U.S. assistance operations to help strengthen the economic trade and stability of these nations once U.S. military support has been withdrawn.

Likewise, we have reviewed various economy and efficiency aspects of such programs as commodity imports, health, refugees, public safety, and rural development and other types of inter-related activities involved in the so-called CORDS "pacification" programs.

Wednesday and Thursday afternoons of this week will be devoted to hearing additional witnesses on the operation of black market currency manipulation and other illegal activities in these countries.

The Assistant Secretary of the Treasury, Eugene Rossides, will be the principal witness on Thursday. Following the hearing that day, I hope to discuss with the other members of the subcommittee the overall plans and timetable for reports on these hearings and the advisability of resuming certain areas of these hearings in September after the recess.

Earlier in our hearings, we discussed various aspects of the pacification program carried on by the CORDS organization. Ambassador Colby, former head of the programs, testified 2 weeks ago today. Members have been disturbed by certain allegations made about the U.S. involvement in the so-called Phoenix program, under which some 22,000 persons of the Vietcong infrastructure were neutralized this past year. We learned that neutralized means killed, imprisoned or rallied.

Ambassador Colby went into some detail about the Phoenix program in a supplemental statement he submitted to the subcommittee. He also {p.288} responded to numerous questions about its objectives and its operational characteristics.

For the record, I would like to include an article in today's New York Times which is headlined: "Rewards up to $11,000 Set for Captured Vietcong."

Without objection it will be made part of the record.

Mr. Uhl. Thank you.

My name is Michael J. Uhl. I am currently listed in the Army records as a retired first lieutenant by virtue of my disability.

Upon arrival in the Republic of Vietnam in November of 1968—

Author's Testimony Before the House Committee 283

Mr. Moorhead. For the record you might give us your address here.

Mr. Uhl. I currently reside in New York City. I am using my parents' address as my address of record: 35 Coppertree Lane, Babylon, New York, Code 11702.

Mr. Moorhead. Thank you.

Mr. Uhl. Upon arrival in the Republic of Vietnam in November of 1968 I was assigned as the team chief of the 1st Military Intelligence Team—1st MIT—11th Brigade, Americal Division. I remained with the 11th Brigade until late May 1969, at which time I was medically evacuated, having contracted pulmonary tuberculosis.

The 1st MIT consisted of three sections: Counter Intelligence (CI), Order of Battle (OB), and Interrogation of Prisoners of War (IPW). My primary function was to administer the team and coordinate its efforts, in order to fulfill our mission of providing the combat brigade with tactical intelligence for immediate exploitation and security from compromise of its operations. By virtue of my military occupational speciality (MOS) I also had direct supervisory control over the CI section.

Through my testimony today I hope to convey, generally, a perspective shared by many of my veteran comrades. This is a perspective gained from the field, of those charged with the responsibility for {p.313} implementing ambiguous and often absolutely misleading directives, policies, and standard operating procedures. Most of these I believe to be based on fallacious analysis of the historical and contemporary Vietnamese situation, not to mention a fundamentally misguided concept of what the role of the United States should be in foreign affairs.

I do not make these charges lightly. For those who have strong beliefs in the many revolutionary concepts that first shaped our Nation, disillusionment does not come easily. Our system has evolved away from the best sentiments of Thomas Paine, Sam Adams, Patrick Henry, and thousands like them throughout our history.

William Jennings Bryan, in spite of his failings, summed up many of these sentiments before this very body {Indianapolis, April 8 1908}. At that time Congress was debating whether or not to withdraw American troops from the Philippines.

And so with the nation. It is of age and it can do what it pleases; it can spurn the traditions of the past; it can repudiate the principles upon which this nation rests; it can employ force instead of reason; it can substitute might for right; it can conquer weaker people; it can exploit their lands; appropriate their property; and kill their people; but it cannot repeal moral law or escape the punishment they decreed for the violation of human rights. * * *

Since this subcommittee is enjoined to hear testimony that bears on the efficiency and funding of governmental operations, I will try to make my comments relevant to these guidelines wherever possible. It is generally fairly obvious that at least with tactical level MI operations, waste and inefficiency are the rule, not exception.

It is not at all unpredictable, given what we have learned from the Pentagon papers, that my operational perspective of MI programs like Phoenix, for example, is diametrically opposed to the administrative perspective of former CORDS chief, Ambassador Colby.

For instance, Ambassador Colby gave the impression that Phoenix targeted specific high level Vietcong infrastructure whose identity had been established by at least three unrelated intelligence sources. In his prepared statement delivered before this committee on July 19, 1971, he cites several interesting statistics. Among these is the number of Vietcong infrastructure (VCI) successfully targeted and "neutralized" during the period 1968—May 1971. 1970 figures show 22,341 VCI "neutralized." Colby thus would have us believe that the vast majority of these people were targeted according to the rules that he outlined.

This capacity on the part of MI groups in Vietnam seems to me greatly exaggerated. A mammoth task such as this would greatly tax even our resourceful FBI, where we have none of the vast cross-cultural problems to contend with.

What types of operations "generate" this supplementary body count then, assuming the figures are accurate? It was my experience that the majority of people classified as VC were "captured" as a result of sweeping tactical operations. In effect, a huge dragnet was cast out in our area of operation (AR) and whatever looked good in the catch, regardless of evidence, was classified as VCI.

MI personnel do not have an "active" combat role. Nevertheless, the 1st MIT had a reputation of being an aggressive unit that did not shy away from initiating and participating in combat patrols. On one {p.314} occasion, shortly after I had joined the team, I was on the land line, land communication, reporting to my commanding officer (CO) at division. In the course of giving him an account of the week's activities, I mentioned that we had staged several MI patrols. He reprimanded me slightly, saying that he did not want to lose "valuable" MI personnel on routine combat patrols; replacements were hard to come by. He further informed me that the only justification for MI people to be on a patrol was for the purpose of hunting down VCI. From that point on, any "body count" resulting from an MI patrol were automatically listed as VCI. To my knowledge, in fact, all those killed by 1st MIT on such patrols, were classified as VCI only after their deaths. There was never any evidence to justify such a classification.

The IPW section, I would estimate—again I stress "estimate"—interrogated an average of 20 people per day.
Mr. Moorhead. Is that your team: 20 per day?
Mr. Uhl. Yes, sir.
These Vietnamese were generally turned over to MI by our various combat units, as VC suspects. There was an extraordinary degree of command pressure placed on the interrogation officer to classify detainees turned over to IPW as civil defendants (CD's). As opposed to innocent civilians (IC's) these are people adjudged to have violated Vietnamese law.

It was a foregone conclusion that the overwhelming majority of detainees could not be classified as prisoners of war (PW's) since the conditions of capture did not meet the rigid criteria set up to make that classification. Therefore, the way that the brigade measured its success was not only by its "body count" and "kill ratio" but by the number of CD's it had captured.

Not only was there no due process, which we as Americans consider to be among man's "natural rights," but fully all the detainees were brutalized and many were literally tortured.

All CD's, because of this command pressure, (the majority of our detainees were classified as CD's) were listed as VCI. To my knowledge, not one of these people ever freely admitted being a cadre member.

And again, contrary to Colby's statement, most of our CD's were women and children.

Mr. Colby, in response to a direct question, denied that Americans actually exercised power of arrest over Vietnamese civilians.

In Duc Pho, where the 11th Brigade base camp was located, we could arrest and detain at will any Vietnamese civilians we desired, without so much as a whisper of coordination with ARVN or GVN authorities.

But the impact of this oversight in Ambassador Colby's testimony pales when compared to his general lack of understanding of what is actually going on in the field.

I mentioned above that in order to be listed as VCI at least three different intelligence agencies had to target the same individual. Even if this were true, which it wasn't in my experience, the most crucial omission in this progression is not even addressed.

That is: what steps are taken to assure that information used to denounce any individual is reliable?

The 1st MIT employed 11 coded sources. These were indigenous subagents paid to provide us with "hot intel" on the VC personalities and movement in our AR.

We had no way of determining the background of these sources, nor their motivation for providing American {p.315} units with information.

No American in the team spoke or understood Vietnamese well enough to independently debrief any "contact." None of us were sufficiently sensitive to nor knowledgeable of the law, the culture, the customs, the history, etc.

Our paid sources could easily have been either provocateurs or opportunists with a score to settle. Every information report (IR) we wrote based on our sources' information was classified as (1) unverifiable and (2) usually reliable source. As to the first, it speaks for itself; the second, in most cases was pure rationale for the existence of the program.

The unverified and in fact unverifiable information, nevertheless, was used regularly as input to artillery strikes, harassment and interdiction fire (H&I), B52 and other air strikes, often on populated areas.

We churned out a dozen IR's per week, not because it was good or reliable information, but it was our mission. Furthermore, it was not possible, given the conditions in Vietnam, for a tactical unit to produce reliable and verified intelligence data.

The intelligence contingency fund (ICF), a classified fund, provides payroll and incentives for these essentially useless subagents. Moral, ideological, and political questions aside, literally millions of dollars must be squandered yearly in operations similar to the one I described extemporaneously, all over Vietnam; all over the world.

If one assumes, as I do, that Phoenix is a hoax—that thousands of Vietnamese are indiscriminately classified as VC—based on no specific targeting procedure—based on no evidence—then this is just one more colossal example of wasted funds and personnel.

So what, a few more millions are wasted among the billions wasted before them.

As the troops return from Southeast Asia, the cost of this war will continue for many years to come. Those addicted to drugs will need extensive rehabilitation.

Those scarred psychologically from having been executioners of brutal policies will not only seek medical and financial relief, but in a real sense, represent a human resource no longer willing or able to believe in the worth of American Institutions.

Mr. Moorhead. Thank you very much, Mr. Uhl.
Before we question you, we will hear from Mr. Osborn.

Index

Abrams, Gen. Creighton 32, 121–123
Abu Ghraib 21–25
Adams, Michael 267
Advanced Research Projects Agency (ARPA) 249
Afghanistan War 22, 30, 100, 161, 170, 179
Agent Orange 56, 1000, 115, 120, 189, 190–192, 209, 210; dioxin 238–240; industrial accident, Sevesso, Italy 239; Vietnam defoliation 238, 247–265
Agent Orange Victims International 272
Ali, Tariq 117
Alien and Sedition Acts 65
Allen, Dr. James 240
Alternatives to Militarism (ATOM, Inc.) 34
American Civil Liberties Union (ACLU) 231
American Dream 156
American Federation of Government Employees (AFGE) 159, 214–216, 217–220, 221–225, 228–230, 233, 234
American Health Foundation 271, 277
American Legion 156
American Psychiatric Association (ASA) 118, 124, 125, 174, 178
Americans Against Union Control of Government 219, 224, 229, 234
Andre, Carl 37
antiwar movements 32, 78, 79, 116; Greek 160; Italian 161–163
antiwar veterans 79, 103
Appy, Christian 102, 118
Arendt, Hannah 47, 51
Army of the Republic of Vietnam (ARVN) 55
Athens, Greece: antiwar mobilization, Feb. 18, 2003 160, 161
Atomic Energy Commission 236, 246
Atomic Test Site, Nevada 236
Australia 157

Baez, Joan 127
The Balkans 160
Bao Dai 129
Berrigan, Phillip 124
Bigart, Homer 66
Black Panthers 63

Black Virgin Mountain 96
Blaylock, Ken 220, 221, 230, 233
body count 23
Born on the Fourth of July 138
Branfman, Fred 131
Brightman, Carol 14, 207
Bring Them Home Now Campaign (BTHN) 161, 195, 196; in Italy 161
British Socialist Workers Party 158
Brooklyn, N.Y. 29, 33
Brown, Harold 222, 228, 233
Brown, Maj. Phil 274
Bundy, McGeorge 49
Bush, George W. 24, 25, 159, 160, 193, 196, 201

Calder, Alexander 35, 36
Calder, Louisa 36
Calley, William L. 22, 25
Calloway, Howard (Bo) 212
Cambodia: invasion 134
Carson, Rachel 245
Carter, Jimmy 220, 269
Casey, Michael 141
Cece, Gerry 263
Central America: U.S. secret war 159
Central Committee for Conscientious Objectors (CCCO) 195, 231
Chomsky, Noam 158, 198
Citizen Soldier 99, 120, 159, 195, 210, 226, 231–235, 269, 271
Citizens Against Toxic Spraying (CATS) 241
Citizens Commission of Inquiry (CCI) 73, 116, 117, 158, 200
Civil War (U.S.) 156; disability entitlements 165
Cleland, Max 271
Clifford, Clark 122
Cline, David 195, 197, 200, 203
Colby, William 123
Commoner, Barry 241, 269
communist witch hunt 65
Cooper, Paul 236, 237
Cortright, David 215
Cox, Paul 187, 190, 199

287

Cranston, Sen. Alan 115
Crumb, Jan Barry 39

Dashiell, Tom 254, 255
Daum, Dr. Susan 271
de Beauvoir, Simone 158
DeBeneditti, Charles 61
Dellums, Ron 72, 73, 116; hearings on war crimes 196
DMZ: demilitarized zone in Vietnam 94
Demilitarized Zones 39
depleted uranium 100
deserters: American 158
Dettinger, Maj. Gen. Garth 273, 274
de Victor, Maude 238, 239, 242, 243, 265–268
Dewey Canyon III (April 1971) 21, 113
Dien Bien Phu 14, 28
Dispatches 133
Douglas, Helen Gahagan 35
Dow Chemical Corporation 240, 256, 267, 277
Duc Pho 22
Duffy, Joan 204

East, John 274
Ehrhart, W.D. 39, 76, 78, 81
Eisenhower, Dwight W. 248
El Salvador: U.S. secret war 159
11th Infantry Brigade 22, 23, 27
Ellsberg, Daniel 204
Engels, Friedrich 35
England: veteran disability policy origins 164
Enlisted Times 231
Ensign, Tod 35–38, 74, 99, 101, 117, 120, 200, 209
Espionage Act 65
Ewell, Gen. Julian 71
ex-servicemen: Australia 157; Britain 158; Greece 160

Fallows, James 60
Font, Louis 101
Ford, Gerald 56
Ft. Benning 27
Ft. Dix 29
Ft. Hamilton 33
Ft. Hood 22
France 157; veteran disability policy origins 164
Franklin, H. Bruce 134
Free Speech Movement 60
Fulbright, Sen. William 103

Georgetown University 18, 22, 26
Gettleman, Marvin 144
G.I. Bill 156
G.I. Coffee Houses 61
G.I. Guinea Pigs 210
G.I. Resistance 61, 157, 184, 201
G.I. Unions 209; Dutch soldiers union 215, 219; soldiers as workers 212–235

Glasser, Ronald J. 138
Golub, Leon 37, 38
Goodbye to All That 167
Goodman, Amy 66, 67
Gore, Al 114
Grand Army of the Republic 166
Grant, John 184
Graves, Robert 167
Great Depression 156
Greeley, Andrew 62, 63
Gulf War syndrome 100

Haber, Dr. Paul 275–277
Halberstam, David 66
Ham Rong Bridge 16
Hanoi 14–20, 94, 95, 123, 187, 190
Harriman, Averell 122
Hartney, Terry 17. 19
Heller, Joseph 56
Hersh, Seymour 21–25
Ho Chi Minh 48, 50, 129
Hoover, Herbert 166
Hoplites of Ancient Greece 163
Hotel Royal des Invalides 164
House Un-American Activities Committee 65
House Veteran Affairs Committee 273
Hubbs, Charley 255, 275
Hunt, Andrew 118
Hussein, Saddam 159
hyphenated immigrants 65

Indochina 157
Infantry Officers School 22
International War Crimes Commission 158
International Workers of the World (IWW) 119
Interrogation Prisoner of War (IPW) 23; civil defendants 23; innocent civilians 23
Iraq War 21–24, 100, 160, 161, 170, 179, 201

Jacobin National Convention 164
Johnson, Lyndon B. 122, 134, 144
Joint Task Force Full Accounting 14, 19
Jurney, Lee 264

Kagan, Leslie 197
Kennedy, Bobby 54, 57, 247
Kennedy, John F. 47, 51, 247, 249, 258
Kennedy, Rory 54–57
Kent State University Student Killings 134
Kernea, Ed 263
Kerrey, Bob: Thanh Phong massacre 105, 106, 109–112
Kerry, John 21, 112, 193, 194; controversy around killing an enemy soldier 102; testimony before the Senate Foreign Relations Committee 103
Ketwig, John 76
King, Dr. Daniel 176, 177
Kinnard, Douglas 51

Kissinger, Henry 55, 56, 122, 128
Klann, Gerhard: Thanh Phong massacre 105, 106, 109–111
Klippen, Artie 26, 27
Kovic, Ron 138
Krendel, Ezra S. 230
Krohn, Herbert 141
Kucinich, Dennis 195
Kunen, James Simon 73
Kurtis, Bill 267
Kuwait: invasion 159, 160

Lamanski, John 252, 253
LaRocque, Adm. Gene 204
League for Industrial Democracy 60
Lembcke, Jerry 119
Lewes, James 61
Lewis, Anthony 131
Lewy, Buenter 73
Lifton, Dr. Robert J. 72, 118, 175, 180
Lippard, Lucy 37
Logevall, Fredrik 58
Louis XIV: policies on disabled and aged veterans 164
LZ Bronco 27

Mao Zedong 50, 51
Martin, Donald 275
Martin, Graham 55
Maugham, Somerset 125, 167
Mazel, Bernie 34
McArthur, Gen. Douglas 166
McCarthy Era 65
McCord Air Force Base 32
McGovern, George 25
McNamara, Robert 46–53, 122, 128
Mekong Delta 31, 102
Metcalfe, Ralph 268
MIAs 14–19, 56; Vietnamese 15–20
Middle Ages 157
Military Families Speak Out (MFSO) 195
Military Intelligence 22, 27
military justice 101
Muller, Bobby 203
Muslim Americans 65
Muste, A.J. 60
My Lai massacre 21–25, 70–78, 117, 187

Nader, Ralph 67, 68, 112
National Academy of Science 175
National Lawyers Guild 231
National Liberation Front (Viet Cong) 103, 104
The National Veterans Law Center 277
New Left 37
New York Review of Books 34
New Zealand 157
Ngo Dinh Diem 129, 249
Nguyen Cao Ky 134
Nguyen Tan Dung 190

Nguyen Van Thieu 32, 55, 122
Nicaragua: U.S. secret war 159
Nick Mazzuco: Biography of an Atomic Vet 210
Nimoy, Leonard 35
9th Infantry Division 29–32, 71
Nixon, Richard M. 15, 24, 25, 32, 35, 122, 128, 135, 157, 159, 192, 218, 248

Obama, Barack 64, 72, 185
O'Brien, Tim 138, 140
Olsen, George 150
Operation Speedy Express 71, 72
Orwell, George 63
Owen, Charles 235; victim of Agent Orange 265
Owen, Ethel (Mrs. Charles) 265, 266

Palmer Raids 65
Paris Peace Accord 1973 15, 55, 191
Pathet Lao 130–132
The Patriot Act 101
Patti, Archimedes 50
Patton, Gen. George S. 153
Pentagon Papers 47, 48, 50, 249
Persian Gulf War 160, 199; Gulf War syndrome 100
Peshkin, Col. Dick 256
Pham Van Dong 39, 192
Phoenix Program 27, 123, 129
Pochurek, Jim 260
Poole, Gordon: on military service in Italy 162
post-traumatic stress disorder (PTSD) 30, 67, 75, 80, 115, 118, 119, 125, 167, 168, 174–182
Powell, Woody 197

Quang Ngai City 22, 187
Quang Ngai Province 14, 187
Qui Nhon 28

R&R (rest and recuperation) 94
Rabe, David 139
Ranch Hands (U.S. Air Force Defoliation Unit) 211, 247–265
Rather, Dan 261
The Razor's Edge 125, 167
Reagan, Ronald 31, 116, 159
recruitment practices: U.S. military 99
Redgrave, Vanessa 158
Reed, Stanley 27, 28
Remarque, Eric Maria 137
Resor, Stanley 32
Reutershan, Paul 272, 277
Rifkin, Jeremy 74, 117
Rinaldi, Matthew 61
Rivera, Geraldo 278
Rivers, William H.R. 167
Robbinson, Col. William "Robbie" 250–253, 265
Roosevelt, Franklin D. 51, 122, 167

Ross, Milton 268
Rostow, Walt 49
ROTC 26
Rottmann, Larry 39, 141
Rousseff, Dilma 186
Rusk, Dean 49, 52
Russell, Bertrand, war crimes tribunal 158, 208

Safe Return Amnesty Committee 34, 35
Saigon 54
Sartre, Jean Paul 158
Sassoon, Siegfried 135
Schell, Jonathan 69–73, 78
Schepers, Dr. Garrit 270, 276
Schlesinger, Arthur 47, 249
Schoenman, Ralph 117
Seattle, Washington 32, 33
7th National Party Congress Vietnam 19
Shatan, Chaim 119
Sheehan, Neil 66
Sheehan-Miles, Charles 199, 204
Sheer, Robert 77
Shoecraft, Billie 244
Silent Spring 245
Singer, Daniel 148
Skocpol, Theda 115
Smith Act 65
Soroka, Paul 264, 265
"spat upon" vet 31
Spay, Jack 250–259, 265
Spock, Dr. Benjamin 60, 63
Starr, Paul 118
Stauber, John: Chaquamego Concerned Citizens 241
Stellman, Dr. Jeanne 271, 277
Stellman, Dr. Steve 270, 271
Stern, Lewis 18
Sticks and Bones 139
Stone, I.F. 34, 35
Stop Loss policy 100
Students for a Democratic Society (SDS) 60
Sturtevant, Tom 198
Sweden, American exiles in 158

Taylor, Maxwell 52, 247, 249, 258
Taylor, Telford 49
Thic Nhat Hanh 126
Thompson, Hunter S. 128
Thompson, Sir Robert 122
Thomson, James 51
365 Days 138
Thurmond, Strom 219, 224, 228, 233

Ton That Tung, Dr. 270
Truman, Harry 50
Turse, Nick 58, 247, 249, 258
Twain, Mark 139

Underwood, Hal 256, 257, 265
UNICEF 189
Uniform Code of Military Justice (UCMJ) 101, 218
U.S. Army War College 76
U.S. Civil War 156, 165

Valenzuela, Aaron 255, 256
veterans: disability policy 164, 165; identity 156–170 (*see also* ex-servicemen); return to Vietnam 93–95, 96–98
Veterans Administration (VA) 174–176, 177, 200, 238
Veterans for Common Sense 199, 203
Veterans for Peace (VFP) 177, 187, 194, 195; founded in Maine 198; operation Dire Distress 197, 202
Vietnam Agent Orange Responsibility and Relief Campaign (VAORRC) 190
Vietnam Agent Orange Victims Association (VAVA) 191
Vietnam Awakening 73, 158
Vietnam Friendship Village 94
Vietnam News 16
Vietnam Overseas News Agency 17
Vietnam Veteran Memorial (The Wall) 26, 28, 30, 98
Vietnam Veterans Against the War (VVAW) 73, 103, 116–119, 134, 194–196, 199, 203
Vietnam Veterans of America (VVA) 19
Vietnam War Commemoration Project 72
Vietnam War Crimes Working Group 75

war crimes in Vietnam (U.S.) 21–24. 69–74, 79, 82–92, 97, 103, 197, 108
Weaver, Dennis 35
Weinberger, Casper 154
Westmoreland, Gen. William C. 32, 122
Whiting, Allen 51
Winning Hearts and Minds 39
Wolfe, Tobias 110
Woodward, Val 239

Yamashita, Tomoyuki 49
Young, Alvin 239, 240, 266, 274

Zhou En Lai 51

www.ingramcontent.com/pod-product-compliance
Ingram Content Group UK Ltd.
Pitfield, Milton Keynes, MK11 3LW, UK
UKHW041927140426
5217IPUK00014B/343